W9-DEL-378

CareWise For Older Adults

CareWise
For Older
Adults
Self-Care
For Lifelong
Health

Third Edition

Acamedica Press
A division of CareWise, Inc. (A SHPS Company)
Seattle, Washington

Reviewed for medical accuracy by a
panel of board-certified physicians

Acamedica Press
A division of CareWise, Inc. (A SHPS Company)
PO Box 34570, Seattle, WA 98124-1570

© 1996, 1999, 2004 by Acamedica Press
All rights reserved. No part of this book may be reproduced or transmitted in any
form, by any means (electronic, photocopying, recording or otherwise) without
the prior written permission of the publisher. First edition 1996
Third edition 2004
Printed in the United States of America
09 08 07 06 05 04   10 9 8 7 6 5 4 3 2 1

Library of Congress Catalog Card Number 2003115363
ISBN 1-886444-07-2

Decision helper charts © 1996, 1999, 2004 Acamedica Press and Reliance Medical
Information, Inc. (RMI)

The medical information in this book was reviewed for accuracy by a panel of
board-certified physicians and was found to be consistent with generally accepted
medical practices at the time of review.

CareWise For Older Adults, intended to provide general information on common
medical topics, is not a comprehensive medical text and does not include all the
potential medical conditions that could be represented by certain symptoms. In
addition, medical practices may change periodically; therefore, this guide cannot
and should not be relied upon as a substitute for seeing an appropriate health care
professional.

Acamedica Press has made every effort to print trademarked product names within this book in initial capital letters to indicate trademark and/or
registered trademark designation.

Design by Michael O'Sullivan
Cover illustration by Deborah Hanley
Interior illustrations by Peter Frazier

Contents

Turn to the first page of each section for specific topics and their page numbers. See the index, pages 381 to 416, for terminology and references as well as specific topics.

Section 3 Health Concerns (continued)

Section 4 Medications 325

How and when to use medications to get the best results

Section 5 Prevention 337

A variety of lifestyle and safety tips for getting and staying healthy

Section 6 Managing Illness 361

Steps for taking charge of your health, whether you are dealing with a temporary illness or a chronic condition

Section 7 Planning for the Future 371

Ways to plan for the years ahead in terms of lifestyle, care and independence

Preface

Managing your own health and that of your loved ones is undoubtedly one of your primary concerns. So it should be especially comforting to know that—through this guide—you have convenient access to the health care information you need to help you make the best possible decisions.

CareWise For Older Adults: Self-Care For Lifelong Health is written especially for men and women approaching and in their later years. It gives you the best available health care information to help you decide when to apply self-care, when to seek professional medical care, how to work more effectively with your doctor and, most important, how to manage your health.

Health care decisions are personal and important, and they can have a tremendous impact on your overall well-being. Think of this resource as a tool you can use to take charge of your health and medical care decisions. For many of you, taking charge may be a new concept. In our era of "managed care" you may be required to take greater control of your medical conditions and assume more responsibility for your health than ever before. And that can often leave you with questions and feelings of uncertainty about treatment methods and your best options for care. But it doesn't have to be this way. It is important for you, as a health care consumer, to take an active role in your health care—and this guide can help.

The guide's focus is on self-care and prevention—making healthy lifestyle decisions, understanding your symptoms and medical concerns, participating with your doctor in shared decision making, and effectively managing your medical conditions. Self-care doesn't mean you'll never get sick. Rather, it improves how you use the medical system and handle illness and injury when they do occur. It's never too late to make important lifestyle behavior changes, and doing so can dramatically improve the quality of your life.

We have taken our extensive health education experience, combined it with leading sources of health and medical information, and presented the material in an easy-to-understand format. This information has been developed by physicians, nurses and health educators in response to consumers' needs, and reviewed by a panel of board-certified physicians.

Our goal is to help you become a wise health care consumer, which means getting in the habit of weighing the benefits, risks and costs of treatment when it comes to your specific medical concerns. As you do, you will experience better health, greater satisfaction when you seek medical care and—ultimately—the highest quality of care.

Acknowledgments

We wish to acknowledge the many medical and communications professionals who contributed to the publication of *CareWise For Older Adults* including:

Editorial Staff
Randi Holland, R.N.
Jan Anderson, R.N.
Charmaine Adsero

CareWise Clinical Content Certification Council
Jesse Samuels, M.D., F.A.C.E.P.
Christopher Scott Stanley, M.D.
Donald E. Stillwagon, M.D.
Kenneth Peterson, M.D.

Research and Review Staff
Juliette A. Dahl, R.N., B.A.
Sandy Staats Evans, R.N., B.A.
Jill Frewing
Lyle Graham, M.D.
Cara Grill
Ross Halliday, M.D.
Christine Jackson, M.D.
William Mantle, M.D.
Margaret M. Regan, R.N., B.S.N.
Amy Schneider, M.D.
Johanna H. Wesneski, R.N.

Contributing Writers
Charmaine Adsero
Lynn Griffes
Jennie Krull Gulian
George Hein
Dick Malloy
Marion Brinkley Mohler
Kip Richards, M.N., R.N.
Ginny Smith

Special thanks to our many readers who are helping us continually improve our quality and who are taking the initiative for their own health.

Introduction

What is Aging?

From the moment of birth, the body begins to age. Physiological and mental changes occur as the years pass. "Aging" is a natural progression driven by the body's changes; however, "growing old" is a state of mind.

There are a number of myths about aging, including the idea that retirement signals the beginning of the end. In fact, the government-selected retirement age of 65 is the result of politics and not the realities of the body or mind.

Your lifestyle may change with retirement; your health doesn't have to. Today nearly eight out of 10 Americans will live beyond age 75—life expectancies are at the highest level in history.

Retirees of today may have 10, 15, 20 or more years ahead of them—time to spend on hobbies, start another career or simply enjoy the fruits of their labors. Quality of life during these years depends on choices you make about your health and lifestyle—choices that can be made with help from this guide.

What does aging mean to my health?

Getting older doesn't have to mean getting sicker. Most older adults are not seriously ill, and very few (4.5 percent) Americans over age 65 are in an institution for long-term health or mental care. The average age of admission is 79.*

The key to improving and maintaining your health is prevention, regardless of your age. According to research by the National Institute on Aging, many of the problems of old age are not due to aging at all, but to improper care of the body over a lifetime. In addition, figures indicate that the vast majority of health problems in older Americans are preventable or postponable. For instance, some can be prevented by periodic health screenings (such as mammograms), and by avoiding health risks (such as smoking). Prevention is just as important now as in your earlier years—in some cases more so, because of the increased risk older adults face for chronic illness. (See *Prevention*, p. 337; *Managing Your Illness*, p. 361.)

* U.S. Department of Health and Human Services, Administration on Aging, "A Profile of Older Americans: 2002."

Finding ways to cope with the effects of aging and manage long-term illness is crucial, too. Prevention will help you avoid some acute illnesses and injuries—and perhaps delay the onset of chronic illness. Once you have a long-term illness, your challenge is to learn self-management skills. This means moving into a new stage of prevention—one that slows a disease's progression, lessens its impact or helps prevent other illnesses from occurring.

If you already have a long-term illness, *CareWise For Older Adults* can help you refine these self-management skills. If you don't, it can help you stay healthier longer—and live a more satisfying life.

A Self-Care Approach

When centenarians are asked about their "secrets for long life," a consistent theme arises: the importance of possessing a positive attitude. In fact, an optimistic outlook on life and the feeling of being in control are essential for healthy aging. Helping you learn how to take charge of your health is one of the primary goals of this book.

There is a common misconception that healthy living is hard work. In truth, a healthy lifestyle is much easier and more rewarding than falling into poor health and struggling to regain good health, or allowing a chronic illness to progress more rapidly than it should.

Successful self-care has three key components: **prevention, participation** and **education**.

Prevention

Making healthy lifestyle and prevention decisions can have an enormous impact on reducing your risk of disease. Start with the basics.

Exercise regularly, eat a healthy diet, kick the habit if you smoke, reduce your alcohol consumption and use of drugs, and control your weight. Immunizations and screening tests are also important. You'll be amazed what a difference these simple steps can make. You won't just feel better, you'll also lower your health risks or manage the onset of disease.

Of course, no amount of prevention can eliminate all disease, which is why your participation in the medical decision-making process is so important. (See *Prevention*, p. 337, to learn more about prevention and recommended immunizations and screenings.)

Participation

Unfortunately, our use of medical services is based on the hope that modern medicine will provide a treatment and cure for all our bad habits. The result is that we often overuse medical services for situations we can better handle at home. (According to current findings, approximately 80 percent of all medical concerns can be effectively treated at home.) Also, our expectations for medical care often go unmet because we don't fully understand the importance of our own active participation in the process.

Whether your doctor suggests putting you on medication, running a few tests, or scheduling a minor procedure or major surgery—it *always* pays to find out what's going on and participate in making decisions about your health care.

Yes, your doctor has years of training and offers invaluable medical advice. But only you can really decide if the benefits outweigh the risks for your particular situation, and if the treatment plan is something you can live with and incorporate into your lifestyle.

In essence, by understanding your options and discussing them with your doctors or health care providers, you become an active partner in the decision-making process.

Here's how to take an active role:

- At the doctor's office, begin the conversation with the topics you are *most* worried about—not your minor complaints—and be as honest and direct as possible about your feelings and concerns. Keep it short and to the point, but take the time you need to describe your problem.
- Ask your doctor to explain the various treatment options—along with the benefits, risks and costs of each—before going ahead with *anything*. Questions to ask include: "What is the official name of the test/procedure/medication?" "Why do I need it?" "What will the procedure involve?" "What are the risks and benefits?" "How much will it cost?" and "What are the alternatives?" Take notes if it helps, and keep them in case you want to refer back to them.
- If you don't understand your doctor's explanations, be persistent and ask: "Could you go over that part again?" "Do you have any material I can read at home?" "Can you show me on paper what will happen?"
- If a prescription drug is suggested, ask about the side effects, and the possibility of using a less expensive but effective generic substitute.

- If a major test or surgery is recommended, ask if there are other treatment options that are equally effective, or if you can watch and wait for a while without putting your health at risk.
- Ask if there will be any restrictions on activity and, if so, how long the restrictions will be necessary. If some treatment is suggested that you know you just can't or won't be able to handle, speak up. Chances are you and your doctor can work out a suitable alternative.
- Find out if there is anything else you can do for yourself—besides or in addition to a prescription or treatment—to help the problem or speed your recovery.

Sort through your options:

- If it's a non-emergency, don't rush into anything! Remember that very few medical procedures are actually emergencies. There is usually time to think about the options and select the one that seems best for you.
- If you find you have more questions for your doctor, or need additional information, call your doctor's office or professional telephone nurse counseling service and ask.

After deciding on treatment:

- Make sure you understand all the treatment instructions. If not, ask more questions!

- Carefully follow your treatment plan. For example, write down your medication schedule and keep a record of each time you take medications. Always fully comply with all instructions, and always talk to your doctor before altering your treatment or medication program.
- Keep track of any side effects and call your doctor if you are worried, have any questions or think something doesn't seem right.

Education

When it comes to the health of you and your family, ignorance is not bliss. Learning what your self-care options are—when it is safe to treat health problems at home and when to see a doctor—saves everyone time and money. Being educated means sidestepping unnecessary treatment and testing, avoiding extra medical charges, and requesting generic drugs when they are less expensive but just as effective as name brands.

Additionally, working to improve your health and decrease your need for medical services is critical to solving our national concern over the growing costs of health care. You can improve the quality of care you receive by combining it with a self-care approach—becoming part of the solution rather than part of the problem.

Using CareWise For Older Adults

Let's say it's 1 a.m. and your throat is raw and sore. Or it's Sunday afternoon and you've pulled a muscle gardening. You're wondering whether to call your doctor or just wait. The problem is, you need help—now!

Open *CareWise For Older Adults,* a book that's designed to serve as your around-the-clock health care guide.

CareWise For Older Adults covers close to 300 topics, ranging from migraines to menopause, from appendicitis to varicose veins. We suggest you take a few moments, now, to browse through the book and familiarize yourself with its format and contents. We think you'll discover that it's filled with helpful information about all kinds of common, day-to-day health concerns—like what to do if you have a funny-looking mole, suddenly hurt your back or sprain your ankle.

Most topics include general information about the medical problem, as well as tips for:

- Prevention
- Treating the problem at home
- When to seek professional medical care
- Managing the condition

Where to find what you need

- *Emergencies* and *Injuries* are covered at the beginning of the book—where they are readily accessible. **In case of an emergency, call 911 or your local emergency services number.**
- *Health concerns* come next, and are organized in a head-to-toe fashion—beginning with neurological problems and working all the way through the body, right down to foot and toe pain. The detailed index in the back of the book is designed to help you look up specific words and references and direct you to related topics.
- Other important sections include *Medications, Prevention, Managing Illness,* and *Planning for the Future.*
- *Decision helper* sections, which accompany most topics, are designed to help you decide when self-care is appropriate, when to call a doctor, and when to apply emergency first aid or seek emergency care. Read on for details on how to use the *Decision helper* sections.

Using the *Decision helper* sections

- First, read all the general information about the topic. It will help you better understand *Decision helper.*

- Next, work your way through *Decision helper*. Don't skip from point to point; each point is based on the assumption that you have answered "yes" or "no" to the previous one. Follow the arrows that apply to each of your answers.
- Take action based on the "yes" arrow that most appropriately applies to your health concern. (See the chart at right.) Or, if *Decision helper* refers you to another topic in the book, turn to that page for additional information. For example, *Decision helper* for nausea and vomiting tells you to "see *Dehydration*, p. 203" for details on that particular side effect of nausea and vomiting.

Need more details?

After reading the section(s) covering your medical concern, you may have questions and want additional information. Ask your health care provider for additional medical information to help you evaluate options for care.

CareWise For Older Adults is not intended to take the place of your doctor or other health care professionals. Instead, it is a resource to help you make the best decisions and get the most from the medical services available to you.

Decision helper:
What does each
action step mean?

 Apply Emergency First Aid
Begin emergency first aid **immediately**.

 Seek Emergency Care
Get professional medical help **immediately**.

 Call Doctor Now
Call your doctor's office **now** and alert the doctor—or a nurse—to the problem. Ask them what you should do next. This is a situation that needs prompt, professional attention, but is not necessarily an emergency.

 Call Doctor
Phone your doctor's office today and talk to the doctor or a nurse about the problem. Make an appointment if it's necessary.

 Apply Self-Care
Follow the directions for self-care (listed in the *What You Can Do* section) carefully. If you become worried about your condition, call your doctor, health care provider, or professional telephone nurse counseling service.

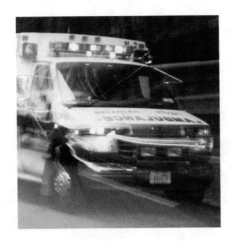

SECTION 1

Emergencies

Introduction

The time to prepare for a medical emergency is now—not at the scene of a car accident or on the doorstep of someone who is having a heart attack. An emergency by definition is an unexpected occurrence that demands immediate action. Staying calm—rather than panicking—is the key, and knowing what to do ahead of time is your best defense against panic.

Seek Emergency Care

Reader's Note: For every medical concern covered in *CareWise For Older Adults,* you'll find information that will help you determine whether you have an emergency. Look for this symbol.

Be Prepared

- Write down the phone numbers of the nearest emergency facility, National Poison Control Center (1-800-222-1222) and rescue squad in the front of this book and your telephone book.
- Know the best way to reach the emergency room by car, in case you need to drive yourself or someone else there.
- Take first-aid and CPR courses. Make both of them family affairs.
- Wear a medical-alert bracelet or necklace or carry emergency medical information in your wallet, especially if you have a condition such as diabetes, epilepsy or serious allergic reactions. This information could save your life if you are unable to speak.

Identifying an Emergency

In general, an emergency is any situation that places a person's health in serious jeopardy. If you think someone's symptoms appear critical or life-threatening, you are probably dealing with an emergency.

Emergency situations include:

- Unconsciousness
- Symptoms of a heart attack, such as chest pain, shortness of breath, nausea, sweating (see *Chest Pain,* p. 184)
- Severe breathing problems
- Severe, uncontrolled bleeding
- Symptoms of shock, such as pale, clammy skin, weakness, rapid heart rate (see *Shock,* p. 39)
- Possible spinal, neck or head injury (see *Head/Spinal Injury,* p. 55)

When to Call an Ambulance

Even if you know a situation is an emergency it may be difficult to determine whether to take the person to an emergency room or call an ambulance.

The American College of Emergency Physicians advises that you ask yourself a few questions before deciding which is appropriate:

- Is the person's situation life-threatening (as in a sudden loss of consciousness)?
- Could the person's condition become life-threatening on the way to the hospital?
- Could moving the person cause further injury?
- Does the person need immediate help from a paramedic or emergency medical technician?
- Would traffic, distance, or unreliable transportation cause a delay in getting the person to the hospital?

If the answer to any of these questions is "yes," or even if you're unsure, it's best to call an ambulance.

Emergencies that you may be able to drive to the emergency room for include:

- Deep wounds (see *Wounds,* p. 42)
- Some severe burns (see *Burns,* p. 28)
- Broken bones (see *Broken Bones,* p. 65)
- Some head injuries
- Sudden, severe pain
- New seizures in an adult

Cardiopulmonary Resuscitation (CPR)

CPR is an emergency first-aid technique for treating a person who is not breathing and has no heartbeat. It's a good idea to encourage each member of your household to learn the techniques. When it's needed, the person who has the most experience and training in CPR should be the one to perform the procedure at the scene of an emergency.

Think ABC—Airway, Breathing and Circulation

In basic life support, remember ABC:

- Airway - Establish an open airway.
- Breathing - Reestablish breathing.
- Circulation - Begin external compressions if the heart has stopped.

> CPR is a complex first-aid procedure. Although we describe all the steps for CPR, this section is not intended to replace a course that allows you to have actual hands-on experience with the procedures. To learn CPR, contact the American Red Cross, American Heart Association or other civic groups in your community for classes.

Step one—Check for consciousness/Call for help:

- Find out if the person is conscious. Shout, "Are you OK?"
- If the person doesn't respond, call 911 or your local emergency services number, then begin CPR.
- CPR must be performed on a hard surface. If you must move the person, do so cautiously to prevent injury to his or her neck and back. If possible, slide a board under the back, keeping the head and spine straight.
- For children and infants, do one minute of CPR before calling 911 or your local emergency services number.

Step two—Check for breathing/Open airway:

If no air is passing through the person's lips (put your cheek next to the mouth to check), and the chest and abdomen are not moving, you will need to open the airway.

- If there is vomit or liquid in the mouth, clean it out with your fingers (cover your fingers with a clean cloth if you have one).
- Push down and back on the forehead and lift the chin by placing your fingers under the jaw bone.
- With an infant, be careful not to extend the head back too far since that can shut off the airway.
- Check the mouth, chest and abdomen again for movement. Sometimes opening the airway is enough to start breathing again.
- If the person does not begin breathing immediately, begin rescue breathing (step three).

Step three—Begin rescue breathing:

- Pinch the person's nostrils shut with the same hand that you have on his or her forehead. (See Figure 1.)
- Place your mouth over the person's mouth, making a tight seal.
- Place your mouth over both the mouth and nose of a small child or infant. Be careful not to blow too hard into an infant since excess air can go into the stomach and cause vomiting or compression of the lungs. Either one will make delivering air more difficult. (See Figure 2.)
- Slowly blow in air until the person's chest rises. Remove your mouth between breaths and allow time for the person to exhale passively before the next breath. Give two full breaths.

Figure 1

Figure 2

Step four—Check for signs of circulation:

- Observe the person for signs of circulation such as normal breathing, coughing or movement in response to stimulation.

If There are Signs of Circulation

Do not do chest compressions on a person who is moving in response to stimulation, coughing or breathing normally. CPR performed on a person whose heart is beating can cause serious injury. Instead:

- If necessary, continue rescue breathing. Blow air into the lungs 12 times per minute (once every five seconds) for an adult and 15 times per minute for a small child (once every four seconds). Breathe 20 times per minute (once every three seconds) for an infant.
- Continue breathing as long as necessary. A person who seems to have recovered needs to be seen by a doctor, since shock is a common occurrence after breathing has stopped. (See *Shock,* p. 39.)

If There are No Signs of Circulation

Step five—Begin chest compressions:

- Find the lower rib cage and move your fingers up the rib cage to the notch where the ribs meet the lower breastbone in the center of the lower part of the chest. (See Figure 3.)
- Place the heel of one hand down on the breastbone and your other hand on top of the one that is in position. (See Figure 4.) In children ages 1 to 8, use the heel of one hand rather than both hands.

Figure 3

- Do not compress the chest with your fingers. This can damage the ribs.
- Lock your elbows into position with your arms straight. Place your shoulders directly over your hands so the thrust of each compression goes straight down on the chest.
- Push down with a steady, firm thrust, compressing the chest one to two inches (2.5 to 5 cm) for an adult.
- Lift your weight from the person and repeat. Do not lift your hands from the person's chest between thrusts.
- Do 15 chest compressions in about 10 seconds.

Figure 4

- After 15 compressions, quickly tilt the head and lift the chin of the person (as previously instructed), pinch the nose and breathe two slow breaths to fill the lungs. The chest must deflate after each breath.
- Continue this cycle (15 compressions and two breaths) at the rate of 80 - 100 compressions per minute. After one minute, check the person for normal breathing or movement in response to stimulation. Continue the compressions and breathing until help arrives if there are still no signs of circulation.
- For children ages 1 to 8, compress the chest one to one-and-one-half inches (2.5 to 4 cm) and give five chest compressions to one breath.

Extra care must be taken when performing CPR on an infant:

- If chest compression is necessary, position your index and middle fingers on the baby's breastbone. (See Figure 5.)

Figure 5

- Gently compress the chest no more than one inch (2.5 cm). Count out loud as you pump in a rapid rhythm— roughly one-and-one-half times a second or about 100 times a minute.
- Gently give one breath (with your mouth covering the baby's mouth and nose) after every fifth compression.
- Continue until help arrives.

Choking

Thousands of Americans choke to death needlessly every year. People of any age can choke on pieces of food, vomit and small objects.

PREVENTION ✓

For Yourself

- Take small bites and chew food thoroughly. Cut meat into small pieces.
- Don't eat too fast, or eat and talk or laugh at the same time.
- Don't drink too much alcohol before eating.
- If you smoke, wait until after you've finished eating to light up.

If You're Caring for a Small Child

- Keep small objects that children might choke on out of reach.
- Do not let children run or jump with food or any other object in their mouths.
- Inspect all toys for small, removable parts that can cause choking. (Follow label guidelines that indicate "appropriate ages.")

WHAT YOU CAN DO ✓

If Someone is Choking

You may have only four to eight minutes to save a choking person's life, so you should know how to administer the Heimlich maneuver. (See the following pages and *CPR,* p. 20.)

A conscious child or adult who is choking will breathe in an exaggerated way. They will be unable to talk or cough, and will probably nod in the affirmative to the question, "Are you choking?" They may grasp their throat. People who can cough or speak are still getting some air into their lungs, and should be encouraged to cough vigorously. The Heimlich maneuver should not be administered in these cases.

Choking Rescue (Heimlich Maneuver) for a Conscious Person

- Establish whether the person can speak or cough by asking, "Are you choking?"
- Stand behind the person.
- Wrap your arms around his or her waist.
- Grasp one of your fists with the other hand and place the thumb-side of the fist just above the navel but below the rib cage.
- Thrust your fist upward in five quick, sharp jabs. (See Figure 6.)
- Repeat until the object is dislodged or the person becomes unconscious.

Figure 6

Choking Rescue for an Unconscious Person

- Call 911 or your local emergency services number.
- Open the airway. (Push down and back on the forehead and lift the chin by placing your fingers on the jaw bone.) Attempt rescue breathing by pinching the nostrils shut, placing your mouth over the person's mouth, and giving two breaths. If needed, open the airway and try again.
- Begin chest compressions as you would in CPR. (See Figure 7 and p. 22.) Chest compression should create enough pressure to eject a foreign body from the airway.

Figure 7

Obstructed Airway in Children Ages 1 to 8

Use the procedure already covered with two important exceptions:

- Look into the airway and use your finger to sweep the object out ONLY if you can see it. DO NOT perform a blind finger sweep. Instead, perform a tongue-jaw lift. (See Figure 8.)
- If the obstruction is not relieved after one minute, call 911 or your local emergency services number. Of course, if someone else is available, have that person call for help immediately. Continue this sequence until the obstruction is dislodged or until help arrives.

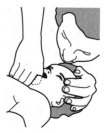

Figure 8

Obstructed Airway in Infant or Child Less Than 1 Year of Age

The following steps are appropriate if there is complete airway obstruction due to a witnessed or strongly suspected obstruction by an object. **DO NOT PERFORM these maneuvers to clear an airway that is obstructed due to swelling caused by infection. SEEK EMERGENCY CARE.**

Infant or child is conscious

- Hold the infant or child face down along your forearm, supporting the head and neck with one hand.
- Give five back blows forcefully between the shoulder blades with the heel of your hand. (See Figure 9.)

Figure 9

- Turn the infant or child face up. Keeping the head supported and lower than the rest of the body, position your index and middle fingers on the baby's breastbone and give five thrusts with two fingers. (See Figure 10.)
- Repeat until the object is dislodged or the infant/child is unconscious.

Figure 10

Infant or child is unconscious

- Place the infant or child on a firm surface.
- Open the airway. (Push down and back on the forehead and lift the chin by placing your fingers under the jaw bone.) With an infant, be careful not to extend the head back too far since that can shut off the airway.
- If the infant or child is not breathing, try to give rescue breaths by covering his or her mouth and nose with your mouth.
- If this doesn't work, reposition the head and try again.
- Turn the child face down and deliver five back blows. (See Figure 9.)
- Deliver five chest thrusts. (See Figure 10.)
- Do the tongue-jaw lift. (See Figure 8.) Remove the object ONLY if you can see it.
- Try again to do rescue breathing. (See p. 21.)
- Repeat back blows, chest thrusts, tongue-jaw lift and rescue breathing attempts until you are successful.
- After one minute of emergency first aid, call 911 or your local emergency services number. Of course, if someone else is available, have that person call for help immediately. Continue the process until success is achieved or help arrives.

If You are Choking and Can't Get Help

- Try not to panic.
- Cough vigorously.
- If this doesn't work, stand behind a chair or beside or over some other object that puts pressure on your abdomen just above your navel (but below your rib cage). (See Figure 11.)
- Thrust yourself on the object in strong, sharp bursts.
- Repeat until the item is dislodged.

Figure 11

For a Pregnant or Obese Person

- Stand behind the person and place your arms under his or her armpits.
- Place your fist on the middle of the breastbone, but not over the ribs.
- Place your other hand on top of it.
- Give five quick, forceful movements. Do not squeeze with your arms, but use your fist.

FINAL NOTES ✓

Call your local hospital or Red Cross chapter for more information and instruction on these procedures. Those who have just had the choking rescue performed on them should see a doctor. The maneuver can cause trauma to the chest or abdomen, and the object may have damaged the throat.

Burns

The skin is the body's largest organ, protecting us against infection and helping to regulate the balance of water and temperature. Burns—whether caused by fire, hot objects or fluids, electricity, chemicals, radiation or other sources—threaten these vital functions. For the very young or old, or those with other medical conditions, burns can be even more serious.

Burns are classified based on their depth of penetration of the skin.

- *First-degree burns* involve only the tough, outer layer of skin. The skin turns bright red and becomes sensitive and painful. It may be dry, but it does not blister.
- *Second-degree burns* are deeper than first-degree burns and are very painful, red and mottled. The burned area may blister and/or be swollen and puffy.
- *Third-degree burns* are still deeper and can involve muscle, internal organs and bone. The skin looks charred and dry and may break open. Underlying muscle or tendons may be visible. Pain may be severe. If nerves have been damaged, however, there may be no pain except around the edges of the burn.

First- and second-degree burns are also called "partial thickness" burns, and third-degree burns are called "full thickness" burns.

WHAT YOU CAN DO ✓

If Someone is on Fire

- Stay calm.
- Help the person drop down and roll in a blanket, rug, coat or some type of covering to smother the flames. Do not let the person run—this will fuel the fire.
- Completely extinguish the fire and stop skin and clothes from smoldering by soaking them with water. Do not remove burned clothing.

- Cover the burn with a cool, damp, sterile bandage or a clean, non-fibrous cloth such as a sheet.
- **Seek emergency care**.

For Severe Burns of Any Kind

Make sure:

- The person is breathing. If not, **call for emergency help and start CPR immediately.** (See *CPR,* **p. 20.**)
- Bleeding is controlled (see *Control Severe Bleeding,* p. 43)
- There are no signs of shock: altered consciousness, faintness, paleness, rapid and shallow breathing, rapid and weak pulse, cool and clammy skin (see *Shock,* p. 39)
- There are no signs of charring in the mouth or of nasal hairs. Check for sooty residue on the face, shortness of breath, a cough or hoarseness. If present, these signs indicate an emergency; the respiratory tract may be damaged. **Seek emergency care.**

For Other Burns

Electrical burns

- Turn off the power before touching someone who is in contact with an electrical wire or appliance. Assume a downed power line is live.
- Try not to move the person.
- If a power line has fallen across a car, passengers remain safest if they stay inside. If they have to leave because of fire or some other reason, they should jump clear of the car.

An electrical burn can appear minor even when it has caused major internal injuries. Generally, there will be wounds at the places of entry and exit of the electrical current, unless the person was in contact with water. All electrical shocks that cause burns or that occurred with water are emergencies.

Chemical burns

- Flush the skin with large amounts of cool, running water for 10 to 15 minutes or until the burning pain has stopped for at least 10 minutes. If the chemical is a dry solid, brush it off first.

- Remove any contaminated clothing, jewelry or other items.
- Cover the area with a cool, damp, sterile dressing or clean cloth and call your doctor.
- If an eye has been burned, flush it immediately with lukewarm water for 20 minutes. Angle the head so the contaminant does not flow into the other eye. After flushing, close the eye and cover it with a loose, moist dressing and **seek emergency care.**

First-degree or partial thickness burns

- Run cool water over the area or soak it in a cool-water bath as often as necessary to control the pain. If this is not possible, apply cold compresses.
- Cover the area with a cool, moist, clean bandage or clean cloth.
- Take pain relievers—such as aspirin, ibuprofen (Advil, Motrin) and acetaminophen (Tylenol)—to help reduce pain. **NEVER give aspirin to children/teenagers unless your health care provider orders it. It can cause Reye's syndrome, a rare but often fatal condition. CAUTION: Talk to your doctor or pharmacist before taking any other medications, including over-the-counter (OTC) medications, vitamins or herbal supplements.**
- Apply a broken aloe vera leaf to the burned area to soothe the pain.
- While caring for your burn at home, be aware of signs of infection (redness around the area or red streaks leading away from it, swelling, warmth or tenderness, pus, fever of 101° F [38.3° C] or higher and tender or swollen lymph nodes), which can develop in 24 to 48 hours. If signs of infection are present, call your doctor now.

Second-degree or partial thickness burns

- Treat like first-degree burns if they are no bigger than 2 to 3 inches (5 to 8 centimeters) in diameter and not on the face, hands, feet, groin, buttocks, a major joint or completely encircling a digit or extremity—in which case you should **seek emergency care.**

Third-degree or full thickness burns

- Cover the burned area with a cool, damp, sterile dressing or clean cloth and **seek emergency care.**

PREVENTION ✓

- Conduct fire drills at home and work. Know the location of fire escapes when you sleep away from home.
- Install smoke detectors in every bedroom and on every floor and test them periodically.
- Keep emergency numbers by the telephone.
- Place a fire extinguisher in the kitchen and check the expiration date on a routine basis.
- Keep a large box of baking soda within easy reach of the stove.
- Keep a potted aloe vera plant in the kitchen (where most burns occur) to use the fresh jelly for treating minor burns.
- Never put lighter fluid on lit charcoal briquettes.
- Only use kerosene or other space heaters that have the UL (Underwriter's Laboratory) seal of approval.
- Always follow safety instructions when using chemicals, and note any warnings or precautions on the container.
- Learn how to deal with an overheated engine, car fire, or live wire on a car.
- Never touch a downed electrical wire.
- Know where all electrical wiring is located before starting construction or renovation. This also applies to any kind of outdoor digging.
- Check with your utility company if you are unsure about the location of power lines in your area.

FINAL NOTES ✓

For all Types of Burns

- NEVER apply ointments, such as Vaseline, sprays, butter, oils or creams. They may slow healing and increase the risk of infection. Use cool water instead.
- NEVER cover a burn with materials such as blankets, towels or tissue, since fibers may become stuck to the wound. Use a clean sheet or sterile dressing.
- NEVER break blisters. Blisters protect the burn from infection and should only be ruptured if swelling constricts circulation.

Heat Exhaustion

Heat exhaustion occurs when your body is not able to cool off and maintain a comfortable temperature. Hot weather, excessive exercise and dehydration can cause the body to overheat. Older adults or people who are frail, obese or have a chronic illness are at risk, as are people in poor condition who overexert themselves.

NOTE YOUR SYMPTOMS ✓

- Headache
- Weakness
- Fatigue
- Dizziness
- Nausea
- Shallow breathing
- Muscle cramps
- Profuse sweating, cool, clammy skin, or a body temperature slightly elevated or lower than normal

WHAT YOU CAN DO ✓

If You are Overheating:

- Move to a cooler place and remain quiet.
- Loosen clothing.
- If you are dizzy, lie down with your head lower than your feet.
- Drink small amounts of liquid frequently.
- Place a cool, wet cloth on your forehead.
- Watch for signs of shock and heatstroke. (See *Shock*, p. 39.)
- Do not consume alcohol or apply it to the skin.

PREVENTION ✓

- Drink more than 10 eight-ounce glasses of water a day if you exercise or work in hot weather.
- Stay in the shade or air-conditioned areas. Avoid sudden changes of temperature.
- Wear loose-fitting, light-colored clothing of natural fibers such as cotton or linen.
- Limit your activity and exercise during the hottest time of the day.
- Never leave a person alone in a closed auto in hot weather.

Decision *helper* Heat Exhaustion
DO THESE APPLY:

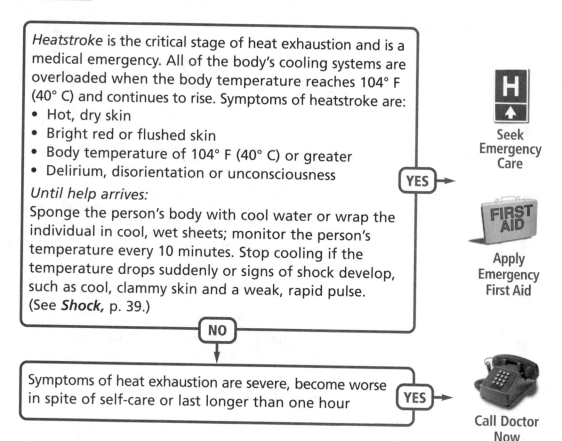

Heatstroke is the critical stage of heat exhaustion and is a medical emergency. All of the body's cooling systems are overloaded when the body temperature reaches 104° F (40° C) and continues to rise. Symptoms of heatstroke are:
- Hot, dry skin
- Bright red or flushed skin
- Body temperature of 104° F (40° C) or greater
- Delirium, disorientation or unconsciousness

Until help arrives:
Sponge the person's body with cool water or wrap the individual in cool, wet sheets; monitor the person's temperature every 10 minutes. Stop cooling if the temperature drops suddenly or signs of shock develop, such as cool, clammy skin and a weak, rapid pulse. (See *Shock,* p. 39.)

YES → Seek Emergency Care

Apply Emergency First Aid

NO

Symptoms of heat exhaustion are severe, become worse in spite of self-care or last longer than one hour **YES →**

Call Doctor Now

Hypothermia and Frostbite

In *hypothermia* your body temperature drops below normal when body heat is lost faster than it can be produced. *Frostbite* is the freezing of the skin or tissue near the skin surface. These conditions usually occur in freezing weather, but hypothermia can also occur when the weather is windy or wet, yet still above freezing. Older adults, especially frail and inactive people, are particularly susceptible. Small children are also at higher risk.

NOTE YOUR SYMPTOMS ✓

Hypothermia

This condition can develop quickly and become a serious problem with little warning. Early symptoms include severe shivering, slurred speech, apathy, impaired judgment and cold, pale skin. As the body temperature continues to drop, shivering may stop; abdomen and chest muscles become hard, and there is slowing of the pulse and breathing. Weakness, drowsiness and confusion may quickly lead to unconsciousness.

Frostbite

Initially the skin feels soft to the touch but is numb and tingly and may turn white. As the skin freezes and becomes hard, blisters may develop. In third-degree frostbite the skin may look blue or blotchy and the underlying tissue is hard and very cold.

WHAT YOU CAN DO ✓

Treat for hypothermia before treating frostbite.

Hypothermia

- Get the person to warm, dry shelter.
- Re-warm the individual slowly. Keep him or her awake.
- Replace wet clothing with dry clothes, sleeping bags or blankets, and apply body heat from another person, if possible.
- If the person is alert, give him or her warm liquids and high-calorie food. **Do not give alcohol.**

Frostbite

- Re-warm the person as soon as possible if refreezing **will not** occur.
- Warm small areas with your breath or by placing your hands next to bare skin.
- Immerse frostbitten areas in warm (not hot) water (104° to 108° F [40° to 42.2° C]) for 20 to 40 minutes.
- Elevate and protect the warmed part.
- Do not rub or massage a frozen area—further damage can occur.
- Protect blisters. Do not break them.
- Aspirin, ibuprofen (Advil, Motrin) or acetaminophen (Tylenol) may ease painful burning. **NEVER give aspirin to children/teenagers unless your health care provider orders it. It can cause Reye's syndrome, a rare but often fatal condition. CAUTION: Talk to your doctor or pharmacist before taking any other medications, including over-the-counter (OTC) medications, vitamins or herbal supplements.**
- Watch for signs of infection. (See *Decision helper,* p. 36.)

PREVENTION ✓

- Dress warmly in layers with wool and polypropylene for insulation and an outer layer that is windproof and waterproof.
- Wear a warm hat with ear protection. Wear mittens rather than gloves.
- Pace your activities. Do not become exhausted or sweaty.
- Avoid alcohol and smoking before spending time in the cold.
- Eat well and carry extra food.
- Plan ahead and carry provisions for emergencies or sudden weather changes.

See *Decision helper,* p. 36.

Decision *helper* Hypothermia and Frostbite
DO THESE APPLY:

- Unconsciousness
- Slowing in pulse and breathing
- Rigid or stiff body
- Dilated pupils
- Weakness, drowsiness or confusion
- Severe shivering or shivering that has stopped without warming having occurred
- Slurred speech
- Cold, blue extremities
- White and very hard skin (like a block of wood)
- No feeling or function in the affected body part

Until help arrives:
see **What You Can Do, Hypothermia,** p. 35

YES →

Seek Emergency Care

Apply Emergency First Aid

NO

- Possible hypothermia and the person is a small child or is elderly or frail
- After the skin thaws:
  - There is considerable pain, numbness or tingling or the skin is mottled red, purplish, blotchy blue or black
  - Blisters develop
- Signs of infection occur 24 to 48 hours after frostbite **YES** →
  (redness around the area or red streaks leading away from it; swelling; warmth or tenderness; pus; fever of 101° F [38.3° C] or higher; tender or swollen lymph nodes)

Until you are seen by a doctor:
see **What You Can Do, Frostbite,** p. 35.

Call Doctor Now

Unconsciousness

When people are unconscious, they are completely unaware of themselves and their surroundings. They have no control over body functions or movement. Usually they are not able to recall or remember any of the time spent in an unconscious state. Causes of unconsciousness include stroke, epilepsy, diabetic coma, head injury, alcohol intoxication, poisoning, heart attack, bleeding, electrocution and shock.

WHAT YOU CAN DO ☑

If Someone has Lost Consciousness

- Call for emergency medical assistance.
- Check for breathing. If necessary, open the airway and begin rescue breathing. (See *CPR*, p. 20 and *Choking*, p. 24.)
- Check for signs of circulation, such as breathing, coughing or movement in response to stimulation. If there are none, begin CPR. (See *CPR*, p. 20.)
- Keep the person warm unless you suspect heatstroke. (See *Heat Exhaustion*, p. 32.)
- Lay the person down face up, with the head below heart level. Move the individual as little as possible and only to provide life support or safety. **DO NOT move the person if you suspect a head or neck injury.** (See *Head/Spinal Injury*, p. 55.)
- If there is vomit in the mouth, turn the person on his or her side to allow fluids to drain out.
- Look for medical identification or a possible cause of unconsciousness.
- Do not give the individual anything to eat or drink.

See *Decision helper*, p. 38.

Decision *helper* Unconsciousness
DO THESE APPLY:

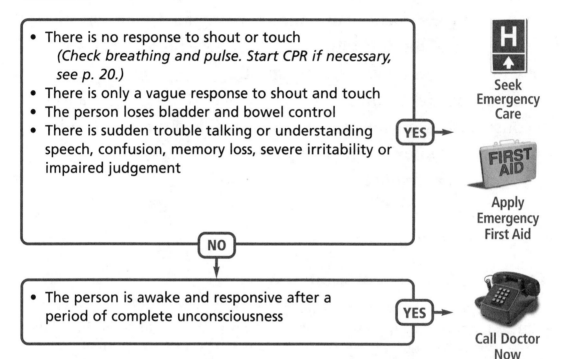

- There is no response to shout or touch
  (Check breathing and pulse. Start CPR if necessary, see p. 20.)
- There is only a vague response to shout and touch
- The person loses bladder and bowel control
- There is sudden trouble talking or understanding speech, confusion, memory loss, severe irritability or impaired judgement

YES ➔

H ↑
Seek Emergency Care

FIRST AID
Apply Emergency First Aid

NO

- The person is awake and responsive after a period of complete unconsciousness

YES ➔

Call Doctor Now

Shock

If your vital organs are unable to get the blood and oxygen they need, your body can go into shock. Many conditions can cause this urgent situation, including an injury, bleeding, pain, poisoning, extremely high or low body temperature, allergic reaction or a severe illness. **Shock is always an emergency and requires professional medical help immediately.**

WHAT YOU CAN DO ✓

Preparing for an Emergency

- Learn your local emergency phone numbers. Post them somewhere handy.
- Wear identification to alert medical help if you have any allergies or chronic medical conditions.

When You See Signs of Shock

- Act immediately when you see any signs of shock. Do not wait to see if the person improves on his or her own.
- Call your local emergency services number. Then, while you wait for help to arrive:
  - Have the person lie down and elevate the legs higher than the heart, with support. **If a head or neck injury is suspected, keep the person flat and do not move him or her.** (See *Head/Spinal Injury*, p. 55.)
  - If vomiting begins, roll the person onto his or her side to allow fluid to drain out.
  - Control bleeding by applying direct pressure to the wound. (See *Control Severe Bleeding*, p. 43.)
  - Keep the person warm unless the cause of shock is heatstroke. (See *Heat Exhaustion*, p. 32.)

- Note the time. Take and record the person's pulse rate every five minutes. (Feel for the heartbeat in the person's wrist or side of the neck with the tips of your index and middle fingers. Count the number of beats in 15 seconds and multiply by four: 30 beats in 15 seconds x 4 = a pulse rate of 120 beats/minute.)
- Do not give the individual anything to eat or drink.
- Comfort and reassure the person while waiting for medical assistance.
- Look for evidence of a cause, such as poison nearby.
- Check for medical-alert identification.

 **Shock**

DO THESE APPLY:

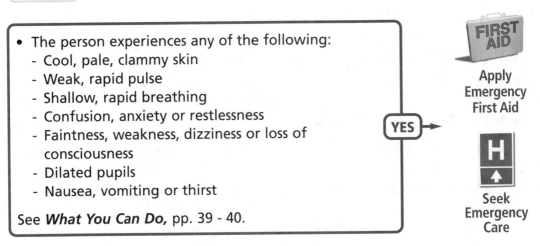

- The person experiences any of the following:
  - Cool, pale, clammy skin
  - Weak, rapid pulse
  - Shallow, rapid breathing
  - Confusion, anxiety or restlessness
  - Faintness, weakness, dizziness or loss of consciousness
  - Dilated pupils
  - Nausea, vomiting or thirst

See *What You Can Do,* pp. 39 - 40.

YES →

FIRST AID

Apply Emergency First Aid

H ↑

Seek Emergency Care

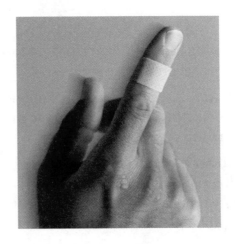

SECTION 2
Injuries

Wounds

As the body ages, the healing process begins to slow. Injuries that might once have been minor may now become more serious.

There are three kinds of wounds: cuts, abrasions and punctures. All of them—no matter how small—should be cared for quickly to promote healing, prevent infection and reduce scarring.

Get a routine tetanus booster every 10 years and keep up-to-date immunization records. If you have a dirty wound or a puncture and have not had a tetanus booster within the last five years, or if you have not completed your primary series, your doctor will probably recommend a booster injection.

Cuts

Shallow, minor cuts (*lacerations*) that are limited to the skin and the fatty tissue beneath, rarely cause permanent damage and usually can be treated at home easily.

In most minor cuts, bleeding is slow and stops on its own after a few minutes. Slightly deeper cuts can reach the veins and cause steady blood flow that is slow and dark red. Pressure on the wound usually stops bleeding after a short period. A cut that strikes an artery causes profuse bleeding and can be difficult to control even with pressure on the wound. Blood is bright red and comes in spurts as the heart beats. A person with severe bleeding can slip into shock. (See *Shock*, p. 39, and *Control Severe Bleeding*, p. 43.)

Stitches are usually not necessary if the edges of the cut can be pulled together with a bandage or sterile adhesive tape—except on the face, where scarring may be a problem. However, your doctor may *suture* (stitch) cuts in areas subject to frequent movement (such as fingers), or cuts more than one inch (2.5 cm) long, deep or having jagged edges. Generally, suturing should take place within eight hours of injury for best results. Call your doctor if you're not sure whether you need stitches.

WHAT YOU CAN DO ☑

Control Severe Bleeding

- **Dial 911 or your local emergency services number.** While waiting for help to arrive:
  - Have the injured person lie down with the head slightly lower than the body. Elevate the legs and the site of the bleeding.
  - Keep the person warm to lessen the possibility of shock. (See *Shock,* p. 39.)
  - Remove large pieces of dirt and debris from the wound, but only if it can be done easily. **DO NOT remove any impaled objects or try to clean the wound.** (See *Punctures,* p. 46.)
  - Place a clean cloth over the wound and apply direct, steady pressure for 15 minutes. To avoid transmission of blood-borne infections, use your bare hands only if necessary. Wash your hands thoroughly after contact with blood.
  - **DO NOT apply direct pressure if there is an object in the wound or a protruding or visible bone.** Apply pressure around the wound instead.
  - If the first cloth becomes soaked with blood, apply a fresh one over it while continuing steady pressure. Do not remove used bandages.
  - If bleeding does not slow or stop after 15 minutes, apply firm, continuous pressure on a pressure point between the wound and the heart to restrict blood flow through the major arteries. Pressure points are located on the inside upper arms and on the upper thighs in the groin area.
  - **DO NOT apply a tourniquet, which can result in loss of a limb due to lack of circulation.**

Give Prompt Attention to Minor Wounds

- Apply pressure on the wound for 10 or 15 minutes to stop bleeding, if necessary.
- Gently clean the cut with soap and water and a clean cloth. Be sure to remove dirt, glass and other particles.
- Keep the cut uncovered and exposed to air, if possible.
- If the wound is slightly gaping, pull its edges together with a regular or butterfly bandage. If necessary, cover the wound with dry gauze and tape. Change the gauze daily, but don't take the butterfly bandage off until the wound has knit together.
- If you must cover a cut that doesn't require a butterfly bandage, apply antibiotic ointment to a gauze pad and tape the pad over the wound. Change the dressing once a day or whenever it gets wet.

Watch for Signs of Infection

Thorough cleansing of the wound is the best way to prevent infection and speed healing. Infection is more likely when a cut occurs in an area that is difficult to keep clean and dry, such as a hand or foot. Signs of infection may begin about 24 to 48 hours after the injury. They include redness around the area or red streaks leading away from it, swelling, warmth or tenderness, pus, fever of 101° F (38.3° C) or higher and tender or swollen lymph nodes.

FINAL NOTES ☑

Deep cuts can sever or damage major blood vessels, nerves or tendons, so it is important to know the signs of a serious laceration. In general, be concerned more with cuts to the face, hands, chest, abdomen or back, which have the potential to be more critical than lacerations to other areas.

See *Decision helper,* pp. 47 - 48.

Abrasions

Scrapes, or *abrasions,* can result from falls or other accidents that scratch and tear the first few layers of skin. The injury is shallow but can be very painful because millions of nerve endings are exposed. The pain usually subsides within a few days as scabs form. These injuries are usually very dirty and must be cleaned thoroughly to prevent infection.

WHAT YOU CAN DO ✓

- Place an ice pack over the wound for a few minutes to alleviate most of the pain. For protection, place a washcloth between bare skin and ice.
- Clean the area with soap and warm water, making sure to remove all dirt and foreign particles.
- Leave skin flaps in place to act as a natural bandage. Dirty skin flaps can be cut away carefully with nail scissors. Stop cutting if it hurts.
- Use a pain reliever such as aspirin, acetaminophen (Tylenol) or ibuprofen (Advil, Motrin) if mild pain persists. **NEVER give aspirin to children/teenagers unless your health care provider orders it. It can cause Reye's syndrome, a rare but often fatal condition. CAUTION: Talk to your doctor or pharmacist before taking any other medications, including over-the-counter (OTC) medications, vitamins or herbal supplements.**
- Watch for signs of infection. (See *Decision helper,* p. 48.)

Large or painful scrapes can be treated with antibiotic ointment and covered with a sterile, nonstick bandage. Put the ointment on the bandage, rather than rubbing it on the scrape. Before trying to remove a dressing that has stuck to the skin, soak the area in warm water.

See *Decision helper,* pp. 47 - 48.

Punctures

A *puncture* wound is a penetrating injury with a sharp-pointed object such as a nail. Seemingly minor puncture wounds sometimes can cause considerable internal damage and—because they can be hard to clean—can become easily infected. If you have not had a tetanus booster within the last five years or if you have not completed your primary series, your doctor will probably recommend a *tetanus* shot to prevent tetanus infection ("lockjaw").

WHAT YOU CAN DO ✓

- **Seek emergency medical care if an object, such as a knife, projects from or is embedded in the skin.** Never try to pull the object out, since this could cause further injury. Very gently place a clean, damp cloth around the wound. (For smaller objects, see *Splinters,* p. 75.)
- Allow the wound to bleed freely to cleanse itself. Don't apply pressure unless blood is spurting out or excessive. (See *Control Severe Bleeding,* p. 43.)
- If the puncture wound isn't serious enough to need emergency medical attention, wash it thoroughly with soap and water. Remove dirt carefully, using tweezers wiped with alcohol to extract debris. Pat the wound dry with a clean cloth. Small wounds will stop bleeding on their own. For others, you may need to apply pressure with a gauze pad or clean cloth and elevate the area above the level of the heart. Avoid contact with blood if possible. Wash your hands thoroughly after touching blood.
- Strong antiseptics, such as Mercurochrome and Merthiolate, aren't necessary and may cause pain. Nonprescription antibiotic ointments, such as Neosporin and bacitracin, may help prevent infection. Apply them to the side of the bandage that touches the wound, rather than to the wound itself.
- Cover the wound with a sterile bandage. Change the dressing at least once a day and keep the area clean and dry.
- Watch closely for signs of infection. (See *Decision helper,* p. 48.)
- Keep a well-stocked first-aid kit on hand. (See *Home Pharmacy,* p. 331.)

FINAL NOTES ☑

Any wound that doesn't heal well within two weeks should be seen by a doctor. Infection is a common and potentially serious complication that can occur even with minor wounds. (See *Decision helper*, p. 48.) An infected wound takes longer to heal and is more likely to scar.

Decision *helper* Cuts/Abrasions/Punctures
DO THESE APPLY:

- Bleeding is steady, profuse, or occurs in rhythmic spurts
- Signs of shock are present: weakness; confusion; cold, pale, moist skin (see **Shock**, p. 39)
- Breathing is shallow and the pulse is weak and rapid
- The wound is deep and penetrates muscle or bone
- An object, such as a knife, projects from or is embedded in the wound (see **What You Can Do, Punctures**, p. 46)

YES →

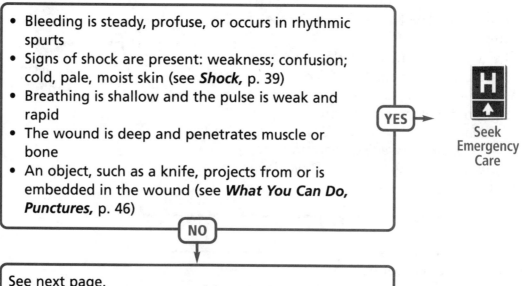

Seek Emergency Care

NO

See next page.

Do these apply: See previous page.

- Bleeding persists despite applying pressure and elevating the wound for 10 to 15 minutes
- The wound is severe and you have difficulty moving the limb or digit, or you have numbness or tingling near the injury
- The wound edges cannot be pulled together easily
- You suspect the wound needs suturing
- The wound involves the head, face, chest, hand or abdomen
- The wound is difficult to clean thoroughly
- The wound is extremely dirty and/or you are uncertain whether there is foreign material in it
- Signs of infection are present
  (redness around the area or red streaks leading away from it; swelling; warmth or tenderness; pus; fever of 101° F [38.3° C] or higher; tender or swollen lymph nodes)

YES →

**Call Doctor
Now**

NO

- The wound has not healed within two weeks
- You have a serious chronic condition and have sustained a wound
- You think you need a tetanus booster or you have not completed your primary series (see *Wounds,* p. 42)

YES →

Call Doctor

NO

See *What You Can Do,* p. 46.

→

**Apply
Self-Care**

Bites/Stings

If you have ever experienced an allergic reaction to a bite or sting, ask your doctor about wearing a medical-alert bracelet and getting a prescription for a kit to prevent *anaphylaxis,* a severe and sometimes fatal allergic reaction. If you're planning outdoor activities such as camping, contact your local health department before you depart to get specific rabies information for the area you will visit.

Animal/Human Bites

The most common type of animal bites involve pets—usually cats and dogs. Overall, about 5 percent of bites become infected. Cat bites become infected 20 to 50 percent of the time. Adult human bites, which become infected in 15 to 30 percent of cases, most frequently result from injuries sustained in fist fights. Bites like these, which break the skin, can cause several types of serious infections:

- Infection caused by various bacteria or microorganisms that can enter the wound
- Pasteurella infection, commonly caused by cat bites
- Tetanus, which can develop after any kind of bite if you have not been inoculated within the last five years or if you have not completed your primary series of tetanus shots
- Rabies, most commonly from bites by skunks, bats, raccoons, coyotes, foxes and other wild mammals and by unvaccinated domestic pets

WHAT YOU CAN DO ✓

Immediately After Being Bitten

- Get emergency care if the bite seems serious or affects the face or hands.

- Rinse and clean the wound immediately.
- Blood flow helps cleanse the wound. Control excessive bleeding by wrapping the wound with a bandage and applying direct pressure. (See *Control Severe Bleeding,* p. 43.)
- Watch for signs of infection, usually within 24 to 48 hours. (See *Decision helper,* p. 53.)
- Report all animal bites to the local health department, especially if the bite is from a wild animal or domestic animal whose rabies vaccination status is unknown. A domestic animal with uncertain rabies vaccination status should be observed for 15 days even if the animal appears healthy.

PREVENTION ✓

- Treat all unfamiliar pets with caution.
- Don't try to touch any wild animal, especially if it appears sick.
- Obey "Beware of Dog" signs.
- Never leave an infant, young child or defenseless person unattended with a pet, especially a large dog.

See *Decision helper,* pp. 53 - 54.

Insects, Spiders and Scorpions

Most insect bites and stings are minor and cause reactions that are *localized* (affecting a limited area). However, a bite from a poisonous spider such as a black widow or brown recluse, or a sting from a scorpion, can cause serious problems.

Even a seemingly harmless bite or sting can be dangerous to people with allergies. Some people are so sensitive to bites and stings that *anaphylaxis* can occur quickly. This potentially life-threatening complication involves extreme breathing difficulty, constriction of the chest, swelling of the mouth, lips, tongue or throat, erratic pulse, severe hives and itching, or violent coughing.

WHAT YOU CAN DO ☑

To know whether you need emergency care, see *Decision helper,* p. 53.

If Emergency Care is Required

Until emergency care can be obtained:

- Use an anaphylactic kit if one is available.
- Apply ice or cold water to the bite for five minutes. For protection, place a washcloth between the bare skin and the ice.
- If the bite is on a hand or foot, keep the limb snugly bandaged above the bite for five minutes (but make sure you can feel a pulse below the bandage). Do not apply a tourniquet.
- Keep the limb below the level of the heart.
- Remove any stinger left in the skin. (See next page.)

When Emergency Care is Not Required

- Scrape or flick out any stinger that may be left in the skin with a credit card or your fingernail. Avoid squeezing the stinger.
- Apply ice for 15 to 20 minutes at a time, more frequently initially, then three to four times a day for up to 48 hours. Leave ice off for at least 15 minutes between applications. For protection, place a washcloth between bare skin and ice and change the cloth if it becomes wet.
- Wash the area with soap and water.
- Use calamine lotion or over-the-counter (OTC) hydrocortisone cream to reduce itching and inflammation.
- If itching becomes severe, try an OTC oral antihistamine such as Benadryl or Chlor-Trimeton. Many antihistamines, especially over-the-counter ones, may cause drowsiness or inattention and lead to accidents. Talk to your physician or pharmacist about the risk of sedation with your antihistamines.

PREVENTION ✓

- Avoid wearing perfume if you'll be spending time outdoors—it attracts bees.
- Get reliable instructions before trying to remove a beehive or nest. Follow directions on commercial products.
- If you are allergic to bees, always carry an anaphylactic kit. You can get one with a prescription from your doctor.

 **Bites/Stings**
DO THESE APPLY:

- You experience symptoms of an allergic reaction following a bite: extreme breathing difficulty, constriction in the chest, swelling of the mouth, lips, tongue or throat, erratic pulse, severe hives and itching or violent coughing
- You are bitten by a black widow or brown recluse spider, poisonous insect or marine animal or reptile
- You have a known sensitivity or allergy to an insect, spider, scorpion, reptile or mammal
- You have a serious bite, especially if it affects the face or hand

YES →

Seek Emergency Care

Apply Emergency First Aid

NO ↓

- An animal or human bite or scratch breaks the skin
- A bite that doesn't break the skin is from a wild animal, a domestic cat or dog that hasn't been vaccinated for rabies or any animal that displays bizarre behavior
- Signs of infection are present
  (redness around the area or red streaks leading away from it; swelling; warmth or tenderness; pus; fever of 101° F [38.3° C] or higher; tender or swollen lymph nodes)

YES →

Call Doctor Now

NO ↓

See next page.

Do these apply: See previous page.

- You are exposed to a bat, but are not bitten or scratched
- You are bitten by a human or animal and you have not had a tetanus shot in five or more years or you have not completed your primary series
- Illness occurs one to two weeks after a cat bite or scratch or a rat bite

YES

Call Doctor

NO

See *What You Can Do,* p. 49, 50, 51, 52.
See *Punctures,* p. 46.

Apply
Self-Care

Other Injuries

Head/Spinal Injury

Any significant trauma to the head or spine is cause for concern because of the potential for injury to the delicate structures within the brain and spinal cord. This can be serious and requires professional medical assistance. Fortunately, most injuries are minor, limited to the surrounding protective tissues, and can be treated with self-care.

WHAT YOU CAN DO ✓

Head Injury

Following an injury to the head, treat any surface injury, protect from additional damage, and watch for signs of internal bleeding. Observation for at least 72 hours is important since bleeding inside the skull may be slow and symptoms may develop gradually.

- If there is external bleeding, apply pressure on the wound for 15 minutes or until the bleeding stops completely. Use a clean cloth; if the blood soaks through, apply additional cloths over the first one.
- Apply ice or cold packs to ease pain and reduce swelling. For protection, place a washcloth between bare skin and ice. A "goose egg" may develop.
- Check for other injuries, especially to the neck and back.
- Keep the person sitting or lying down with the head slightly elevated to decrease swelling.
- Check for signs of bleeding inside the skull immediately after the injury, then every two hours for the first 24 hours, every four hours for the following 24 hours, and every eight hours through the third day. Signs include:
  - **Changes in mental state** that may include unconsciousness, confusion, a decrease in alertness, abnormally deep sleep, or difficulty waking up

- Unequal pupil size after the injury; some people normally have different
  pupil sizes, but a change after an injury can be a serious sign
- **Severe, forceful vomiting** that is repeated or continuous (one single
  episode of vomiting may be a reaction to the pain)
- **Weakness in the arms or legs or difficulty moving** parts of the body or a
  change in the ability to see, smell, hear, taste or touch
- Watch for bleeding or clear drainage from the nose or ears, and for fever.
- Avoid heavy exercise or exertion for at least 72 hours.
- Be alert to chronic headache or changes in personality for weeks to months
  after a head injury. These may be signs of very slow internal bleeding, which
  can cause pressure on the brain much later.

Spinal Injury

Injury to the spine can occur in any accident involving the head, neck or back.
Self-care is directed toward preventing additional damage and permanent
paralysis, decreasing symptoms and eliminating future injury.

WHAT YOU CAN DO ✓

If you suspect an injury to the spine:
- **DO NOT MOVE THE PERSON** unless there is an immediate threat to life,
  such as a fire.
- Call for professional medical help to move the person. Keep the person still
  and warm. Do not give the individual anything to eat or drink.
- If there is immediate danger and you must move the person, **immobilize the
  neck and back.** Slide a board or other firm surface under the person's head
  and back without moving either from the position it was in. Place soft, bulky
  material on each side of the head to prevent rotation.
- In a diving or surfing accident, do not pull the person from the water unless
  his or her life is endangered. Float the person face up. If you must move the
  individual, use a board that supports the area from the head to the buttocks.
  Lift him or her out of the water on the board.
- If there is much bleeding from the nose or mouth, roll the person onto his
  or her side (the entire body needs to roll in one, even movement) without
  twisting the neck or back. If the bleeding is minor, wipe out the mouth and
  nose without moving the individual.

PREVENTION ✓

- Wear your seat belt while in all motor vehicles.
- Wear a helmet while skating or riding a bicycle, motorcycle or horse.
- Don't dive into shallow or unfamiliar water.

Decision *helper* Head/Spinal Injury
DO THESE APPLY:

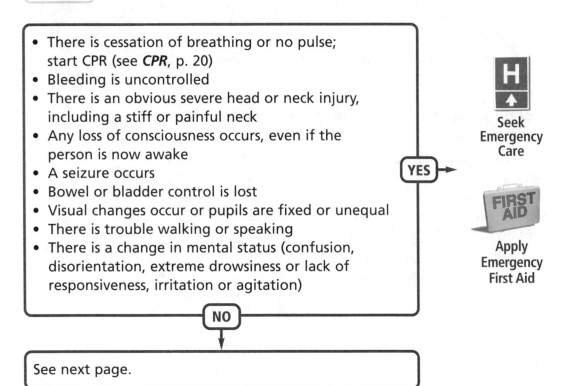

- There is cessation of breathing or no pulse; start CPR (see *CPR*, p. 20)
- Bleeding is uncontrolled
- There is an obvious severe head or neck injury, including a stiff or painful neck
- Any loss of consciousness occurs, even if the person is now awake
- A seizure occurs
- Bowel or bladder control is lost
- Visual changes occur or pupils are fixed or unequal
- There is trouble walking or speaking
- There is a change in mental status (confusion, disorientation, extreme drowsiness or lack of responsiveness, irritation or agitation)

YES →

H ↑
Seek Emergency Care

FIRST AID
Apply Emergency First Aid

NO ↓

See next page.

Do these apply: See previous page.

- A laceration may need stitches
- Fluid drains from the nose or an ear
- Vomiting occurs more than twice
- You have a severe headache
- You receive a forceful impact with a very hard object
- A fall results in a forceful impact on the head or neck
- New bruising appears around the eyes or behind both ears
- You have a past head injury with later increasing or recurrent headache, difficulty concentrating, memory loss, or personality change

YES

Call Doctor Now

NO

- You have a minor injury and no immediate signs of brain or spinal injury

See *What You Can Do, Head Injury,* p. 55.
See *What You Can Do, Spinal Injury,* p. 56.

Apply Self-Care

Accidental Tooth Loss

When a tooth is knocked out, your dentist may be able to re-implant it successfully if the tooth tissue is kept alive. Your chances of saving a tooth are good up to one hour after injury.

WHAT YOU CAN DO ✓

When You Injure or Lose a Tooth

- Avoid touching the root end of the tooth.
- As long as the tooth is not contaminated or dirty and you feel alert, place the tooth back in the gum socket or hold it in the pouch of your cheek where saliva and blood will protect it.
- If you are unable to place the tooth in your mouth, put it in cold milk or water.
- Do not clean, wash or scrape the tooth; this may cause more damage.

PREVENTION ✓

- Wear a helmet when riding a bicycle or motorcycle.
- Know how to reach your dentist in an emergency.

Decision helper Accidental Tooth Loss
DO THESE APPLY:

- A tooth is knocked out with no other signs of head or facial injury

See **What You Can Do,** this page.

Request an emergency appointment for re-implantation by your dentist. Bring the tooth with you.

YES →

Call Dentist

Bruises

Bruises (*contusions*) usually result from a blow or fall that causes small blood vessels to rupture under the skin and blood to seep into the surrounding tissues. Bruises usually appear as red or purple areas and then change color—to green, yellow and brown—before disappearing. The process typically takes 10 to 14 days.

As you become older, you are increasingly susceptible to bruising. This is because you lose thickness in the layer of fat that protects your skin and tissue, and your *capillaries* (small blood vessels connecting arteries and veins) are more fragile. People who regularly take *anticoagulants* (medicine that prevents or delays the blood from clotting), aspirin or other medications may bruise even more easily.

Soft Tissue Injury

A soft tissue injury is similar to a bruise but involves damage to muscles and larger blood vessels, resulting in oozing of blood and swelling within the muscles or damaged tissues under the skin. Don't be misled into thinking these injuries can be ignored just because they may not result in discoloration like bruises. They can be serious and may require a doctor's care.

WHAT YOU CAN DO ✓

- Apply ice for 15 to 20 minutes at a time, more frequently initially, then three to four times a day for up to 48 hours. Leave ice off for at least 15 minutes between applications. For protection, place a washcloth between bare skin and ice and change the cloth if it becomes wet.
- Elevate the bruised area to reduce swelling and discomfort.

- Use a pain reliever such as aspirin, acetaminophen (Tylenol) or ibuprofen (Advil, Motrin) if mild pain persists. **NEVER give aspirin to children/teenagers unless your health care provider orders it. It can cause Reye's syndrome, a rare but often fatal condition. CAUTION: Talk to your doctor or pharmacist before taking any other medications, including over-the-counter (OTC) medications, vitamins or herbal supplements.**
- Apply a bandage only if the skin is broken.

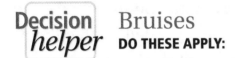

Decision **Bruises**
helper **DO THESE APPLY:**

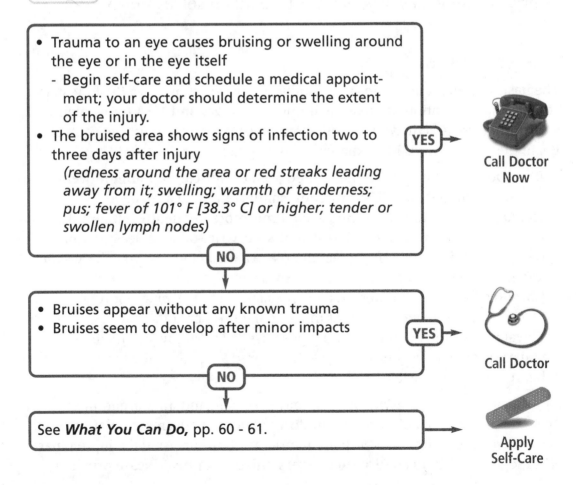

- Trauma to an eye causes bruising or swelling around the eye or in the eye itself
  - Begin self-care and schedule a medical appointment; your doctor should determine the extent of the injury.
- The bruised area shows signs of infection two to three days after injury
  (redness around the area or red streaks leading away from it; swelling; warmth or tenderness; pus; fever of 101° F [38.3° C] or higher; tender or swollen lymph nodes)

YES → **Call Doctor Now**

NO

- Bruises appear without any known trauma
- Bruises seem to develop after minor impacts

YES → **Call Doctor**

NO

See *What You Can Do,* pp. 60 - 61.

→ **Apply Self-Care**

Strains and Sprains

A *strain* is an injury to a muscle caused by over-stretching. Also called a "pulled muscle," a strain occurs when a muscle's elastic fibers are overextended and contract, tear and bleed. A *sprain* is an injury to a ligament and other soft tissue around a joint. *Ligaments* are bands of fiber that connect the bones at a joint. They can be stretched or torn when a joint is twisted, "jammed" or overextended. With either injury, bleeding may produce a bruise that resolves slowly.

WHAT YOU CAN DO ✓

The basic treatment for strains and sprains is a two-part process: **RICE** (rest, ice, compression, elevation) to treat the immediate injury and **MSA** (movement, strength, alternate activity) to help the injury heal and prevent further problems. Begin the RICE process **immediately** following the injury:

- **Rest.** Do not put weight on the injured joint or muscle, and limit movement in the area of the injury. Use crutches, splints or a sling as needed.
- **Ice.** Apply ice for 15 to 20 minutes at a time, more frequently initially, then three to four times a day for up to 48 hours. Leave ice off for at least 15 minutes between applications. For protection, place a washcloth between bare skin and ice and change the cloth if it becomes wet.
- **Compress.** Wrap the injured area in an elastic bandage for support and protection. Don't wrap it so tight that circulation is cut off.
- **Elevate.** Place the injured part on pillows while you apply ice and anytime you are seated or lying down. Raise the injured area above the level of your heart whenever possible.

Aspirin and ibuprofen (Advil, Motrin) may ease pain and inflammation. Acetaminophen (Tylenol) eases discomfort but does not decrease inflammation. Do not use other drugs to mask pain in order to continue using the injured part. **NEVER give aspirin to children/teenagers unless your health care provider** orders it. It can cause Reye's syndrome, a rare but often fatal condition. CAUTION: Talk to your doctor or pharmacist before taking any other medications, including over-the-counter (OTC) medications, vitamins or herbal supplements.

The **MSA** process can be started only if the initial swelling is gone:

- **Movement**. Begin gently moving the joint to resume full range of motion.
- **Strength**. After the swelling is gone and full range of motion is restored, gradually begin to strengthen the injured part. Slow, gentle stretching during the healing process will make scar tissue flexible and prevent limited movement later.
- **Alternate activities**. Resume regular exercise through activities and sports that do not place a strain on the injured area. Go slowly and stop any activity that causes discomfort.

Any increase in pain or return of swelling is a sign to stop **MSA** and resume **RICE**.

Heat can be applied once swelling stops increasing to relieve muscle spasm and increase circulation. Place a warm washcloth, water bottle or heating pad directly on the injured area for 20 minutes at a time. Use caution with heat to prevent burns.

PREVENTION ✓

- Use correct form in all work and play activities.
- Adjust equipment and furniture to fit your needs.
- Go slowly when starting a new activity or sport.
- Use warm-up and cool-down exercises to help your body prepare and recover safely. Don't forget to stretch.
- Take frequent breaks when performing any continuous activity.
- Do not push beyond your strength or ability; advance your skill level gradually.

See *Decision helper,* p. 64.

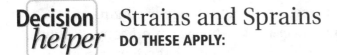

Decision *helper* — Strains and Sprains

DO THESE APPLY:

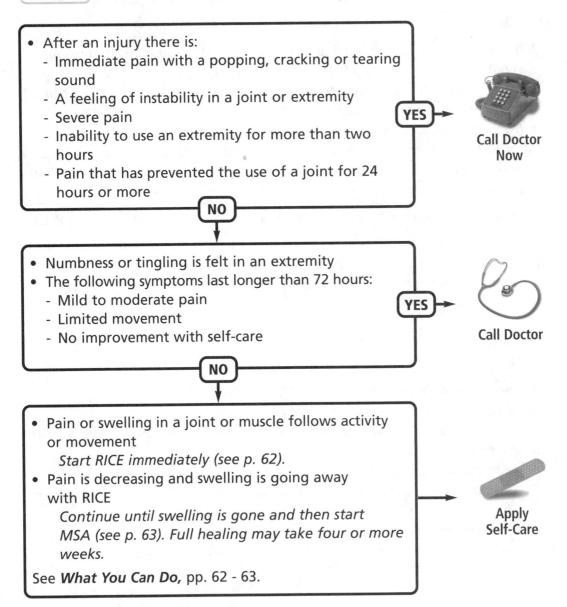

- After an injury there is:
  - Immediate pain with a popping, cracking or tearing sound
  - A feeling of instability in a joint or extremity
  - Severe pain
  - Inability to use an extremity for more than two hours
  - Pain that has prevented the use of a joint for 24 hours or more

YES → Call Doctor Now

NO

- Numbness or tingling is felt in an extremity
- The following symptoms last longer than 72 hours:
  - Mild to moderate pain
  - Limited movement
  - No improvement with self-care

YES → Call Doctor

NO

- Pain or swelling in a joint or muscle follows activity or movement
  Start RICE immediately (see p. 62).
- Pain is decreasing and swelling is going away with RICE
  Continue until swelling is gone and then start MSA (see p. 63). Full healing may take four or more weeks.

See **What You Can Do,** pp. 62 - 63.

→ Apply Self-Care

Broken Bones

Through the years your bones lose density, or thickness, which weakens them and sometimes makes them brittle. Aging bones grow and heal more slowly. Fortunately, weight-bearing exercise and a calcium-rich diet can work wonders for maintaining healthy bones.

Exaggerated loss of bone density is called *osteoporosis.* (See *Osteoporosis,* p. 238). Even a minor injury or difficult movement can result in a broken bone or *fracture* (break). Wrist and hip fractures are especially common. (See *Hip Pain,* p. 260; see *Leg Pain,* p. 256; for tips on preventing falls, see *Falls,* p. 355.)

It is often difficult to tell if a bone has been fractured in an injury. Unless the fracture is obvious, an x-ray may be needed to be sure. The break may be a small crack such as a *stress fracture* caused by overuse, a *simple fracture* in which the bone ends separate but stay in alignment, or a *compound fracture,* in which the soft tissue in the area is torn and the bone protrudes through the skin. The seriousness of a break varies depending on which bone is broken, the type of break involved and whether there are associated injuries.

Suspect a Fracture if

- The injured part is bent or deformed
- A bone pokes through the skin
- There is a bump or irregularity along the bone
- A cracking or snapping sound is heard at the time of injury
- There is rapid swelling or bruising immediately after the injury

WHAT YOU CAN DO ☑

- Assume there may be a fracture.
- Immobilize and support the injured area with a splint. To splint, attach a stiff object (such as a rolled magazine or newspaper or a cane) to the injured limb with a rope or belt. Position the splint so the injured limb cannot bend.

- Do not attempt to move an abnormally bent or displaced bone back into place. Splint it as it is.
- Apply ice for 15 to 20 minutes at a time, more frequently initially, then three to four times a day for up to 48 hours. Leave ice off for at least 15 minutes between applications. For protection, place a washcloth between bare skin and ice and change the cloth if it becomes wet.
- To immobilize and support a possible fractured toe, gently tape it to an adjacent toe.
- Wrap the injury with an elastic bandage to immobilize and compress the area. Loosen the bandage if it becomes too tight.
- Elevate the injured area.
- Avoid any unnecessary movement. Rest the injury for at least 24 to 48 hours.

Use aspirin or ibuprofen (Advil, Motrin) to ease pain and inflammation. **NEVER give aspirin to children/teenagers unless your health care provider orders it. It can cause Reye's syndrome, a rare but often fatal condition. CAUTION: Talk to your doctor or pharmacist before taking any other medications, including over-the-counter (OTC) medications, vitamins or herbal supplements.**

Decision *helper* | Broken Bones
DO THESE APPLY:

- The limb is cold, blue or numb
- The pelvis or thigh is injured
- Signs of shock occur (cool, clammy, pale skin; dizziness or lightheadedness; thirst)

  Keep the person lying down and covered to stay warm. Do not give him or her anything to eat or drink.

- Shortness of breath or difficulty breathing occur after a chest injury

  Keep the person quiet and place in a seated position to assist breathing.

- Bone protrudes through the skin
- You suspect a fracture near a joint
- The injured part is crooked or deformed
- Heavy bleeding occurs or blood spurts out

  Cover an open wound with a clean, dry cloth. Apply direct pressure on the bleeding with a sterile or clean cloth. Apply only enough pressure to stop the bleeding. If blood soaks through, apply another bandage. Do not remove the first one or apply a tourniquet.

YES →

Seek
Emergency
Care

Apply
Emergency
First Aid

NO

See next page.

Do these apply: See previous page.

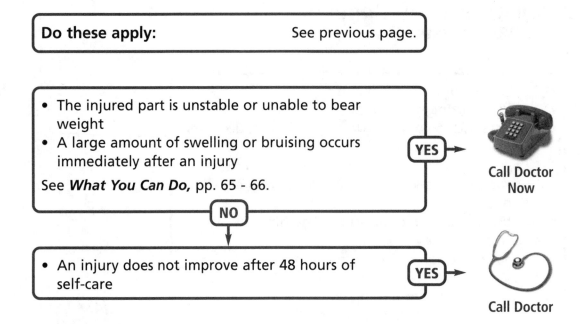

- The injured part is unstable or unable to bear weight
- A large amount of swelling or bruising occurs immediately after an injury

See *What You Can Do,* pp. 65 - 66.

YES →

Call Doctor Now

NO

- An injury does not improve after 48 hours of self-care

YES →

Call Doctor

Smashed Fingers

Fingers often get smashed, pinched or jammed during daily activities. Most finger injuries are not serious. Although they may be quite painful and inconvenient, these injuries heal well with self-care at home. Serious injuries with possible bone fractures, severe bleeding or severed parts require professional medical help.

WHAT YOU CAN DO ✓

- Immediately insert the fingers into ice-cold water to decrease the pain and reduce swelling. Then, apply ice for 15 to 20 minutes at a time, more frequently initially, then three to four times a day for up to 48 hours. Leave ice off for at least 15 minutes between applications. For protection, place a washcloth between bare skin and ice and change the cloth if it becomes wet.
- Remove any jewelry if you can do so without causing additional pain.
- If the skin is broken, wash the injured finger with soap and water, then dry. Apply a soft, clean dressing.
- Splint and support an injured finger by taping it to a finger splint.
- Rest and elevate the hand for 24 to 48 hours. Immobilize it in a sling or use it as little as possible.
- Take aspirin or ibuprofen (Advil, Motrin) to reduce swelling and pain. **NEVER give aspirin to children/teenagers unless your health care provider orders it. It can cause Reye's syndrome, a rare but often fatal condition. CAUTION: Talk to your doctor or pharmacist before taking any other medications, including over-the-counter (OTC) medications, vitamins or herbal supplements.**
- Once swelling stops, apply warm compresses at intervals for comfort.
- Keep the limb elevated above the level of the heart.
- Stop any activity that causes pain.

"Torn" or "Torn Off" Fingernails

- Keep the area clean; watch for signs of infection. (See *Decision helper,* p. 72.)
- Protect the tip of the finger with a soft cloth or covering to which antibiotic ointment has been applied. A new nail will take one to two months to grow back.
- If a nail is still partially attached, seek care. However, if it is held on by just a thin band of tissue, snip it off to remove the nail.

Blood Under a Nail

- Apply ice as soon as possible. For protection, place a washcloth between bare skin and ice.
- Clean the nail with soap and water.
- Make a hole in the nail to relieve pressure and pain:
  - Straighten a paper clip and hold it with a pair of pliers in a flame until it is red hot.
  - Place the tip of the paper clip on the nail and let it melt through. You need not push. A thick nail may take several tries. As soon as the hole is complete, blood will escape and the pain and pressure will ease.
- If the blood and pressure build up again, repeat the procedure using the same hole.
- Soak the finger three times a day for 15 minutes in a solution of equal parts warm water and hydrogen peroxide to keep the hole open.

Decision *helper* Smashed Fingers
DO THESE APPLY:

- The finger is severed
  Apply direct pressure with a sterile bandage to control bleeding. Wrap the finger in clean or sterile gauze and place it in a plastic bag. Place the bag in cold water; do not let the tissue freeze. Bring the severed finger with the injured person.
- Severe bleeding or hemorrhage occurs
  Apply direct pressure with a sterile bandage.
- A finger is deformed or bent into an abnormal shape or bone protrudes through the skin
  Immobilize the hand. Avoid unnecessary movement. Do not move or reposition the finger.
- You have a penetrating finger injury
  Do not attempt to remove an object that is stuck in a finger. Control bleeding and immobilize the hand.

YES →

H ↑

Seek
Emergency
Care

FIRST AID

Apply
Emergency
First Aid

NO

See next page.

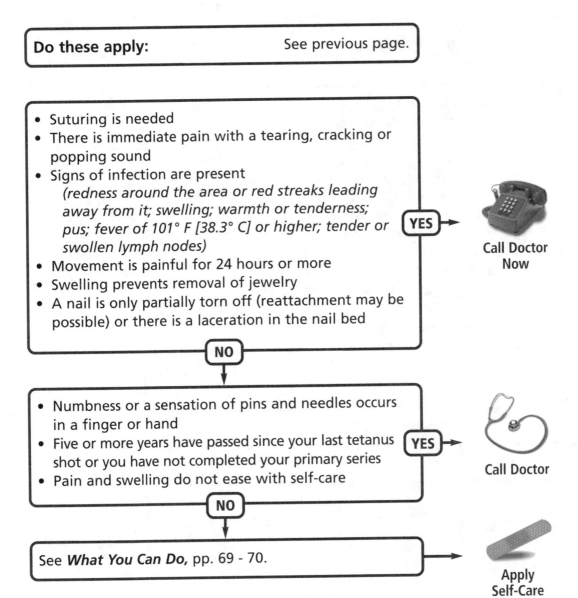

Do these apply: See previous page.

- Suturing is needed
- There is immediate pain with a tearing, cracking or popping sound
- Signs of infection are present
  (redness around the area or red streaks leading away from it; swelling; warmth or tenderness; pus; fever of 101° F [38.3° C] or higher; tender or swollen lymph nodes)
- Movement is painful for 24 hours or more
- Swelling prevents removal of jewelry
- A nail is only partially torn off (reattachment may be possible) or there is a laceration in the nail bed

YES →

Call Doctor Now

NO

- Numbness or a sensation of pins and needles occurs in a finger or hand
- Five or more years have passed since your last tetanus shot or you have not completed your primary series
- Pain and swelling do not ease with self-care

YES →

Call Doctor

NO

See *What You Can Do,* pp. 69 - 70.

Apply Self-Care

Fishhooks

Fishhooks are designed with a barb to keep the fish hooked. Unfortunately, the barb works the same way on people once the skin is punctured. It is useful to know how to remove a fishhook for yourself or a companion, especially if you are any distance from medical help.

WHAT YOU CAN DO ✓

If the Hook is Near the Skin Surface

- **Step 1:** Clean the hook and skin with soap and water.
- **Step 2:** Apply ice or cold water to provide temporary numbing.
- **Step 3:** Loop a piece of fishing line through the hook (Figure 12). Make the line long enough to grasp with your hand.
- **Step 4:** Grasp the eye or shaft of the hook with one hand and press down about one-eighth inch (.3 cm) to disengage the barb.
- **Step 5:** While still pressing down on hook, pull the line parallel to the skin's surface so the hook shaft leads the barb out of the skin (Figure 13).
- **Step 6:** Wash the wound thoroughly with soap and water. Treat it as you would a puncture wound. (See *Punctures*, p. 46)

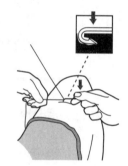

Figure 12

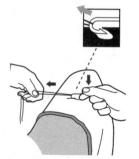

Figure 13

If the Hook is Deeply Embedded

Note: only attempt a difficult hook removal if medical care is unavailable.

- **Step 1:** Clean the hook and skin with soap and water.
- **Step 2:** Apply ice or cold water to provide temporary numbing.
- **Step 3:** Push the hook through the skin.

- **Step 4:** Cut off the barb with wire cutters.
- **Step 5:** Pull the hook back out.
- **Step 6:** Wash the wound thoroughly with soap and water. Treat it as you would a puncture wound. (See *Punctures*, p. 46.)

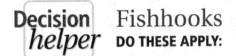

Decision **Fishhooks**
helper **DO THESE APPLY:**

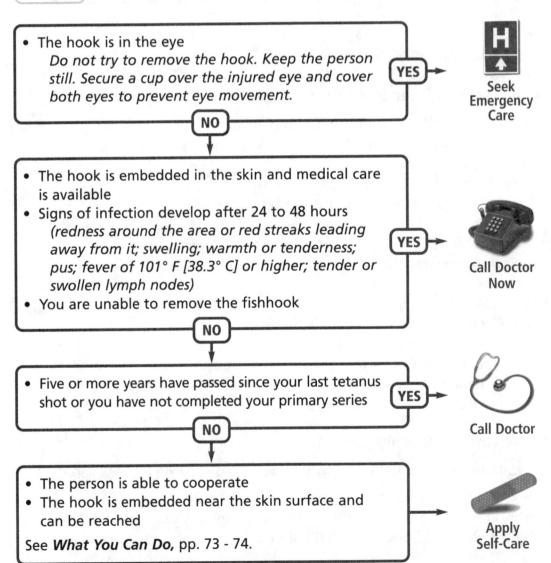

- The hook is in the eye
  Do not try to remove the hook. Keep the person still. Secure a cup over the injured eye and cover both eyes to prevent eye movement.

YES → **H** ↑ Seek Emergency Care

NO ↓

- The hook is embedded in the skin and medical care is available
- Signs of infection develop after 24 to 48 hours *(redness around the area or red streaks leading away from it; swelling; warmth or tenderness; pus; fever of 101° F [38.3° C] or higher; tender or swollen lymph nodes)*
- You are unable to remove the fishhook

YES → Call Doctor Now

NO ↓

- Five or more years have passed since your last tetanus shot or you have not completed your primary series

YES → Call Doctor

NO ↓

- The person is able to cooperate
- The hook is embedded near the skin surface and can be reached

See **What You Can Do**, pp. 73 - 74.

→ Apply Self-Care

Splinters

A sharp, slender piece of wood, metal or glass can easily pierce the skin and become lodged. This type of injury usually can be treated at home. In some instances, infection may develop or a nerve may be damaged, both of which require medical evaluation.

WHAT YOU CAN DO ✓

If the Splinter Can be Reached

- Grasp the end of the splinter with tweezers and gently pull it out along the entry track.
- Cleanse the area with soap and water.
- Keep the area clean and dry; apply a dry bandage if necessary.
- Watch for signs of infection (*redness around the area or red streaks leading away from it; swelling; warmth and tenderness; pus; fever of 101° F [38.3° C] or higher; tender or swollen lymph nodes*).

If the Splinter is Deeply Embedded

- Clean a needle by dipping it in alcohol or holding it in a match flame.
- Cleanse the skin with soap and water, then pick the skin over the end of the splinter and make a small hole.
- Lift the splinter with the tip of a needle until it can be grasped by tweezers. Withdraw it along the entry track.
- Cleanse again and care for the wound, as outlined above.

See *Decision helper,* p. 76.

Splinters
DO THESE APPLY:

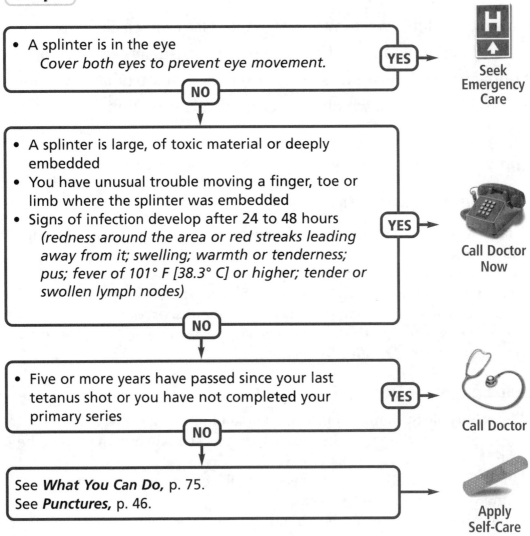

- A splinter is in the eye
  Cover both eyes to prevent eye movement. **YES** →

Seek Emergency Care

NO ↓

- A splinter is large, of toxic material or deeply embedded
- You have unusual trouble moving a finger, toe or limb where the splinter was embedded
- Signs of infection develop after 24 to 48 hours *(redness around the area or red streaks leading away from it; swelling; warmth or tenderness; pus; fever of 101° F [38.3° C] or higher; tender or swollen lymph nodes)* **YES** →

Call Doctor Now

NO ↓

- Five or more years have passed since your last tetanus shot or you have not completed your primary series **YES** →

Call Doctor

NO ↓

See *What You Can Do,* p. 75.
See *Punctures,* p. 46. →

Apply Self-Care

SECTION 3
Health Concerns

Neurological

It is a fact that neurological functions of the body change over time. For example, blood flow to the brain tends to decrease.

Occasionally forgetting things is another common change in brain function that occurs with age. If you've ever forgotten a name or neglected to unplug the iron, don't automatically assume you're suffering from serious conditions like *dementia,* a significant, ongoing decline in intellectual capacity, or Alzheimer's disease, a type of dementia.

Although certain changes in the neurological system are a natural function of aging, some of the conditions in this chapter (even those involving disease) can be avoided—or at least well managed—through healthy lifestyle choices related to diet, exercise and the decision to stop smoking.

Fever

As the body ages, its immune system also changes so that it doesn't fight inflammation or infection as efficiently as it once did. Fever may now become an inaccurate gauge of serious illness. You can be seriously ill and have a very low fever or no fever at all.

Fever is a rise in body temperature above "normal." However, normal body temperatures can vary in individuals, and a person's body temperature varies throughout the day. A person is considered to have a fever if the oral temperature is higher than 99.5° F (37.5° C).

Fever can occur as a result of exercise, dehydration or injury to the *hypothalamus* (the temperature regulator in the brain); from a reaction to certain chemicals (such as caffeine); or as a symptom of the body's immune system fighting inflammation or infection.

NOTE YOUR SYMPTOMS ✓

Generally, fever is caused by viruses, bacterial infections, fungi or parasites. It can also result from inflammatory diseases (like lupus and rheumatoid arthritis) and from cancers (such as Hodgkin's disease and kidney cancer).

Physical signs of fever include:

- Feeling hot or cold
- Shivering
- Headache
- Muscle aches
- Joint pains
- General *malaise* (feeling lousy)

WHAT YOU CAN DO ✓

- Take acetaminophen (Tylenol), aspirin or ibuprofen (Advil, Motrin) to lower temperature and minimize discomfort. **NEVER give aspirin to children/teenagers unless your health care provider orders it. It can cause Reye's syndrome, a rare but often fatal condition. CAUTION: Talk to your doctor or pharmacist before taking any other medications, including over-the-counter (OTC) medications, vitamins or herbal supplements.**
- Practice good hygiene, particularly handwashing, which is important in preventing infectious illnesses that cause fever.
- Take warm (but never cold) baths or showers to help lower fever. Cool sponge baths may help in the case of a high fever.
- Dress lightly and keep the room temperature cool.
- Drink plenty of fluids, unless you're on a fluid-restricted diet.

See *Decision helper,* p. 80.

Decision *helper* Fever
DO THESE APPLY:

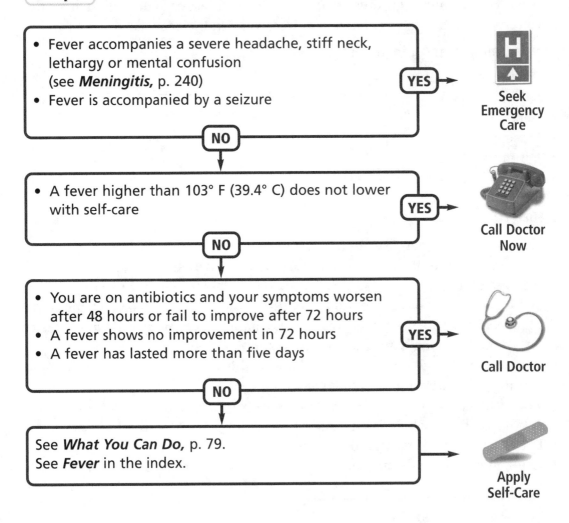

- Fever accompanies a severe headache, stiff neck, lethargy or mental confusion (see *Meningitis,* p. 240)
- Fever is accompanied by a seizure

YES → **Seek Emergency Care**

NO

- A fever higher than 103° F (39.4° C) does not lower with self-care

YES → **Call Doctor Now**

NO

- You are on antibiotics and your symptoms worsen after 48 hours or fail to improve after 72 hours
- A fever shows no improvement in 72 hours
- A fever has lasted more than five days

YES → **Call Doctor**

NO

See *What You Can Do,* p. 79.
See *Fever* in the index.

→ **Apply Self-Care**

Headaches

Headaches can range in intensity from a dull ache to unbearable pain and last from hours to days. Although many factors can contribute to headaches, they all involve the pain-sensitive nerve fibers of the head.

Tension-type Headaches

Tension-type headaches are extremely common. Almost everyone has had one at some point. For some, episodes might occur just a few times a year; for others, they may recur more frequently. They apparently are caused by reactions of the pain pathways in your head and may be triggered by a number of factors, including stress. The pain of a tension-type headache may feel like a band around your head and is generally dull and continuous, with fluctuations in intensity.

Tension-type headaches are frequently triggered by emotional or physical factors. Figuring out what triggers your headaches may help you reduce or avoid them in the future. Situations that make you grit your teeth, tighten your shoulders or clench your fist, for example, may cause them. Other causes could include fighting traffic, loud noises, dealing with a difficult person, sitting in an uncomfortable position, or getting too much or too little sleep.

Migraine Headaches

Migraine headaches can cause excruciating pain and prevent sufferers from carrying out daily activities. Migraines account for 2 to 7 percent of all headaches, affect more women than men and usually begin between the ages of 7 and 30. Some people experience fewer episodes as they grow older and may even enjoy a complete remission after age 50. Migraines often run in families.

Migraines are believed to occur when pain pathways to the brain are triggered easily, resulting in inflammation and blood vessel changes in the head. Researchers have found that *serotonin,* a chemical that transmits messages in the brain, is involved in migraines. Migraine medications can bind to serotonin sites, called *receptors,* and relieve headache symptoms. Migraine symptoms include pain (which can be one-sided), sensitivity to light or noise, nausea, vomiting, or visual changes.

Factors that trigger migraines include glare from harsh light, stress, hunger, climatic changes, certain foods and beverages, hormones and medications, physical or mental exhaustion, or too much or too little sleep.

If you are susceptible to migraines, you will generally experience several headaches a year (each lasting one to three days). If your headaches increase in severity or frequency, you may want to call your doctor. Many medications are now available to prevent headaches or control pain.

The good news is that with the right combination of self-care techniques and appropriate medication, you can make a significant difference in your ability to manage, and possibly eliminate, this painful disorder.

The key is to identify your triggers. Keeping a diary of your symptoms, possible triggers and which self-care techniques work and don't work provides helpful information for both you and your doctor.

WHAT YOU CAN DO ☑

- Take over-the-counter (OTC) painkillers such as aspirin, acetaminophen (Tylenol) or ibuprofen (Advil, Motrin). **NEVER give aspirin to children/ teenagers unless your health care provider orders it. It can cause Reye's syndrome, a rare but often fatal condition. CAUTION: Talk to your doctor or pharmacist before taking any other medications, including over-the-counter (OTC) medications, vitamins or herbal supplements.** Avoid taking OTC pain medications more than twice a week and limit the amount of caffeine found in food or beverages. Both can cause rebound headaches.
- Lie down in a cool, dark, quiet room.
- Put an ice bag on your head. For protection, place a washcloth between bare skin and ice.
- Soak in a hot bath.
- Take a nap.
- Exercise regularly and consider stretching, meditation or other muscle-relaxation techniques.

Cluster Headaches

Cluster headaches are similar to migraines with a few differences. They occur mostly in men and are not necessarily inherited. They are usually one-sided like a migraine, but the throbbing, burning pain behind or above the eye intensifies rapidly and lasts from 10 minutes to several hours.

One to three attacks can occur in a 24-hour period, nausea and vomiting are rare, and nasal stuffiness also may occur. Treatment requires prescription medication, which may include oxygen. Studies indicate that cluster headaches originate from the *hypothalamic* area of the brain, which governs many *autonomic* activities, such as body temperature and hormone regulation.

Decision *helper*   Headaches
DO THESE APPLY:

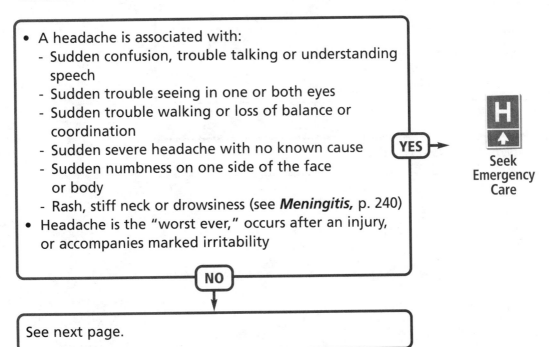

- A headache is associated with:
  - Sudden confusion, trouble talking or understanding speech
  - Sudden trouble seeing in one or both eyes
  - Sudden trouble walking or loss of balance or coordination
  - Sudden severe headache with no known cause
  - Sudden numbness on one side of the face or body
  - Rash, stiff neck or drowsiness (see **Meningitis**, p. 240)
- Headache is the "worst ever," occurs after an injury, or accompanies marked irritability

YES → **H** Seek Emergency Care

NO

See next page.

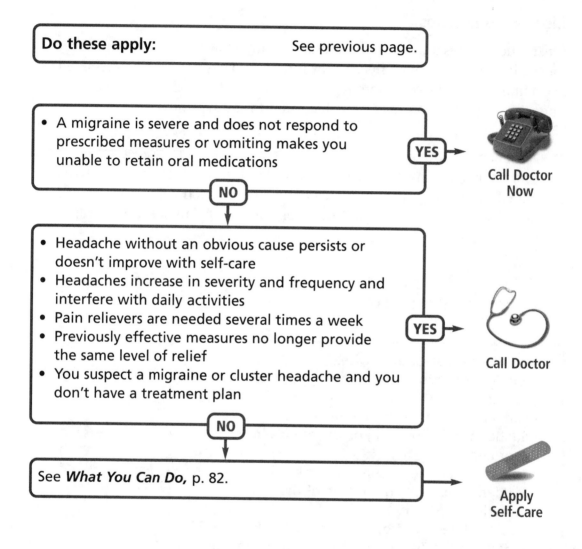

Do these apply: See previous page.

- A migraine is severe and does not respond to prescribed measures or vomiting makes you unable to retain oral medications

YES →

Call Doctor Now

NO

- Headache without an obvious cause persists or doesn't improve with self-care
- Headaches increase in severity and frequency and interfere with daily activities
- Pain relievers are needed several times a week
- Previously effective measures no longer provide the same level of relief
- You suspect a migraine or cluster headache and you don't have a treatment plan

YES →

Call Doctor

NO

See *What You Can Do,* p. 82.

Apply Self-Care

Dizziness and Vertigo

Dizziness involves difficulty maintaining balance while you stand or sit. It is a generally mild feeling, sometimes described as wooziness or lightheadedness. Dizziness that creates the sometimes disabling sensation that you or your surroundings are spinning uncontrollably is called *vertigo.*

Fainting (*syncope*) is a brief loss of consciousness that lasts for a minute or less, usually resulting from a temporary drop in blood flow to the brain. A number of conditions can contribute, including *hypotension* (low blood pressure) or *hypovolemia* (diminished blood plasma volume).

Both dizziness and vertigo are related to your sense of balance, which is maintained by a complex interaction between the following elements of the nervous system:

- **Eyes:** Your eyes tell you where your body is in space, and how and where it's moving.
- **Inner ears:** The inner ears monitor the directions of motion and help detect back-and-forth motion.
- **Sensory nerves:** Sensory nerves are located in your muscles and joints; they transmit information from these areas to your brain about movement, positioning and stimulation from the environment.

Maintaining good balance depends on the function of at least two of these three sensory systems. Dizziness can occur when the sensory systems send the central nervous system conflicting messages. For example, if damage occurs on one side of the inner ear, the brain receives a mixed message about your body's movements. Your eyes and sensory nerves may coordinate as they should, but the inner ear injury may create a sensation of spinning or rotation.

Sensations such as these can be brought on by hunger, exhaustion, emotional upsets, severe pain, hot stuffy environments, laughing, drugs, alcohol, dehydration, variations in heart rhythm, a drop in blood pressure, standing up suddenly, or anything that momentarily decreases blood flow to your brain.

WHAT YOU CAN DO ✓

If you currently feel dizzy, take the following steps to keep yourself and those around you out of potentially dangerous situations:

- Tell someone you are in need of help.
- Move away from any stairs or glass, or other potentially hazardous locations.
- Keep yourself warm.
- Sit or lie down and rest quietly until the feeling passes.
- Do not drive or operate heavy machinery.

The following self-care tips can help relieve symptoms of dizziness or vertigo:

- Loosen any restrictive clothing.
- If you are in a stuffy or hot environment, move to a cool area.
- Drink liquids frequently (in small amounts).
- If sitting, place your head between your knees.
- Lie down and rest.
- Change position slowly; this allows time for your body and blood flow to adjust slowly.
- Try lying on one side versus the other to help ease vertigo.

See *Decision helper,* p. 87.

PREVENTION ✓

Although you usually can't anticipate dizziness, you can do a number of things to help prevent the sensation:

- Eat well-balanced meals at regular intervals and snacks between meals if you are hungry.
- Work and exercise in moderate amounts. Stop and rest at intervals to avoid becoming exhausted.
- Drink eight glasses of water daily unless you're on a fluid-restricted diet. Drink more during hot conditions.
- Limit your alcohol intake, especially in warm weather.
- Learn about the side effects of all the medications you take; discuss any new medications with your doctor or pharmacist, including over-the-counter medicines, vitamins and herbal supplements.

- Get up slowly after sitting or lying in one position for a long time.
- Treat motion sickness with appropriate medications such as dimenhydrinate (Dramamine) or meclizine (Bonine).
- Try to identify the cause of dizziness and avoid that activity in the future.

FINAL NOTES ✓

Everyone occasionally feels faint or dizzy. These feelings can be caused by anything from not having enough to eat to being slightly dehydrated. Fortunately, there are a number of safe, easy steps you can take at home to prevent dizzy spells and to ease symptoms, should they occur.

Decision helper — Dizziness and Vertigo
DO THESE APPLY:

- Loss of consciousness occurs (see *Unconsciousness*, p. 37)
  - Lay the person down in a safe place. Check for breathing and pulse. Start CPR, if necessary. (See *CPR*, p. 20)
- Symptoms of a possible stroke occur:
  - Sudden confusion, trouble talking or understanding speech
  - Sudden trouble seeing in one or both eyes
  - Sudden trouble walking or loss of balance or coordination
  - Sudden severe headache with no known cause
  - Sudden numbness on one side of the face or body
- Symptoms of a possible heart attack occur:
  - Chest, jaw, neck shoulder or arm discomfort, along with dizziness, weakness or a faint feeling

YES → **H** Seek Emergency Care

NO

See next page.

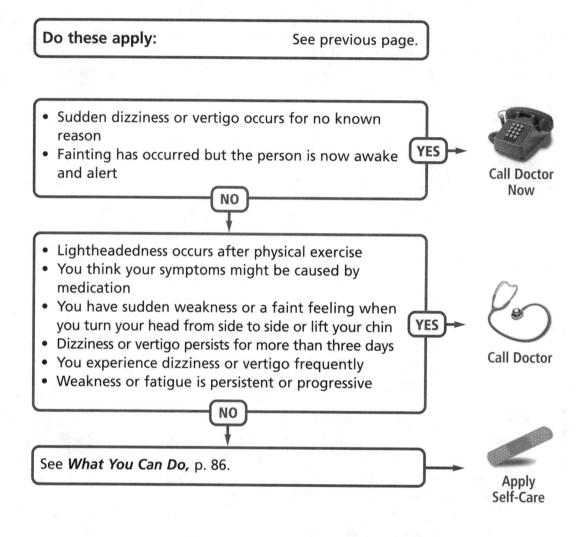

Do these apply: See previous page.

- Sudden dizziness or vertigo occurs for no known reason
- Fainting has occurred but the person is now awake and alert

YES → **Call Doctor Now**

NO ↓

- Lightheadedness occurs after physical exercise
- You think your symptoms might be caused by medication
- You have sudden weakness or a faint feeling when you turn your head from side to side or lift your chin
- Dizziness or vertigo persists for more than three days
- You experience dizziness or vertigo frequently
- Weakness or fatigue is persistent or progressive

YES → **Call Doctor**

NO ↓

See *What You Can Do,* p. 86.

→ **Apply Self-Care**

Weakness/Fatigue

Although they are often discussed together, weakness and fatigue are two distinctly different problems.

Weakness is a decrease in your physical ability or an increase in difficulty moving your muscles. It is usually the more serious symptom, especially when it involves a large group of muscles such as an arm or a leg, or one whole side of the body. Temporary or prolonged weakness in one part of the body may be a warning of injury to the nervous system or a stroke.

Fatigue is a feeling of weariness, exhaustion or a decrease in energy. Causes may include stress, a sudden change in one's physical activity level, a change in medication, limited or altered sleep, exposure to toxic chemicals, recovery from a major health or emotional event, depression, poor nutrition or excessive alcohol intake. In many cases, symptoms can be treated and relieved through self-care within two months.

Anemia

Prolonged or extreme fatigue that does not respond to self-care may be a sign of a more serious problem. Occasionally, fatigue can be the result of gastrointestinal bleeding (see *Peptic Ulcer*, p. 212; *Colon Cancer*, p. 224), resulting in *anemia*, a decrease in the number of red blood cells.

With anemia, adequate amounts of oxygen do not get to all of the tissues of the body. If the brain and heart receive less oxygen, you may feel tired or weary. Less oxygen to the muscles may cause weakness.

Anemia may be caused by an iron deficiency, a lack of certain nutrients, a serious illness or a disease of the bone marrow (such as leukemia or the spreading of breast or prostate cancer).

If your doctor suspects anemia, you will be given blood tests to help determine the cause and treatment. Treatment can range from taking iron or nutrient supplements to, in the most serious cases, having a blood transfusion. If the anemia results from a serious illness, your doctor will treat the illness rather than the anemia.

PREVENTION ✓

Prevention and self-care for problems related to weakness and fatigue include:

- Exercising regularly; include exercises that strengthen and tone muscle and improve aerobic endurance (see *Staying Active,* p. 343)
- Eating a well-balanced diet that is high in fiber and low in fat (see *Eating Right,* p. 338)
- Improving your sleeping habits (see *Insomnia,* p. 323)
- Dealing with any feelings of depression (see *Depression,* p. 319)
- Limiting your intake of alcohol, caffeine and nicotine
- Providing variety in your activities and interests
- Avoiding exhaustion by scheduling time for rest and relaxation

WHAT YOU CAN DO ✓

- Follow the prevention guidelines listed above.
- You can help your doctor diagnose the cause of your fatigue by keeping track of your symptoms. Include when the feelings started, when they occur or are most intense, anything that seems to make them worse or better, whether others in your home or work setting have similar problems, etc.
- Listen to your body. Notice the effect drugs, activities and stress have on you.
- Be patient. It may take six to eight weeks of practicing prevention and self-care guidelines regularly before you feel strong and energetic again.

FINAL NOTES ✓

Prolonged or extreme fatigue that does not respond to self-care may be a sign of a more serious problem. Chronic fatigue is a symptom often associated with diseases such as diabetes, hypothyroidism, lupus, heart disease and rheumatoid arthritis, to name a few.

Decision *helper* Weakness/Fatigue
DO THESE APPLY:

- There is a complete loss of consciousness (see *Unconsciousness,* p. 37)
  - Lay the person down in a safe place. Check for breathing and pulse. Start CPR if needed (see p. 20)
- Any of the following have occurred:
  - Sudden confusion, trouble talking or understanding speech
  - Sudden trouble seeing in one or both eyes
  - Sudden trouble walking or loss of balance or coordination
  - Sudden severe headache with no known cause
  - Sudden numbness on one side of the face or body
- Symptoms follow a head injury (see *Head/Spinal Injury,* p. 55)

YES →

Seek Emergency Care

Apply Emergency First Aid

NO

- Sudden dizziness or vertigo has no known cause
- Irregular heartbeat is accompanied by dizziness or lightheadedness (see *Palpitations,* p. 188)
- Fainting has occurred but the person is now awake and alert
  The patient should not drive him or herself to the medical appointment.

YES →

Call Doctor Now

NO

See next page.

Do these apply: See previous page.

- Dizziness or vertigo persists after three days
- Symptoms may be caused by a prescribed medication
- Weakness or fatigue is persistent or progressive

YES →

Call Doctor

NO ↓

See *What You Can Do, Dizziness/Vertigo,* p. 86.
See *What You Can Do, Weakness/Fatigue,* p. 90.

→

**Apply
Self-Care**

Stroke/TIA

A *stroke* is the death of brain tissue, caused by blockage of the brain's blood supply or by severe bleeding in or near the brain. A *transient ischemic attack* is a temporary interruption in blood flow to the brain.

Stroke

The most common type of stroke is *ischemic* or *embolic*, involving the blockage of the blood supply to the brain by a blood clot. Ischemic strokes are usually the result of *atherosclerosis*, the buildup of fatty plaques and other deposits within blood vessels, narrowing them and making them prone to blockage. Cell death occurs within a few hours if blood flow to the brain is not restored.

Hemorrhagic strokes, also known as *cerebral hemorrhages*, occur when a blood vessel in the brain ruptures and blood leaks into the brain. Most cerebral hemorrhages are associated with high blood pressure, but some are the result of *aneurysm* (the abnormal weakening or *dilation* [opening] of a blood vessel).

Transient Ischemic Attack (TIA)

TIA symptoms can be identical to those of stroke, but they last for less than 24 hours. Normal cell function usually resumes once the blockage clears. Brain cells generally do not die during a TIA; they malfunction for a short period. However, a TIA is a warning sign that a stroke is likely. Nearly one-third of all strokes are preceded by a TIA. It is impossible to tell the symptoms of TIA from those of stroke.

NOTE YOUR SYMPTOMS ✓

Depending on the part of the brain affected, a stroke can impair memory, speech, comprehension, the senses and behavior. Strokes usually involve a sudden loss of muscle control, causing weakness or paralysis—typically on one side of the body.

Many stroke patients lose control of their emotions. They laugh or cry inappropriately or get very angry. Many also develop post-stroke depression, which is believed to be both a physical and psychological response to stroke.

Aphasia is another common complication of stroke. It is the inability to speak or write or to make sense of spoken or written language. It does not affect intelligence, however. Those with aphasia can be mentally alert even if their speech is jumbled or incoherent.

Warning signs of stroke and TIA are always sudden and often affect only one side of the body. Symptoms may involve:

- Changes in normal consciousness or severe drowsiness
- Weakness or numbness in the face or in one arm or leg
- Severe headache
- Visual changes such as dimness, loss of vision or double vision (especially in one eye)
- Difficulty speaking or understanding speech
- Unsteadiness or dizziness
- Seizures

RISK FACTORS ☑

Hypertension (high blood pressure) is the greatest risk factor for stroke. The risk can be lowered significantly if blood pressure is controlled. Other risk factors you may be able to control are diabetes, high cholesterol levels, heart disease, obesity, smoking, drug abuse, high stress levels and inactivity.

Risk factors that cannot be controlled are age (people over the age of 55 are at increased risk); personal or family history of stroke or cardiovascular disease; history of migraines (especially for women); ethnicity (African Americans are at higher risk); and certain chronic illnesses, such as sickle cell disease.

PREVENTION ☑

When brain cells die, they cannot be regenerated. That's why stroke prevention is so important. To lessen the risk of stroke:

- Control high blood pressure.
- Control diabetes.
- If you smoke, start taking steps to kick the habit. Quitting at any age significantly reduces the risk of stroke.
- Improve cardiovascular fitness through regular exercise and a low-fat, low-cholesterol diet that is high in fruits, vegetables and fiber.

TREATMENT ✓

A stroke is a medical emergency. Emergency care is required to prevent permanent brain damage. Remember, the sooner medical treatment is started, the better your chances are for recovery. Follow-up treatment usually involves a combination of medication therapy and lifestyle measures (such as dietary improvements, mild-to-moderate exercise, and if necessary, weight loss, smoking cessation and/or alcohol restriction). Occupational or physical therapy is often also necessary. In severe cases, surgery may be required.

FINAL NOTES ✓

Prompt medical attention following a stroke can save your life or the life of a loved one. It can also mean the difference between recovery and long-term disability. Even though dead brain tissue cannot be repaired, in many cases, with proper treatment, other parts of the brain can assume some or all of a person's lost function.

Decision *helper* Stroke/TIA
DO THESE APPLY:

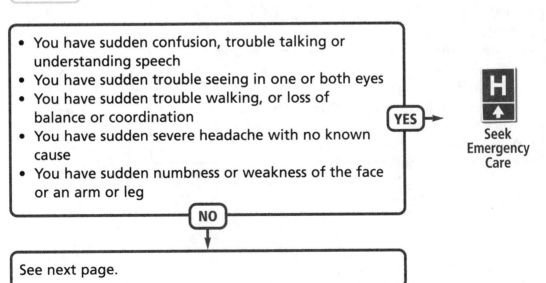

- You have sudden confusion, trouble talking or understanding speech
- You have sudden trouble seeing in one or both eyes
- You have sudden trouble walking, or loss of balance or coordination
- You have sudden severe headache with no known cause
- You have sudden numbness or weakness of the face or an arm or leg

YES → **H** ↑ Seek Emergency Care

NO

See next page.

> **Do these apply:**   See previous page.

- You experience any of the above symptoms, but recover completely within a few minutes.
- You have had a stroke or TIA and experience pain or swelling in a leg
- You are taking anticoagulant medication and any of the following occurs:
  - Unexplained bruising over a large area or multiple areas
  - Tiny red spots on the skin
  - Bleeding of any mucous membranes (such as bloody nose, bleeding gums)
  - Blood in the urine
  - Bloody stools or unusually dark stools

 YES →

Call Doctor Now

 NO

- Medication you take to prevent stroke is causing side effects
- You have difficulty performing everyday tasks following a stroke
- You need emotional support following a stroke
- You have no post-stroke rehabilitation plan
- You are at risk of stroke and need to discuss preventive measures with your doctor

YES →

Call Doctor

Memory Loss

Mild memory loss is a normal part of the aging process. Many people find themselves occasionally struggling to remember the name of a person they just met or the words of a once familiar song.

These occasional feelings of confusion or forgetfulness are different from *dementia,* a serious decline in mental function. And while the terms dementia and senility are often used interchangeably, they are not the same thing. In fact, senility actually just means "old age."

Many adults find that their ability to recall events or facts declines somewhat as they age. This is due in part to a gradual decrease in the chemicals that affect memory. Stress, depression and other factors can also impact memory.

Dementia

Dementia is a serious and progressive loss of *cognitive* (intellectual) function. Those with dementia forget whole events, not just minor details. In the early stages, symptoms may be subtle. Over time, loss of mental powers becomes obvious and progressive. Recognition of people, places or objects becomes difficult and recalling words or numbers can be lost over time. Disorientation and changes in personality are common.

If dementia is related to an underlying cause such as poor nutrition, medications or certain conditions (such as *hypothyroidism,* or underactive thyroid), treating that condition may improve symptoms. Even the dementia associated with certain diseases, such as Parkinson's disease, can be improved somewhat with medical treatment.

However, dementia is often related to Alzheimer's disease or *multi-infarct* dementia, for which there are so far no effective medical treatments. Alzheimer's involves the slow, steady deterioration of mental and, often, emotional function. It can occur at any age but is more common in older adults. While there is no cure for this ultimately fatal disease, a great deal of research is underway to discover the underlying causes of and possible treatments for Alzheimer's.

Multi-infarct dementia is the result of damage to the *cerebral* (brain) blood vessels from stroke or *hypertension* (high blood pressure).

Mental decline occurs in stages. For people with these types of dementia, medical treatment consists of assisting the patient and his or her caregiver to maintain a safe and comfortable home environment for as long as possible.

WHAT YOU CAN DO ✓

Memory Loss

While there is no "cure" for memory loss, there are a number of steps you can take to help you sharpen your memory; just like the rest of your body, your brain needs regular activity to keep it healthy.

- Exercise your brain with word games, crossword puzzles, and card games and other activities that require memory skills; Concentration, cribbage and bridge are good choices.
- Exercise your body to improve circulation, which can affect memory.
- Build your day around a routine, using "things-to-do" lists to help.
- Make associations between events, people and dates. Think of a significant or particularly pleasant event in your life and recall the people you shared it with, the small details that made it special, etc.
- Practice. When you meet a new person, pay attention to his or her name. Try to use the name right away: "Nice to meet you, Hank!"
- Relax. Excessive worrying about whether you're losing your memory can be distracting and actually make your memory worse. Relaxation techniques may be helpful. (See *Stress,* p. 313.)

Dementia

Most people can be cared for at home in the early stages of dementia. The following tips can help you maintain a safe and orderly home environment if someone in your family has some form of dementia:

- Lock away chemicals, drugs and other potentially harmful substances.
- Put bells on doors or door knobs.
- Provide the person with an ID bracelet to wear.
- Use signs to identify the bathroom, bedroom, etc.

- Provide healthy foods and plenty of fluids.
- Stimulate the senses with touch, songs, hugs and exercise.
- Review all medications and dosages with a doctor or pharmacist since some drugs can add to mental fogginess or confusion.

FINAL NOTES ✓

Memory loss is not necessarily serious. However, if your memory seems to get increasingly worse over time, or if cognitive problems are interfering with your ability to carry on normal daily activities, talk to your doctor about having a medical evaluation.

Decision helper Memory Loss **DO THESE APPLY:**

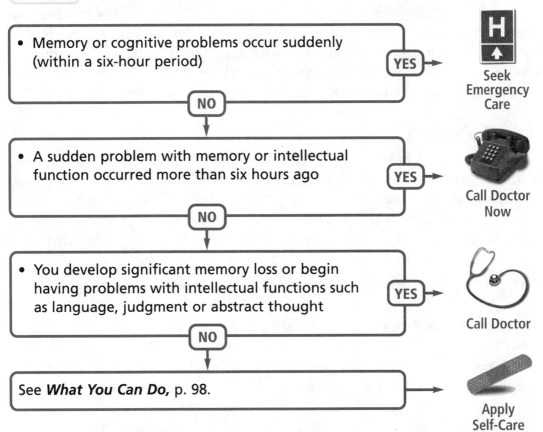

- Memory or cognitive problems occur suddenly (within a six-hour period)

YES → **H ↑** Seek Emergency Care

NO

- A sudden problem with memory or intellectual function occurred more than six hours ago

YES → Call Doctor Now

NO

- You develop significant memory loss or begin having problems with intellectual functions such as language, judgment or abstract thought

YES → Call Doctor

NO

See *What You Can Do,* p. 98.

→ Apply Self-Care

Parkinson's Disease

Parkinson's disease is caused by the degeneration of the part of the brain that produces a chemical called *dopamine,* a *neurotransmitter* that allows brain cells to communicate with one another. This deficiency in dopamine accounts for the uncoordinated movements, tremor and stiffness commonly seen in people with Parkinson's.

Early in the disease, the facial muscles responsible for expression do not respond normally, giving the person a flat or expressionless look. Often, this is mistaken for depression. The second noticeable effect is usually a change in the person's walk. Movement starts slowly, and the ability to change direction is often affected. The *tremor* (or bodily shaking) often associated with Parkinson's disease does not affect everyone, but when present, usually occurs when an arm or leg is at rest. As the disease progresses, symptoms worsen and the muscles that coordinate swallowing are affected. This makes choking a likely possibility. Dementia also occurs in up to one-third of those with advanced Parkinson's. (See *Dementia,* p. 97.)

WHAT YOU CAN DO ✓

Although scientists have various theories about the cause of Parkinson's, treatments are available. The most commonly used medication (*L-dopa*) is a chemical that changes into dopamine within the brain. **CAUTION: Talk to your doctor or pharmacist before taking any other medications, including over-the-counter (OTC) medications, vitamins or herbal supplements.** Physical and occupational therapy can be beneficial. In some cases, surgery is an option.

Caring for a person with Parkinson's disease takes careful monitoring of medications. It's important to encourage self-reliance as much as possible when you assist a Parkinson's patient with eating, personal hygiene and daily activities. Support for the caregiver is also available and highly recommended. Many communities have associations to help the patient, caregiver and family members better understand the disease. (See *Care for the Caregiver,* p. 377.)

Shingles

Shingles is caused by the same virus that causes chickenpox (*varicella-zoster herpes*). Once chickenpox runs its course, the virus takes up residence in a person's *dorsal root ganglion* (a bundle of sensory nerve cells connected to the spinal cord), where it usually remains dormant. However, it can be reactivated, causing shingles—a painful inflammation of the nerves and skin along the ganglion's path.

Shingles generally erupts along one side of the body, most commonly the trunk, although it can occur elsewhere as well. The infection is most common in older adults, especially those over the age of 50.

Among the many triggers that can reactivate the herpes virus are trauma, acute or chronic illness, fatigue, emotional stress, or weakened immune function from conditions such as Hodgkin's disease or *immunosuppressive* therapy (medications given to block the body's immune response to such things as organ transplants).

NOTE YOUR SYMPTOMS ✓

Symptoms that precede an active outbreak of shingles—starting three to four days before the blisters appear—include chills, fever, *malaise* (feeling lousy), upset stomach, and pain and/or itching along the site of the future eruption.

On the fourth or fifth day, the symptoms of shingles appear, including:

- Pain (which can be severe) or a tingling sensation, often along the nerve pathway or one side of the torso
- Itching (which may be intense)
- A rash of small, fluid-filled blisters, frequently following a defined pattern along one side of the body. The blisters begin to dry and scab in about five days. Blisters may be large; when they rupture, a clear, sticky fluid is released that forms yellow, crusty scabs. Crusts usually fall off two or three weeks after the initial symptoms.

WHAT YOU CAN DO ☑

At the first sign of possible shingles, discuss whether antiviral medication might be a treatment option for you.

The following measures may help relieve symptoms:

- Over-the-counter analgesics, such as acetaminophen (Tylenol), ibuprofen (Advi, Motrin) or aspirin can be used for pain. **NEVER give aspirin to children/ teenagers unless your health care provider orders it. It can cause Reye's syndrome, a rare but often fatal condition. CAUTION: Talk to your doctor or pharmacist before taking any other medications, including over-the-counter (OTC) medications, vitamins or herbal supplements.**
- If pain relief is not sufficient, your doctor may prescribe a stronger pain reliever.
- Wear soft cotton clothing over affected skin (clothing may stick to the skin as the blisters ooze). Avoid tight clothing or anything that rubs against the skin.
- Apply cool compresses for temporary relief.

To relieve itching, apply cool wet compresses of plain water or Burow's solution. (Be sure to follow package instructions.) An oatmeal bath (1/2 to 1 cup [115 to 230 mL] of oatmeal in a tub of lukewarm water) may also be soothing; to avoid clogging the tub drain put the oatmeal in an old nylon or sock, tie a knot in it and let it soak in the tub. A commercial oatmeal bath, called Aveeno, is also available. Other measures to relieve itching include baking soda baths (1/2 cup [115 mL] to 1 tub of warm water) and Calamine or Caladryl lotion.

Although the infection may be very uncomfortable, most people make a complete recovery from shingles within one month and do not experience any complications. However, for some, pain may persist for months after the blisters have healed (*postherpetic neuralgia*). Talk to your doctor or pharmacist about additional treatment strategies for pain.

It is important to note that you cannot get shingles from exposure to a person with chickenpox. However, shingles blisters contain the live herpes virus and a person who has never had chickenpox can catch it from contact with the fluid in a shingles blister.

FINAL NOTES ✓

Shingles can be very painful, but symptoms often pass after a month or so and complications are uncommon. If pain persists after your rash has healed, talk to your doctor or pharmacist about treatment options.

Decision **Shingles**
helper **DO THESE APPLY:**

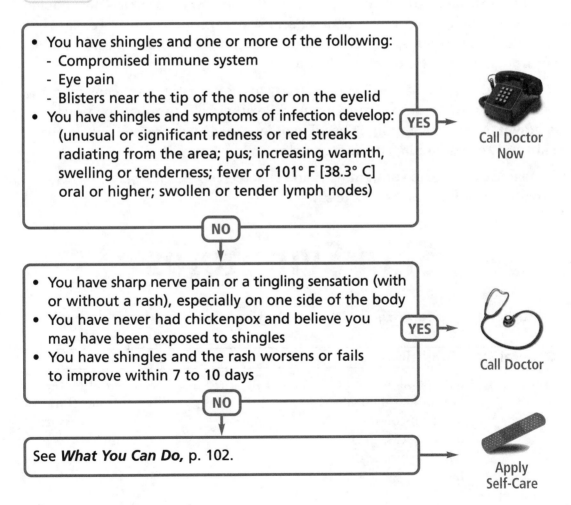

- You have shingles and one or more of the following:
  - Compromised immune system
  - Eye pain
  - Blisters near the tip of the nose or on the eyelid
- You have shingles and symptoms of infection develop: (unusual or significant redness or red streaks radiating from the area; pus; increasing warmth, swelling or tenderness; fever of 101° F [38.3° C] oral or higher; swollen or tender lymph nodes)

YES → Call Doctor Now

NO

- You have sharp nerve pain or a tingling sensation (with or without a rash), especially on one side of the body
- You have never had chickenpox and believe you may have been exposed to shingles
- You have shingles and the rash worsens or fails to improve within 7 to 10 days

YES → Call Doctor

NO

See *What You Can Do,* p. 102. → Apply Self-Care

Skin Concerns

As the body ages, the skin undergoes many changes. The loss of thickness in the layer of *subcutaneous* fat (a layer of fat under the skin) leaves the deeper layers of skin unable to support the top layer, forming folds—or wrinkles. This loss of fat also causes older adults to become more readily chilled.

The skin itself also becomes thinner and the small blood vessels that supply it provide less nutrition. Bruises and cuts occur more easily and heal more slowly. The pressure of sitting or lying in one position for more than two hours at a time can damage the skin by preventing blood flow to the area. Older adults who are not able to move frequently because of injury, disease or weakness may develop bed sores, or pressure ulcers, on the skin. All skin ulcers should be brought to the attention of a doctor.

With aging, some skin cells lose the ability to produce pigment (causing hair, which is part of the skin, to turn gray) while other cells produce too much pigment (causing age spots). The oil in older skin also decreases, causing dry skin and *xerosis* (itching, burning, cracking or scaling skin).

Repeated exposure to sunlight without sunscreen speeds the skin's aging process and increases the risk of skin cancer.

Skin Symptoms

Condition	Appearance/ Location	Itching	Fever	Other Symptoms/ Comments
General Skin Conditions				
Boil p. 119	Red, swollen, painful bump (like a large pimple); common on buttocks, groin, waist, armpits, neck, face	No	No	Occurs in infected hair follicles that are under pressure or chafed

Condition	Appearance/ Location	Itching	Fever	Other Symptoms/ Comments
General Skin Conditions *continued*				
Dandruff	White to yellow to red, some crusting; on scalp, eyebrows, groin	Occasional	No	Fine, oily scales and flaking; to treat, use anti-dandruff shampoo
Eczema p. 114	Red; cracking and thickening of dry areas; on elbows, wrists, knees, cheeks	Moderate to intense	No	Moist, oozing, water-filled blisters
Psoriasis p. 114	Thick, silvery skin patches; often on knees, elbows, scalp	Moderate to intense	No	Symptoms come and go over weeks to months
Shingles p. 101	Small, fluid-filled blisters, accompanied by sharp nerve pain; usually on one side of body (most often the torso)	Intense	Maybe	Blisters rupture, forming yellow, crusty scabs
Skin Cancer p. 111	Change in size or shape of mole	Occasional	No	Skin irregularity that is smooth, shiny or waxy; mole that scales, oozes or bleeds
Warts p. 268 (plantar warts)	Raised, grainy, lump anywhere on the body	No	No	Can be flat in areas of pressure, like soles of feet
Fungal Rashes				
Athlete's Foot p. 121	Colorless to red; between toes	Mild to intense	No	Cracks, scaling, oozing blisters

chart continues next page

Condition	Appearance/ Location	Itching	Fever	Other Symptoms/ Comments
Fungal Rashes *continued from previous page*				
Jock Itch p. 121	Patches of redness, scaling and raised areas that ooze; on groin	Mild to intense	No	Penis and scrotum usually not involved
Ringworm p. 121	Red, slightly raised rings; located any-where, including nails, scalp	Occasional	No	Fungus can cause hair loss and patchy bald spots
Allergic Reactions				
Hives p. 123	Welt-like elevations, surrounded by redness; located any-where	Intense	No	Reaction to an allergen; many possible causes
Poison Ivy/ Poison Oak	Red, elevated blisters on any exposed area; oozing, some swelling; rash begins 12 to 48 hours after contact with plant and may persist for up to two weeks	Intense	No	Also spread by pets, contaminated clothing, smoke from burning plants; to treat, clean affected skin area with soap and water, bathe with Aveeno powder (OTC); Ivy Block can be used for prevention
Rashes caused by chemicals	Redness, possible blisters; on any exposed area	Moderate to intense	No	Oozing and/or swelling

Age Spots and Dry Skin

Age Spots

Age spots are pigment changes in the skin that don't cause any medical problems. Some skin cells lose the ability to produce the pigment *melanin,* while other cells produce too much. Age spots or adult freckles are generally not raised above the skin's surface.

Seborrheic keratosis is a common skin growth that appears grayish, raised or flat and scaly, and can be darker than the surrounding skin (but not black). These growths generally require no treatment. However, any spot or growth that you can feel should be examined by your doctor. (See *Skin Cancer,* p. 111.)

Dry Skin

As the body ages, skin produces less oil, causing dry skin. Although it is the water in skin cells that keeps skin moist, the natural oil in skin keeps the water from evaporating. Very dry skin may itch, burn, crack or scale. This is called *xerosis.*

WHAT YOU CAN DO ✓

- Bathe or shower no more than once or twice a week, to preserve the natural oils in your skin.
- Take short showers, or tub or sponge baths, and use warm, not hot, water.
  - Wash the cleanest areas first and use soap only in areas that need it, such as the genitals, underarms, hands, feet and face.
  - Use moisturizing soaps, such as Aveeno or Dove.
  - Avoid bubble baths and drying or deodorant soaps such as Ivory or Dial.
  - Use a soft natural sponge or soft washcloth, instead of a brush or rough washcloth.

- Pat skin dry—don't rub it.
- Pay special attention to cleaning and drying skin folds and creases such as under the breasts or abdomen. To prevent chafing in those areas try a powder made of cornstarch instead of a moisturizer.
- Apply moisturizer generously and frequently, particularly after handwashing.
- Increase your fluid intake. (Check with your health care provider first if you're on a fluid-restricted diet.)
- Stay out of the sun, which ages the skin; when you are outside, wear a sunscreen with a sun protection factor (SPF) of 15 to 30.
- Use a humidifier.
- If you smoke, stop.

Sunburn

A *sunburn* is a true burn of the outer layer of your skin. A *first-degree* burn causes skin redness and moderate discomfort. Severe sunburns with blisters, pain and swelling are *second-degree* burns and involve the deeper skin layer. Repeated sunburning and tanning speed the skin's aging process and increase the risk of some cancers. (See *Burns,* p. 28 and *Skin Cancer,* p. 111.)

PREVENTION ✓

- Use sunscreen on all skin surfaces with a sun protection factor (SPF) of at least 15. Apply sunscreen 15 minutes before exposure and reapply it every two hours. Use a sunscreen that protects against both UVA and UVB light. Ask your pharmacist for recommendations.
- Check with your doctor or pharmacist to find out if any of your medications increase your skin's sensitivity to sunlight. If they do, use extra caution in the sun.
- Wear long sleeves and a hat with a broad brim or visor while you are in the sun.
- Drink extra fluids on sunny days, even if the temperature is not hot, unless your fluid intake has been limited by your doctor.
- Avoid the sun between 10 a.m. and 3 p.m., when the sun's rays are strongest. Cloudy conditions do not screen out the rays that can burn your skin.
- Take sunburn precautions at high altitudes, in tropical climates, and around snow or water.

WHAT YOU CAN DO ✓

- Try cool compresses or baths to ease sunburn discomfort. Adding one cup (230 mL) of baking soda or finely ground oatmeal to the bath water may increase the soothing effects.
- Take aspirin or ibuprofen (Advil, Motrin) to ease the pain and decrease inflammation. **NEVER give aspirin to children/ teenagers unless your health care provider orders it. It can cause Reye's syndrome, a rare but often fatal**

condition. CAUTION: Talk to your doctor or pharmacist before taking any other medications, including over-the-counter (OTC) medications, vitamins or herbal supplements.

- Apply aloe vera gel or lotion to make your skin more comfortable.
- Avoid oil-based products, such as petroleum jelly, for 24 hours after a sunburn. They may actually retain the heat.
- Avoid products that contain anesthetic "caines" such as benzocaine. They may cause an allergic reaction in sensitive skin.
- Drink extra water and watch for signs of dehydration, unless your fluid intake has been limited by your doctor. (See *Dehydration,* p. 203.)
- Get extra rest and avoid exertion for 24 hours.

Decision *helper*   Sunburn
DO THESE APPLY:

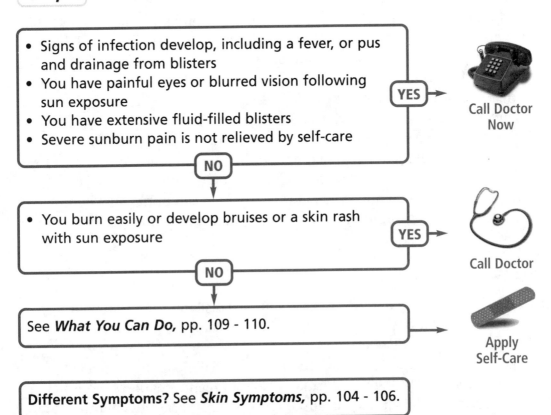

- Signs of infection develop, including a fever, or pus and drainage from blisters
- You have painful eyes or blurred vision following sun exposure
- You have extensive fluid-filled blisters
- Severe sunburn pain is not relieved by self-care

YES →   Call Doctor Now

NO

- You burn easily or develop bruises or a skin rash with sun exposure

YES →   Call Doctor

NO

See *What You Can Do,* pp. 109 - 110.   →   Apply Self-Care

Different Symptoms? See *Skin Symptoms,* pp. 104 - 106.

Skin Cancer

The American Cancer Society estimates that by the age of 65, 40 to 50 percent of all Americans have had at least one episode of skin cancer.

There are many types of skin cancer, but the three most common are basal cell carcinoma, squamous cell carcinoma and malignant melanoma.

Basal cell carcinoma, the most common type, is a slow-growing cancer that forms in the outermost layer of the skin. If treated early, it is usually completely curable. If untreated, it can ultimately spread (*metastasize*) and cause extensive skin damage.

Squamous cell carcinoma, the second most frequent type, may appear as a scaly, slightly raised patch that bleeds or crusts. It can double in size within weeks.

Malignant melanoma is the third most common and deadliest type of skin cancer. This is cancer of the *melanocytes,* the pigment cells of the skin. Unlike most other types of skin cancer, malignant melanoma can spread through the lymph system and the bloodstream. That's why it is very important that it be detected in the earliest possible stage. More than 90 percent of cases of very early melanoma can be cured. However, the prognosis is not as favorable for cases that are treated in later stages. Other factors that influence the outcome of treatment include age and general health.

Some Causes

The primary known cause of all types of skin cancer is exposure to the ultraviolet (UV) radiation contained in sunlight. People who live in sunny climates and those with fair skin, freckles, blond or red hair, or blue eyes are at greatest risk. However, people with dark skin also can develop skin cancer. Some people with many moles (*nevi*) that contain abnormal (*dysplastic*) cells have an increased risk of developing melanoma.

Other factors that increase the risk of skin cancer include exposure to artificial sources of UV radiation (such as commercial tanning devices and phototherapy for certain skin disorders), concurrent use of certain drugs or cosmetics, immunosuppressive treatment, AIDS, hereditary disorders, and exposure to x-rays, uranium and a variety of chemicals.

NOTE YOUR SYMPTOMS ☑

Skin cancer forms without causing any symptoms of illness. Therefore, it's extremely important to be aware of the signs, especially in people with known risk factors.

Check your skin once a month for any skin irregularities. If you have any suspicious growths on your skin, have them checked by your doctor. A skin *biopsy,* in which part or all of the tissue from a mole or suspicious growth is removed for analysis, may be required. Biopsy is the only definitive test for melanoma and other skin cancers.

Melanoma

The "hallmark" sign of melanoma is a change in the size or shape of a mole. "ABCD" is an abbreviation used to make it easy to remember the four basic signs of possible melanoma:

- Asymmetry—The shape of one half of a mole doesn't match the other.
- Border—The edges are ragged, notched or blurred.
- Color—The color is uneven and shades of black, brown or tan are present. Areas of white, red or blue may also be seen.
- Diameter—There is a change in size. The mole may be raised or flat, round or oval.

Other signs include a mole that scales, oozes, bleeds or changes in the way it feels. Some moles will become hard, lumpy, itchy, swollen or tender. Melanoma may also appear as a new mole.

Other Skin Cancers

Watch for skin irregularities that:

- Have a smooth, shiny or waxy surface
- Are small in size
- Bleed or become crusty
- Are flat or lumpy, red or pale

PREVENTION ✓

The best approach to skin cancer is preventing it in the first place:
- Stay out of the sun as much as possible, especially if you have fair skin, a history of sunburns or a current diagnosis of skin cancer.
- If you can't avoid sun exposure, wear protective clothing (hats and long sleeves) and gradually build up exposure to sunlight.
- Avoid or limit sunlight exposure between 10 a.m. and 3 p.m., when the sun's rays are the most direct.
- Some medications can greatly increase the likelihood of sunburn. Check all prescription and over-the-counter (OTC) medications for precautions about sun exposure.
- ALWAYS use sun block, even on overcast, cloudy days. Sunscreens are rated by a sun protection factor (SPF); the higher the SPF number, the greater the protection.
- Check your skin regularly.

Decision *helper* **Skin Cancer**
DO THESE APPLY:

- You are concerned about a skin lesion or growth
- There is a change in the size, shape or feel of a mole

YES →

Call Doctor

Eczema and Psoriasis

Eczema is more a symptom than a disease. It involves dry, irritated patches of skin that usually result from contact with a harsh or irritating substance. Psoriasis, sometimes mistaken for eczema, is a chronic and sometimes serious skin condition.

Eczema

Eczema, also known as *dermatitis,* is common on the face, neck, hands, elbows, wrists and/or knees. Dry, scaly, irritated, itchy skin patches or rashes are its signs. Causes range from contact with detergents or cleaning solvents (also called *contact dermatitis*) to emotional stress. The cause of eczema may be unknown, however.

A common form of eczema is called *atopic* (allergic) dermatitis. You're a likely candidate if you have a personal or family history of asthma, hay fever or some other allergy. Recent studies suggest that certain foods—such as citrus fruits, wheat, eggs and nuts—may also be responsible in some cases.

Psoriasis

Eczema can be confused with other skin conditions, such as *psoriasis,* another chronic skin condition. Psoriasis appears as silvery skin patches or *plaques,* often located on the knees, elbows and scalp. Normally, skin cells mature and are shed once a month. With psoriasis this occurs at a much faster rate—every three to four days. Because the *dermis* (lower layer of skin cells) is dividing so rapidly, dead cells accumulate in thicker-than-normal patches on the *epidermis* (skin's outermost layer). The symptoms of this chronic disease typically come and go over weeks or months and then may disappear altogether.

As many as 4 to 5 million Americans cope with psoriasis. Although there is no cure, the right therapy can help control symptoms. Care is individualized and based on the severity of symptoms. Treatment may consist of self-care, *phototherapy* (exposure to ultraviolet or infrared light) and a variety of medications to help relieve the scaling.

WHAT YOU CAN DO ✓

- Avoid drying out the skin. Limit the use of soap and bathe or shower in cool or lukewarm water. Follow with an unscented moisturizer.
- Use *hypoallergenic* (non-allergy causing) makeup, or none at all. Wear rubber gloves for dishwashing and other household chores. Wear lightweight, loose-fitting cotton clothing, especially during exercise. (Wool and synthetic materials may be irritating.)
- Trim nails to minimize the effects of scratching.
- Do not apply anesthetic lotions or antihistamine creams unless your doctor prescribes them; they can actually increase irritation. For the worst areas, try using a cool gauze dressing soaked in diluted aluminum acetate solution (Domeboro, Bluboro, Burow's). Follow package directions.
- Try topical corticosteroid creams to control symptoms if other self-care measures fail; use infrequently to lower risk of side effects.
- Try medicated shampoos, such as Head & Shoulders, Selsun Blue and Neutrogena.

If you think you have psoriasis, consult your doctor for a treatment plan that is best for your symptoms. If you've been diagnosed with psoriasis and your current treatment is no longer working, call your doctor. New products are being developed that may help.

See *Decision helper,* p. 116.

Decision **Eczema and Psoriasis**
helper **DO THESE APPLY:**

- Signs of infection are present
  (redness around the area or red streaks leading away from it; swelling; warmth or tenderness; pus; fever of 101° F [38.3° C] or higher; tender or swollen lymph nodes) **YES** →

Call Doctor
Now

NO

- The whole body, or the eyelids, face or genitals are involved
- Eczema sores become crusty or develop a weepy discharge
- No improvement occurs or symptoms worsen after one week of treatment
- Itching makes sleeping difficult despite self-care
- Eczema or psoriasis interferes with daily functions or causes emotional stress

YES →

Call Doctor

NO

See *What You Can Do,* p. 115.
History of allergies? See *Allergic Reaction,* p. 123.

Apply
Self-Care

Different Symptoms? See *Skin Symptoms,* pp. 104 - 106.

Hair Loss

Hair is constantly lost and replaced by your body. By far the most common reason for hair loss, or *alopecia,* is male-pattern baldness, in which hair replacement fails to keep up with hair loss.

Causes

The cause of hair loss is often indicated by the way it falls out and the condition of the scalp. In *male-pattern baldness,* typically the hair loss starts with a receding hairline, continuing until only a horseshoe-shaped area of hair remains around the head. The scalp looks healthy. Both aging and genetics play a part in balding, with as many as 60 percent of men over age 50 affected. *Female-pattern baldness,* which is a general thinning of hair at the crown or hairline, is also genetic and influenced by hormonal changes during or after menopause.

Sudden loss of hair in patches is called *alopecia areata.* The hair generally grows back normally within several months.

Hair that falls out in large clumps and uncovers a normal-looking scalp may be due to a rare condition called *generalized alopecia.* It can be alarming to see clumps of hair in the shower drain or on a pillow. Causes usually involve physical or emotional stress such as surgery, trauma, high fever or burns. The hair usually falls out three to four months after the stressful event and eventually grows back.

Chemotherapy can cause complete or partial hair loss on the body, with hair almost always growing back when treatment ends. Some common medications that can cause significant hair loss include heparin, oral contraceptives, amphetamines and beta blockers.

Hair loss that develops over weeks, months or even years can be due to autoimmune diseases (such as systemic lupus), infectious diseases (such as syphilis) or endocrine disorders (such as thyroid disease).

Hair loss that is accompanied by an inflamed or scaly scalp may be caused by psoriasis (see *Psoriasis,* p. 114) or dandruff. The hair usually thins because of the intense scratching or applied treatment. If hair loss leaves bald spots with a gray-green scale, *ringworm* (a fungal infection) may be suspected. (See *Ringworm,* p. 121.)

Some people may develop a nervous hair-pulling habit that can also lead to hair loss.

WHAT YOU CAN DO ✔

Male- and female-pattern baldness can't be prevented, but the over-the-counter (OTC) drug minoxidil (Rogaine) has been used with mixed results. When rubbed on the scalp, this expensive lotion has sometimes slowed hair loss and generated new hair growth, but many people have been disappointed with the results.

Other alternatives include a variety of hair restoration surgeries and the oral prescription medication finasteride (Propecia and Proscar).

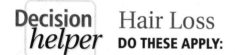

Decision *helper*   Hair Loss   **DO THESE APPLY:**

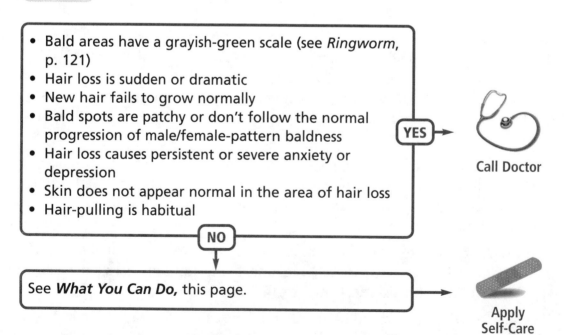

- Bald areas have a grayish-green scale (see *Ringworm,* p. 121)
- Hair loss is sudden or dramatic
- New hair fails to grow normally
- Bald spots are patchy or don't follow the normal progression of male/female-pattern baldness
- Hair loss causes persistent or severe anxiety or depression
- Skin does not appear normal in the area of hair loss
- Hair-pulling is habitual

YES ➡

Call Doctor

NO

See *What You Can Do,* this page.

Apply Self-Care

Boils

A *boil* is a red, swollen, painful bump that looks like a large pimple. It is usually caused by an infected hair follicle in an area of the body that is under pressure or chafed.

Common sites for boils are the buttocks, groin, waistline, armpits, neck and face. Bacteria, most often *staphylococcus,* get blocked in the follicle and develop an abscess. The tissue around the follicle becomes tender and inflamed as it tries to wall off the infection. This forces the abscess outward until it ruptures on the skin surface and drains. If the wound is kept open and clean, it can heal; if it closes off too soon, the pus pocket can form again.

PREVENTION ✓

- For areas that are prone to boils, wash and dry well.
- Avoid clothing that is too tight. Eliminate chafing and ease pressure against your skin whenever possible.
- Keep clothes and personal linen of someone with a boil separate from the rest of the household to prevent spreading the infection.

WHAT YOU CAN DO ✓

- Wash the area frequently to prevent boils from spreading.
- Apply warm, moist compresses to the boil for 15 to 20 minutes, four times a day. The moist heat helps bring the boil to a head and soften the skin to ease the rupture. This may take up to a week of compress treatments.
- **Do not squeeze, scratch, cut or force the boil to drain.** Any pressure or forced opening can push the bacteria deeper into the skin and spread the infection.
- Once the boil begins to drain, keep the wound open and clean, and:
  - Continue applying compresses at least three times a day.
  - Wash the area thoroughly with soap and water twice a day or as needed.
  - Apply antibacterial ointment and a sterile bandage after each compress treatment or whenever the old dressing becomes moist.

- Take aspirin or ibuprofen (Advil, Motrin) to ease pain and inflammation (follow the directions on the package). **NEVER give aspirin to children/teenagers unless your health care provider orders it. It can cause Reye's syndrome, a rare but often fatal condition. CAUTION: Talk to your doctor or pharmacist before taking any other medications, including over-the-counter (OTC) medications, vitamins or herbal supplements.**

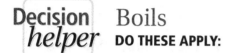

Boils

DO THESE APPLY:

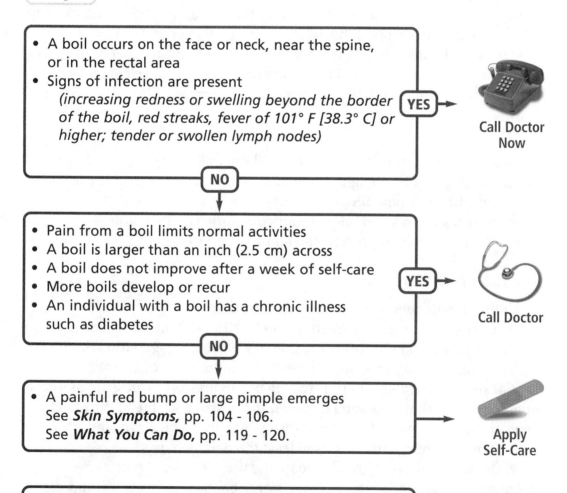

- A boil occurs on the face or neck, near the spine, or in the rectal area
- Signs of infection are present
  (increasing redness or swelling beyond the border of the boil, red streaks, fever of 101° F [38.3° C] or higher; tender or swollen lymph nodes)

YES → **Call Doctor Now**

NO

- Pain from a boil limits normal activities
- A boil is larger than an inch (2.5 cm) across
- A boil does not improve after a week of self-care
- More boils develop or recur
- An individual with a boil has a chronic illness such as diabetes

YES → **Call Doctor**

NO

- A painful red bump or large pimple emerges
  See *Skin Symptoms,* pp. 104 - 106.
  See *What You Can Do,* pp. 119 - 120.

→ **Apply Self-Care**

Different Symptoms? See *Skin Symptoms,* pp. 104 - 106.

Fungal Infections

Fungus requires moisture to grow. That's why common fungal infections develop in the folds of skin that trap moisture. They tend to spread from person to person in public areas such as showers and swimming pools.

Ringworm, an infection of the nails, skin or scalp, has nothing to do with worms, but gets its name from its characteristic red rings.

Athlete's foot, a form of ringworm, makes feet red, itchy and irritated.

Jock itch mainly affects men. Symptoms include minor to intense itching in the groin area and, in more serious cases, patches of redness, scaling and raised areas that ooze. The penis and scrotum (the skin "sac" that holds the testes) are usually not involved.

PREVENTION ✓

- Always use your own towels.
- Wear sandals in public showers, pools or locker rooms.
- Wear cotton socks to absorb moisture and change them every day.
- Have all pets checked for ringworm before bringing them into your home. Avoid touching stray dogs or cats.
- Launder secondhand clothing.

WHAT YOU CAN DO ✓

Keep the infected area clean and dry. Wear loose, cotton clothing and clean all clothes in hot water and detergent. Avoid damp public areas, such as shower rooms.

Many over-the-counter (OTC) anti-fungal medications applied to the skin are effective treatments for these infections. Follow all directions on the container.

See *Decision helper,* p. 122.

Decision helper

Fungal Infections
DO THESE APPLY:

- Signs of infection develop
  (redness around the area or red streaks leading away from it; swelling; warmth or tenderness; pus; fever of 101° F [38.3° C] or higher; tender or swollen lymph nodes)

YES →

Call Doctor Now

NO ↓

- Symptoms of athlete's foot or other foot problems occur in a person with diabetes and/or peripheral vascular disease
- Toenails are thickened, distorted, yellowish or crumbly (possible fungal infection of nails)
- Symptoms of ringworm occur on the scalp or on large areas of the chest or abdomen
- Jock itch spreads to the anal area
- Symptoms of any fungal problems persist or worsen after self-care
- Ringworm is not completely gone after four weeks of treatment

YES →

Call Doctor

NO ↓

- Signs of ringworm develop
  - The rash begins as small, round, pink patches
  - Patches turn red and grow into a ring shape
  - The center of the ring clears as it enlarges
- Groin itching is mild to intense
- Feet are red, itchy and irritated

See **What You Can Do,** p. 121.

Apply Self-Care

Allergic Reaction

An *allergic reaction* occurs when the body's immune system reacts to a foreign substance in an extreme way. Substances that trigger such an immune response are called *allergens*. Common allergens include pollen, animal dander, foods, medications, molds, insect venom and house dust, to name only a few. Literally anything you inhale, eat, drink or touch can cause an allergic reaction.

When your body encounters an allergen, it releases protective chemicals called *histamines*. While this process is part of your body's normal defense system, excess histamines can cause a runny nose, watery eyes and itching of the throat, nose, eyes and roof of your mouth. You may also experience hives and other rashes, stomach cramps, diarrhea, or nausea and vomiting. If the respiratory system is involved, wheezing, coughing and shortness of breath can occur.

Anaphylactic Reaction

If the reaction is severe enough, life-threatening *anaphylaxis* may take place. During an anaphylactic reaction, the airways of the lungs constrict, making it difficult to breathe; blood vessels dilate, making blood pressure drop, and the heart beats erratically. Swelling, hives, *cyanosis* (bluish skin) and convulsions may also occur. Anaphylactic reactions, untreated, may lead to unconsciousness or even death.

PREVENTION ✓

The most effective way to treat an allergy is to:

- Avoid exposure to the offending substance. This is particularly true of food allergies, which can get worse with each exposure.
- If you notice a reaction to a specific food, try eliminating it from your diet and watch for improvement in your symptoms.

- Use insect repellent and extra caution when you're in an area with a lot of insects.
- If you have hay fever, stay indoors when pollen counts are high; keep windows and doors closed.
- Make sure your home, car and workplace are as clean and dust-free as possible. Use a vacuum with a HEPA filter for cleaning.

WHAT YOU CAN DO ✓

If you have had a life-threatening allergic reaction in the past, ask your doctor about whether an allergic reaction kit (Anakit or EpiPen) is appropriate for you.

For insect stings, remove the stinger if you can see it by flicking it out with a driver's license or credit card. Do not squeeze the stinger, which can release more venom into the skin. Apply an ice bag to slow your body's absorption of venom.

For itching, avoid scratching the area, which can lead to infection. To relieve discomfort:

- Apply cool wet compresses of plain water or Burow's solution, according to package directions.
- Take an oatmeal bath (1/2 to 1 cup [115 to 230 mL] of oatmeal in lukewarm water) or bathe in the commercial form called Aveeno.
- Bathe in a baking soda tub (1/2 cup [115 mL] baking soda in lukewarm water).
- Try Calamine or Caladryl lotion on your skin to combat the itch.
- Use over-the-counter (OTC) hydrocortisone cream or ointment. However, apply the hydrocortisone sparingly and do not use it on infected skin or near your eyes.
- Take an oral antihistamine such as Benadryl or Chlor-Trimeton for symptom relief. Talk to your doctor about which ones may cause drowsiness. **CAUTION: Talk to your doctor or pharmacist before taking any other medications, including over-the-counter (OTC) medications, vitamins or herbal supplements.**

Decision *helper* Allergic Reaction

DO THESE APPLY:

- Someone loses consciousness during an anaphylactic reaction
- You have a sudden and severe onset of any of the following:
  - *Cyanosis* (bluish discoloration of the skin or lips)
  - Coughing, wheezing or shortness of breath
  - Confusion or agitation
  - Dizziness
  - Hives or itching
  - Nausea, vomiting, diarrhea or abdominal cramping
  - Swelling or tingling of the lips, mouth, tongue or throat

YES →

Seek
Emergency
Care

NO ↓

- You develop hives or any other rash after being stung or bitten by an insect or after eating or taking a medication

YES →

Call Doctor
Now

NO ↓

- You have swelling of the eyelids, face or genitals
- You have severe itching that does not respond to self-care measures
- A severe allergic reaction has occurred in the past, and you have no plans or medications for handling future attacks (such as an Anakit)

YES →

Call Doctor

Tick Bites

Ticks are small parasites related to spiders that embed themselves in the skin. Although tick bites are rarely harmful, ticks may transmit serious diseases such as *Rocky Mountain spotted fever* and *Lyme disease.*

Ticks are common in all outdoor areas of the United States and may be passed to people by their pets. Ticks frequently lodge in the scalp, nape of the neck, ankles, genital area or skin folds. Although small, ticks embedded in the skin are usually visible.

Tick bites often go unnoticed. They are characterized by itching, a small, hard lump on the skin, and redness surrounding the bite.

PREVENTION ✓

- Avoid tick-infested areas, such as thickly wooded brush, whenever possible.
- Use an insect repellent on your skin and clothing whenever you plan to be outdoors for any length of time, especially in the warm months of spring and summer.
- Wear light-colored clothing, long-sleeved shirts and long pants. Make sure your shirt is tucked inside your pants, and tuck your pants inside your boots or socks.
- After being in a known tick-infested area, check your body thoroughly and remove any ticks you find.

WHAT YOU CAN DO ✓

Never scratch a tick bite. The body of the tick may break off, leaving the head embedded in the skin.

Ticks should be removed carefully and promptly to help prevent the diseases they carry.

- With small tweezers, grip the tick as close to the surface of the skin as possible. Pull straight up and out using gentle, steady pressure. Do not squeeze the body of a tick, since this can increase the chance of getting a tick-borne disease.
- Extract the tick slowly and firmly to assure complete removal.
- Clean the area of the tick bite with soap and water, then apply antiseptic.

FINAL NOTES ✓

Lyme disease is usually transmitted by small deer ticks, common in summer and early fall. Symptoms develop up to three weeks after a bite.

Rocky Mountain spotted fever is usually transmitted by wood ticks in the West and by dog ticks and lone star ticks in the East and Southeast. This disease generally occurs in warm weather and symptoms begin suddenly, two to 14 days after the bite.

See *Decision helper,* p. 128.

Decision helper   Tick Bites
DO THESE APPLY:

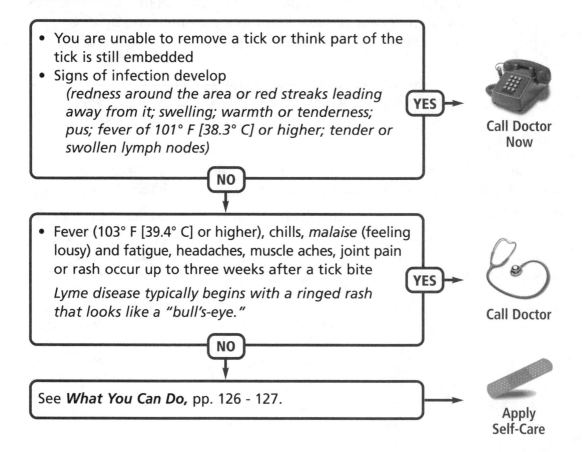

- You are unable to remove a tick or think part of the tick is still embedded
- Signs of infection develop
  (redness around the area or red streaks leading away from it; swelling; warmth or tenderness; pus; fever of 101° F [38.3° C] or higher; tender or swollen lymph nodes)

YES → **Call Doctor Now**

NO ↓

- Fever (103° F [39.4° C] or higher), chills, *malaise* (feeling lousy) and fatigue, headaches, muscle aches, joint pain or rash occur up to three weeks after a tick bite

  Lyme disease typically begins with a ringed rash that looks like a "bull's-eye."

YES → **Call Doctor**

NO ↓

See **What You Can Do,** pp. 126 - 127. → **Apply Self-Care**

Eye Concerns

After about age 40, the lens and functions of the eye become less flexible. This is called *presbyopia,* which makes focusing on close objects difficult. The eyes of older adults often adjust less easily to changes in light and many people experience drooping eyelids from a loss of elasticity in the skin surrounding the eyes. This drooping may even obstruct vision. Eyes may also tear less as you age, making them feel dry and sometimes itchy. Protect your eyesight with proper care and regular checkups. Many vision problems can be treated with early diagnosis and treatment.

Glaucoma/Cataracts/ Macular Degeneration

Three of the most common eye problems affecting older adults are glaucoma, cataracts and macular degeneration. (Also see *Diabetic Retinopathy,* p. 229.)

Glaucoma

Glaucoma, the second leading cause of blindness in the U.S., involves high pressure inside the eye. This gradually destroys nerve fibers in the *retina,* the area at the back of the eyeball that receives and transmits images to the brain. Glaucoma can cause "tunnel vision" (a loss of peripheral vision). Blindness may eventually occur.

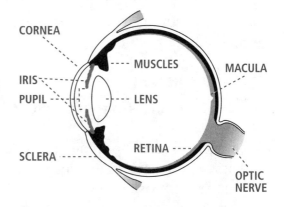

Figure 14

Glaucoma is usually painless and has no early symptoms, so regular checkups are important. Testing is painless; treatment involves medicated eye drops or surgery to reduce pressure.

Cataracts

Opaque or cloudy areas in the eye lens, known as *cataracts,* gradually make vision dull and fuzzy, increase discomfort from glare and may eventually make it impossible to read. Cataracts occur in more than 50 percent of people over age 75. Cataracts are most common in individuals with diabetes (see *Diabetes,* p. 226) or who have had years of unprotected exposure to sunlight, and those who have taken steroids long-term.

Reducing your exposure to glare both indoors and outdoors will lessen how much a cataract affects your vision. Use indirect lighting (light that bounces off walls and ceilings) in the home and wear sunglasses that provide 99 to 100 percent UV (ultraviolet ray) protection outdoors.

Once the cataract begins to severely affect your vision, surgical removal should be considered. Cataracts can be removed in a relatively simple surgical procedure that does not require an overnight stay in a clinic or hospital.

Macular Degeneration

The *macula* is the central area of your retina and contains the largest portion of light-sensitive nerves. (See Figure 14, p. 129.) With age, some degeneration of the macula is normal, causing a blurring of central vision, but peripheral vision is not affected. Macular degeneration, the leading cause of blindness in the United States, involves serious deterioration of the macula and loss of central vision.

Good glasses, strong lighting and magnifying lenses can help you cope with the condition.

WHAT YOU CAN DO ✓

- Be alert for changes in your vision such as:
  - Blurring
  - Inability to focus on small or faraway objects or printed type
  - Loss of peripheral vision, leading to "tunnel vision"
  - Dull or fuzzy vision
  - Inability to tolerate bright sunshine
- See your eye doctor for regular checkups, especially if any of the above symptoms are present.
- Wear sunglasses to protect your eyes from the harmful rays of the sun.

Red, Irritated Eyes

Eye discomfort ranges from simple itching, which can be caused by a common cold or an allergic reaction, to pain that may signify a much more serious eye disease.

Conjunctivitis (pinkeye) refers to an inflammation of the *conjunctiva*—the outermost membrane that covers the eye and inner part of the eyelid—and is the most common eye disease. Pinkeye can be caused by viruses, bacteria, allergies, pollution or other irritants such as cigarette smoke. The most common symptoms are redness of the whites of the eyes, gritty or itchy eyes, tearing, swelling, eye discharge that is matted in the morning, and sensitivity to light.

It's best not to rub your eyes, which may aggravate symptoms and increase the risk of spreading infection to the other eye or to other people. Most forms of eye discomfort respond well to self-care.

PREVENTION ✓

Some preventive measures can reduce your risk of eye problems:

- Avoid infection: wash hands frequently and don't share towels.
- Never use anyone else's makeup.
- Discard your mascara after a couple of months.
- Wear goggles to protect your eyes when you use tools or swim in chlorinated swimming pools.
- Air condition your home and/or car to reduce allergens. Be sure to change filters regularly. Do not use an evaporative (swamp) cooler.
- Use vacuum cleaners and heating and air systems with HEPA filters, which reduce airborne allergens.

WHAT YOU CAN DO ✓

Conjunctivitis

- Avoid rubbing or touching your eyes.
- Wash your hands frequently with soap and water, especially if you're around a child who has pinkeye.
- Don't share washcloths or towels.
- Change bed linens and pillowcases daily.
- Apply warm or cool compresses.
- If you wear contact lenses, remove them until the infection subsides.
- Try over-the-counter (OTC) eye drops to relieve itchiness.
- Try antihistamines to help relieve allergic eye discomfort. Read the precautions on the label regarding drowsiness. **CAUTION: Talk to your doctor or pharmacist before taking any other medications, including over-the-counter (OTC) medications, vitamins or herbal supplements.**

FINAL NOTES ✓

Eye pain sometimes is caused by injury, infection or some other disease. Sensitivity to bright light is common with viral infections such as flu and disappears once the infection clears up. Injury to the eye by a foreign object also can cause pain. This type of eye pain should be treated by your doctor. (See *Object in Eye,* p. 136.)

Decision *helper* Red, Irritated Eyes
DO THESE APPLY:

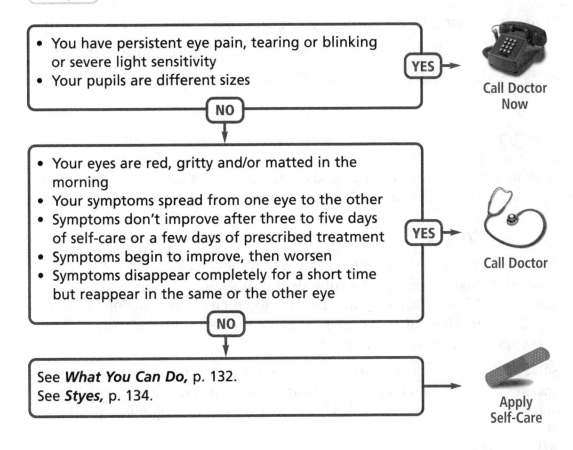

- You have persistent eye pain, tearing or blinking or severe light sensitivity
- Your pupils are different sizes

YES → Call Doctor Now

NO

- Your eyes are red, gritty and/or matted in the morning
- Your symptoms spread from one eye to the other
- Symptoms don't improve after three to five days of self-care or a few days of prescribed treatment
- Symptoms begin to improve, then worsen
- Symptoms disappear completely for a short time but reappear in the same or the other eye

YES → Call Doctor

NO

See *What You Can Do,* p. 132.
See *Styes,* p. 134.

→ Apply Self-Care

Styes

Styes are caused by a bacterial infection of the tiny glands near the base of the eyelashes. They almost never result in damage to the eye or sight, and should not be confused with blocked tear ducts.

A *stye* typically starts out looking like a pimple on the eyelid—a small, red, tender and swollen bump—and grows to full size over a day or so. The stye then fills with pus and ruptures within a few days. If the bacteria spread, more than one stye may occur. Styes can also form inside the eyelid, but this is less common.

WHAT YOU CAN DO ☑

Wring out a clean cloth soaked in warm or hot water. Place it directly on the affected (closed) eye. For best results, do this three or four times a day for about 10 to 15 minutes each time. The stye will then rupture and drain, which usually occurs after about two days. Sometimes a stye may fade away without ever coming to a head and draining.

Since styes can be spread from one eye to another, and from one person to another through close contact, wash your hands frequently. Never pinch the stye to try to remove the pus, since this may spread infection deeper into the tissue.

FINAL NOTES ☑

Styes are common enough that many people can identify them on their own. Occasionally, they are confused with a *chalazion,* a swelling caused by a blocked gland within the eyelid. Unlike a stye, a chalazion is painless and is not helped by self-care. It may require minor surgery.

For a stye, a doctor may prescribe an antibiotic solution applied directly to the eyelid. Oral antibiotics are usually reserved for styes that do not respond to other treatment, are very large, or are located inside the eyelid. A particularly stubborn stye may need to be lanced and drained by a surgeon. Never try to do this on your own.

A stye can be extremely unpleasant because of its pain and appearance. Properly treated, it will disappear soon after it comes to a head and drains.

Decision *helper*   Styes
DO THESE APPLY:

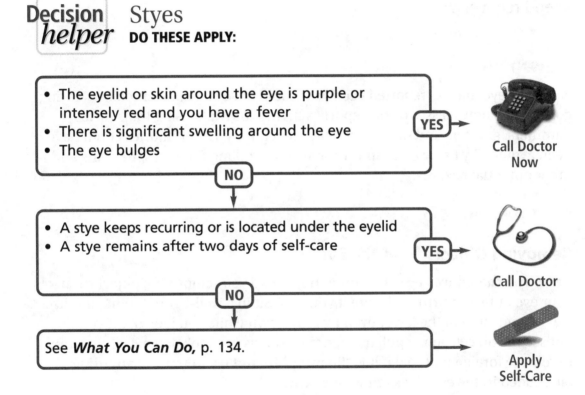

- The eyelid or skin around the eye is purple or intensely red and you have a fever
- There is significant swelling around the eye
- The eye bulges

YES → Call Doctor Now

NO

- A stye keeps recurring or is located under the eyelid
- A stye remains after two days of self-care

YES → Call Doctor

NO

See *What You Can Do,* p. 134.

→ Apply Self-Care

Object in Eye

Tears and blinking are your natural defenses against sand, dust and other particles that enter the eye. But when something larger injures the eye, other steps are necessary to protect your vision and speed recovery.

PREVENTION ✓

Nearly all eye injuries reported each year could have been prevented by wearing goggles or safety glasses during sports activities or while using tools (drills, hammers, grinders and saws) and heavy machinery. Other injuries could have been avoided by using common sense when handling fireworks, BB guns and other potential hazards.

WHAT YOU CAN DO ✓

Removing Objects from the Eye

Never rub the injured eye. Ask someone to help you remove the object from your eye or use a mirror to locate it yourself. Sit in a well-lighted room and use clean hands to pull the lower eyelid gently down while you look up. If you do not see the object, gently pull the upper lid out as you look down. Only attempt to remove foreign material if it is "floating." **Do not try to remove anything embedded in the eye. Seek emergency care.**

If you cannot readily see the object, grasp the lashes of your upper lid and pull down. Blink several times. This sometimes removes small particles.

- Flush the eye with clean water by pressing the rim of a small glass against the eye socket and tilting your head back. Open and close the eye.
- If flushing with water proves unsuccessful, moisten a cotton swab and gently lift off the object. Flush the eye with water afterward.
- Do not use ointments or *anesthetic* (pain relief) drops in the eye.

Handling Possible Complications

- If a trip to the doctor is necessary (see *Decision helper,* below), cover the eye with a sterile pad or clean cloth and keep it still. Close both eyes to prevent involuntary movement.
- If you can't close your eye, tape a paper cup over it.

FINAL NOTES ☑

An object in the eye can scratch the *cornea* (covering of the eye) and may cause significant vision loss. Your recovery depends on how deeply the object penetrates the eye, how quickly the injury is treated and whether an infection develops.

 **Object in Eye**
DO THESE APPLY:

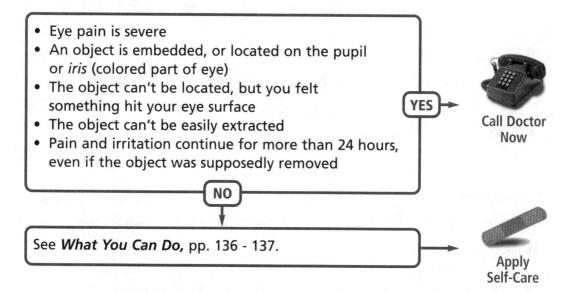

- Eye pain is severe
- An object is embedded, or located on the pupil or *iris* (colored part of eye)
- The object can't be located, but you felt something hit your eye surface
- The object can't be easily extracted
- Pain and irritation continue for more than 24 hours, even if the object was supposedly removed

YES → **Call Doctor Now**

NO

See *What You Can Do,* pp. 136 - 137.

Apply Self-Care

Ear/Nose/Throat

As we age, so do our senses; sight, hearing, taste and smell are altered by the effects of time. Taste buds decrease in number, for example, dulling our ability to perceive salty and sweet flavors. Thus, foods naturally begin to take on a different flavor. (See *Mouth Concerns,* p. 161.) The sense of smell—connected to taste—also begins to fade a bit.

The ability to hear high-frequency tones decreases, making the range of spoken words harder to understand.

Because the *immune system* responds more slowly, we are less able to fight off common infections, such as cold or flu, that affect the ears, nose and/or throat. The good news, though, is that with a healthy diet and exercise, you can fight back against many common complaints.

The Common Cold

A cold is a viral illness that can cause a sore throat, runny nose and other symptoms. Most colds are caused by *rhinoviruses* ("rhino" refers to the nose), which are transmitted through sneezes, coughs or handling virus-contaminated objects.

PREVENTION ☑

Since there's no cure, avoiding the cold virus is the best way to beat the bug.

- Wash your hands frequently.
- Avoid touching your eyes, nose or mouth after touching objects that could be contaminated with the cold virus, such as doorknobs or stair railings.

NOTE YOUR SYMPTOMS ☑

Cold symptoms develop suddenly within two to six days of exposure. A runny, stuffy nose is a very common symptom. However, runny noses are also caused by hay fever or *allergic rhinitis*. (See *Hay Fever,* p. 141.)

Foul-smelling, yellow or gray-green discharge from the nose usually indicates a bacterial infection. A foreign object in a nostril can prompt a runny nose, as well. In this case, the nose runs from one nostril and the discharge is foul-smelling.

The excess mucus produced by a runny nose can cause postnasal drip, which triggers a nighttime cough and can lead to a sore throat. Ear or sinus infections also may develop if mucus plugs the *eustachian tube* between the nose and ear or the sinuses. (See *Sinusitis*, p. 143; *Middle Ear Infection*, p. 154.)

Other cold symptoms include:

- Scratchy or sore throat
- Sneezing
- Watery eyes
- Headache
- Swollen glands
- Cough that fails to bring up sputum
- Fever, usually below 101°F [38.3°C]

A cold usually runs its course in one to two weeks.

WHAT YOU CAN DO ✓

Simple Steps to Relief

- Get plenty of rest.
- Drink lots of fluids.
- Use a cool-mist vaporizer to relieve congestion. Change the water daily and rinse the vaporizer with a weak bleach and water solution.

Medication Considerations

Over-the-counter (OTC) medications will not shorten the course of a cold, but they may offer temporary relief from some symptoms. All have minor side effects. (See *Using Medications*, p. 326; *Home Pharmacy*, p. 331.) **CAUTION: Talk to your doctor or pharmacist before taking any other medications, including over-the-counter (OTC) medications, vitamins or herbal supplements.**

- Nose drops or nasal sprays are effective decongestants, but they can increase stuffiness if they are used for more than three days in a row. Instead, substitute a homemade saline solution of one-fourth teaspoon (1.2 mL) of salt to eight ounces (230 mL) of water. Discard any unused saline daily.

- Oral decongestants may act as stimulants and make you restless or unable to sleep. Often they are combined with antihistamines (which tend to cause drowsiness) to lessen this side effect.
- Antihistamines appear to be more effective against allergy symptoms than cold-related complaints. Some of them cause drowsiness, which can help you sleep, but are dangerous to use while driving or operating heavy machinery.
- Pain relievers, such as aspirin, ibuprofen (Advil, Motrin) and acetaminophen (Tylenol) can lessen aches, pains and fevers. **NEVER give aspirin to children/ teenagers unless your health care provider orders it. It can cause Reye's syndrome, a rare but often fatal condition.**

FINAL NOTES ✓

In some cases, the common cold can lead to ear or sinus infections, laryngitis, bronchitis or pneumonia. Other conditions—such as strep throat and allergies— produce symptoms which mimic a cold. Monitor the cold's progress and watch for increasing fever, rashes, ear pain or breathing difficulty that can signal a more serious illness. (See index, pp. 381 - 416.)

Decision *helper* Common Cold

DO THESE APPLY:

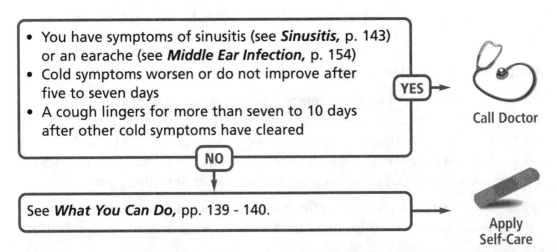

- You have symptoms of sinusitis (see *Sinusitis,* p. 143) or an earache (see *Middle Ear Infection,* p. 154)
- Cold symptoms worsen or do not improve after five to seven days
- A cough lingers for more than seven to 10 days after other cold symptoms have cleared

YES → Call Doctor

NO

See *What You Can Do,* pp. 139 - 140.

→ Apply Self-Care

Hay Fever

Hay fever sufferers can blame pollen for the sneezing, watery eyes and runny nose that mark this common allergy. Some form of pollen is almost always in the air, whether from trees in the spring, summer grass or fall ragweed. The severity of your symptoms can depend on the time of year and the airborne pollen present on a particular day.

NOTE YOUR SYMPTOMS ✓

Hay fever occurs when your body's *antibodies* (protective agents) react to pollen and prompt the release of *histamine*. Histamine inflames the lining of nasal passages and eyes and causes sneezing, itching, runny nose and watery eyes. Headaches, irritability and insomnia are possible, too.

Hay fever can be confused with the common cold, but you can suspect you have allergies if your symptoms last for long periods and return during the same season each year. If hay fever runs in your family, chances are your sneezes are based on allergies, too. If necessary, your doctor can test your nasal secretions to confirm whether you have hay fever, and allergy testing can identify which pollens cause the most problems for you.

WHAT YOU CAN DO ✓

- Stay indoors on dry, windy days or when pollen counts are high. Pollen counts are often reported daily in the media.
- Rid your home of pollen traps, such as carpeting or dirty air filters.
- Try over-the-counter (OTC) antihistamines to relieve mild symptoms. If your antihistamines make you drowsy, never use them when driving or using heavy machinery. Nasal decongestant sprays will help dry up your runny nose, but overuse can cause the symptoms to worsen so you should never use them for more than three days in a row. (See *Home Pharmacy,* p. 331.) **CAUTION: Talk to your doctor or pharmacist before taking any other medications, including over-the-counter (OTC) medications, vitamins or herbal supplements.**

FINAL NOTES ✓

Hay fever can develop at any age. While irritating, hay fever symptoms will go away when the offending pollen disappears at the end of the season.

Hay Fever
DO THESE APPLY:

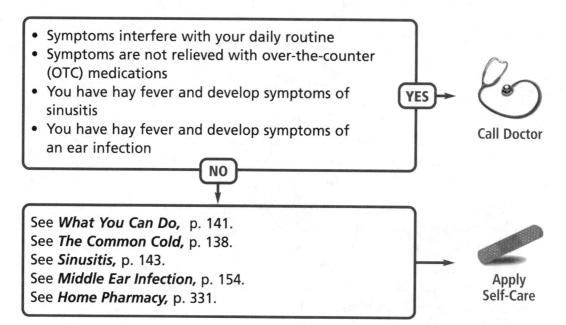

- Symptoms interfere with your daily routine
- Symptoms are not relieved with over-the-counter (OTC) medications
- You have hay fever and develop symptoms of sinusitis
- You have hay fever and develop symptoms of an ear infection

YES → Call Doctor

NO

See *What You Can Do,* p. 141.
See *The Common Cold,* p. 138.
See *Sinusitis,* p. 143.
See *Middle Ear Infection,* p. 154.
See *Home Pharmacy,* p. 331.

→ Apply Self-Care

Sinusitis

Sinusitis is an inflammation of the *sinuses,* the four pairs of empty chambers in the facial bones surrounding the nose and eyes. These chambers are located near the cheekbones, above the eyebrows, behind or between the eyes and near the temples. Inflammation can be caused by viral, bacterial or fungal infection, or by allergies.

The condition is usually brought on by an upper respiratory tract infection, hay fever (see *Hay Fever,* p. 141) or a *deviated septum* (a deformity in the structure between the nostrils that divides the inside of the nose into right and left sides). About 25 percent of chronic sinusitis cases that occur in the area near the cheekbones are related to dental infections. (See *Dental Care,* p. 161.)

NOTE YOUR SYMPTOMS ✓

- Tenderness and swelling
- Pain around the eyes or cheeks
- Difficulty breathing through the nose
- Redness and swelling inside the nose
- Yellow or gray-green nasal discharge
- *Malaise* (general feeling of illness and fatigue)
- Fever (may or may not be present)

WHAT YOU CAN DO ✓

- Inhale steam to promote nasal drainage. Try sitting in a steamy bathroom.
- Stay indoors and keep rooms at an even temperature.
- Drink plenty of fluids (a glass of water or juice every one to two hours), which may help open the nasal passages and promote sinus drainage.
- Try decongestant nasal sprays (such as phenylephrine 0.25 percent); do not use them for more than three days in a row. **CAUTION: Talk to your doctor or pharmacist before taking any other medications, including over-the-counter (OTC) medications, vitamins or herbal supplements.**

- Apply hot and cold compresses to the forehead and cheeks (alternately, one minute each, for 10 minutes) to aid sinus drainage.
- Increase home humidity.

Anyone with a history of recurring sinusitis should use self-care treatment at the first sign of a cold, other respiratory tract infection or allergic reactions.

A doctor may prescribe antibiotics to treat chronic sinusitis or sinusitis caused by a bacterial infection. On rare occasions, surgical repair of the sinuses may be necessary.

 **Decision** *helper* **Sinusitis**
DO THESE APPLY:

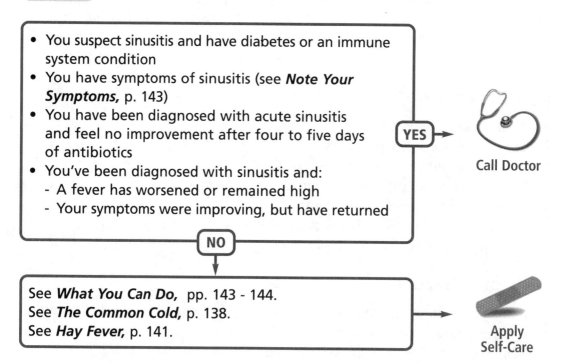

- You suspect sinusitis and have diabetes or an immune system condition
- You have symptoms of sinusitis (see **Note Your Symptoms,** p. 143)
- You have been diagnosed with acute sinusitis and feel no improvement after four to five days of antibiotics
- You've been diagnosed with sinusitis and:
  - A fever has worsened or remained high
  - Your symptoms were improving, but have returned

YES →

Call Doctor

NO

See **What You Can Do,** pp. 143 - 144.
See **The Common Cold,** p. 138.
See **Hay Fever,** p. 141.

Apply
Self-Care

Nosebleeds

Nosebleeds are usually messier and more embarrassing than they are serious, and can almost always be stopped with self-care. They are usually caused by trauma or by things that irritate nasal tissues, such as dry air, allergies, or by picking or blowing the nose.

PREVENTION ✓

Frequently, nosebleeds are related to the common cold, when blood vessels in the nose are irritated by a virus or by constant nose blowing. Treating cold symptoms may reduce these nosebleeds.

Nosebleeds tend to occur more often in the winter when people spend more time indoors where the air is dry and heated. Turning the heat down and using a cool-mist vaporizer to put moisture back into the air sometimes brings relief.

Finding the cause of recurrent nosebleeds is, of course, the first step in preventing them.

WHAT YOU CAN DO ✓

When you have a nosebleed:
- Sit in a chair, keeping your head level rather than tilted back. This prevents the blood from running down your throat.
- Blow the nose to remove any remaining blood or clots.
- Squeeze the nostrils shut between your thumb and forefinger.
- Breathe through your mouth and apply pressure for 15 full minutes without letting go of your nose.
- If the bleeding doesn't stop, repeat these measures, but before applying pressure, gently insert a gauze pad or a cotton ball or pad saturated with nasal decongestant spray (Afrin, Neo-Synephrine); do not use facial tissue. An alternate method is to use one or two sprays of nasal decongestant in each nostril before pinching the nose again for 15 minutes.

When the bleeding stops, try to remain quiet for a few hours. Don't blow your nose, laugh or talk loudly.

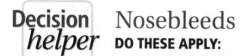

Decision *helper*   Nosebleeds
DO THESE APPLY:

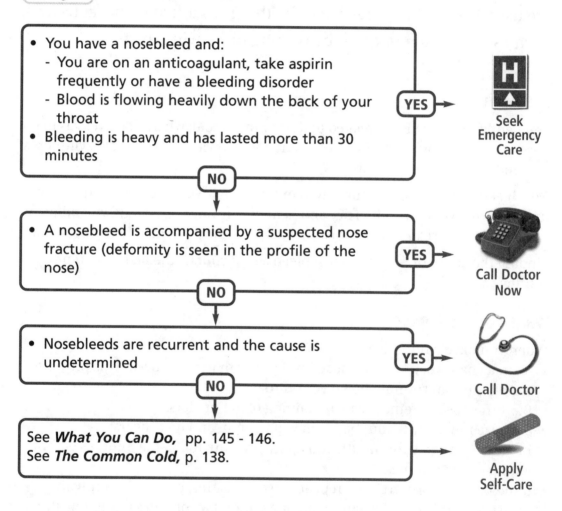

- You have a nosebleed and:
  - You are on an anticoagulant, take aspirin frequently or have a bleeding disorder
  - Blood is flowing heavily down the back of your throat
- Bleeding is heavy and has lasted more than 30 minutes

YES → **Seek Emergency Care**

NO

- A nosebleed is accompanied by a suspected nose fracture (deformity is seen in the profile of the nose)

YES → **Call Doctor Now**

NO

- Nosebleeds are recurrent and the cause is undetermined

YES → **Call Doctor**

NO

See *What You Can Do,* pp. 145 - 146.
See *The Common Cold,* p. 138.

→ **Apply Self-Care**

Coughs

A cough is nature's way of sounding an alarm when something interferes with free breathing. It's a natural reflex designed to clear your breathing tubes of mucus and foreign particles.

NOTE YOUR SYMPTOMS ✓

Coughs are usually referred to as "productive" or "nonproductive." A productive cough jars loose phlegm and helps expel it from the body. You'll probably be advised to let a productive cough do its work and avoid cough suppressants. A nonproductive cough is dry or hacking and you may need to take steps to quiet it. Learning to spot a cough's characteristics can help you pinpoint the appropriate steps for relief.

Some common causes of dry, nonproductive coughs are dry air, smoking and postnasal drip. Productive coughs, meanwhile, may signal viral or bacterial infections. Mucus is usually yellow or white with a viral infection, but it can be yellow, gray-green or rust-colored and contain pus with a bacterial infection. Bacterial infections usually require antibiotics.

WHAT YOU CAN DO ✓

- Drink lots of water to loosen phlegm and soothe your irritated throat.
- Use a cool-mist vaporizer to increase humidity.
- Use throat lozenges or hard candies to relieve the "tickle" and throat irritation.
- If postnasal drip is causing the dry, hacking cough, try an over-the-counter (OTC) decongestant. Avoid medications with antihistamines, which thicken the secretions you are trying to dislodge. **CAUTION: Talk to your doctor or pharmacist before taking any other medications, including over-the-counter (OTC) medications, vitamins or herbal supplements.**
- Try a nonprescription cough medication containing *guaifenesin*, which can thin secretions. OTC cough suppressants with *dextromethorphan* may help

quiet the cough at night so you can get some rest. Use cough suppressants only as directed. (See *Home Pharmacy,* p. 331.)

- Use pillows to elevate your head at night.
- If you smoke, stop.

Decision *helper* Coughs
DO THESE APPLY:

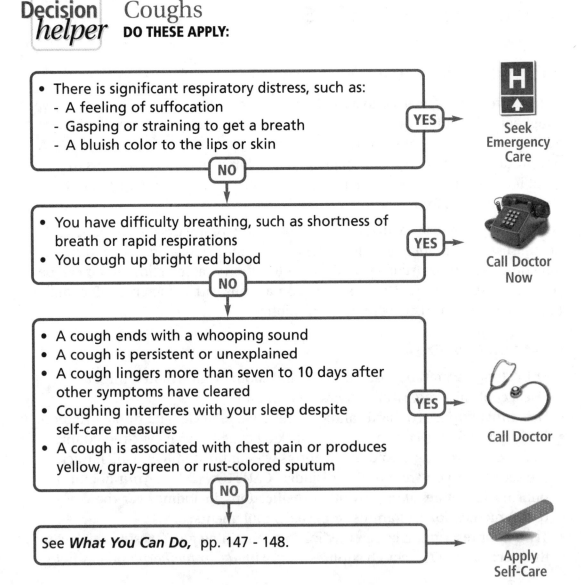

- There is significant respiratory distress, such as:
  - A feeling of suffocation
  - Gasping or straining to get a breath
  - A bluish color to the lips or skin

YES → Seek Emergency Care

NO

- You have difficulty breathing, such as shortness of breath or rapid respirations
- You cough up bright red blood

YES → Call Doctor Now

NO

- A cough ends with a whooping sound
- A cough is persistent or unexplained
- A cough lingers more than seven to 10 days after other symptoms have cleared
- Coughing interferes with your sleep despite self-care measures
- A cough is associated with chest pain or produces yellow, gray-green or rust-colored sputum

YES → Call Doctor

NO

See *What You Can Do,* pp. 147 - 148.

→ Apply Self-Care

Sore Throat and Laryngitis

A sore throat, or *pharyngitis,* is often the result of a viral or bacterial infection, although dry or polluted air, tobacco smoke or excessive alcohol use can also cause irritation. Typically, a sore throat is part of a cold or the flu, or the result of postnasal drip from allergies. However, in some cases it can be the symptom of a more serious condition that requires a doctor's care.

Strep Throat

Strep throat is caused by an infection of *streptococcal* bacteria, and if left untreated can cause serious complications. Symptoms usually include a bright red and severely sore throat, swollen tonsils and glands, and a fever.

WHAT YOU CAN DO ☑

Most sore throats are viral in origin, so antibiotics are of little help. Time and patience are the greatest healers. Other tips:

- Use over-the-counter (OTC) pain relievers, such as aspirin, ibuprofen (Advil, Motrin) and acetaminophen (Tylenol), to ease the soreness. **NEVER give aspirin to children/teenagers unless your health care provider orders it. It can cause Reye's syndrome, a rare but often fatal condition. CAUTION: Talk to your doctor or pharmacist before taking any other medications, including over-the-counter (OTC) medications, vitamins or herbal supplements.**
- Gargle with warm salt water (one-fourth teaspoon [1.2 mL] of salt added to eight ounces [230 mL] of water) several times a day.
- Use throat lozenges to soothe inflamed mucous membranes.
- Eat a soft or liquid diet to avoid irritating the throat.
- Drink plenty of liquids, unless your fluid intake has been limited by your doctor.
- Get plenty of rest.
- If you smoke, see *Smoking Cessation,* p. 346, for ways to kick the habit.

Laryngitis

Laryngitis is an inflammation of the *larynx* (voice box), which is located at the top of the windpipe. When the vocal cords, which are part of the larynx, become inflamed, they swell and cause hoarseness and distortion of the voice.

Laryngitis may be caused by illnesses such as the common cold, bronchitis or the flu, or by:

- Excessive talking, singing or shouting
- Reflux of irritating stomach contents into the throat (GERD)
- Allergies
- Inhaling irritating chemicals
- Benign polyps or tumors on, or paralysis of, the vocal cords
- Heavy smoking or excessive alcohol intake

NOTE YOUR SYMPTOMS ✓

Laryngitis is usually identified by its primary symptom, hoarseness. Other symptoms can include loss of voice, tickling, rawness or pain in the throat, or a constant need to clear your throat.

WHAT YOU CAN DO ✓

There is no specific medical treatment for laryngitis. To relieve symptoms:

- Rest your voice.
- Inhale steam. (Sit in the bathroom with the shower turned on hot to make steam.)
- Drink lots of liquids, especially warm, soothing ones, unless your fluid intake has been limited by your doctor.
- Don't smoke.
- Gargle with warm salt water (one-fourth teaspoon [1.2 mL] of salt added to eight ounces [230 mL] of water) to soothe the throat.
- Take antihistamines to relieve symptoms caused by allergy. **CAUTION: Talk to your doctor or pharmacist before taking any other medications, including over-the-counter (OTC) medications, vitamins or herbal supplements.**

If laryngitis is caused by GERD, polyps, exposure to irritants or excessive alcohol intake, the cause must be dealt with directly before the symptoms can be eliminated.

Decision *helper* Sore Throat and Laryngitis
DO THESE APPLY:

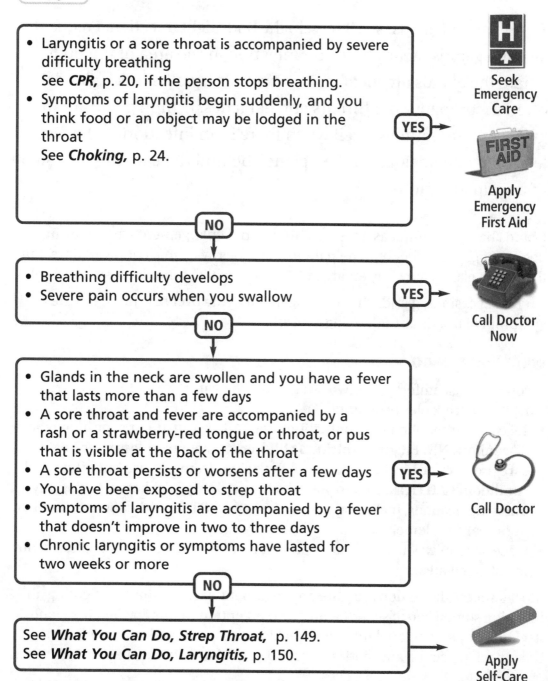

- Laryngitis or a sore throat is accompanied by severe difficulty breathing
  See **CPR,** p. 20, if the person stops breathing.
- Symptoms of laryngitis begin suddenly, and you think food or an object may be lodged in the throat
  See **Choking,** p. 24.

YES →

Seek Emergency Care

Apply Emergency First Aid

NO

- Breathing difficulty develops
- Severe pain occurs when you swallow

YES →

Call Doctor Now

NO

- Glands in the neck are swollen and you have a fever that lasts more than a few days
- A sore throat and fever are accompanied by a rash or a strawberry-red tongue or throat, or pus that is visible at the back of the throat
- A sore throat persists or worsens after a few days
- You have been exposed to strep throat
- Symptoms of laryngitis are accompanied by a fever that doesn't improve in two to three days
- Chronic laryngitis or symptoms have lasted for two weeks or more

YES →

Call Doctor

NO

See **What You Can Do, Strep Throat,** p. 149.
See **What You Can Do, Laryngitis,** p. 150.

Apply Self-Care

Swollen Glands

Lymph nodes (glands) swell to help the body fight infection. Frequently, swollen glands mean there's an infection in the area of the body where the glands are located. For example, swollen neck glands often accompany sore throats and earaches. Lymph glands in the groin area sometimes swell when there is an infection in the feet, legs or genital region. Swollen glands behind the ears can be a sign of a scalp infection.

Glands become painful as a result of their rapid enlargement when they first begin to fight an infection. The pain usually goes away in a couple of days, but the lymph glands may stay enlarged for quite a while, sometimes several weeks.

On rare occasions, glands that have been enlarging over several weeks are a symptom of a serious underlying cause.

WHAT YOU CAN DO ✓

If you have discomfort from swollen glands, you can:
- Rest and drink plenty of fluids.
- Take acetaminophen (Tylenol), ibuprofen (Advil, Motrin) or aspirin to relieve discomfort. **NEVER give aspirin to children/teenagers unless your health care provider orders it. It can cause Reye's syndrome, a rare but often fatal condition. CAUTION: Talk to your doctor or pharmacist before taking any other medications, including over-the-counter (OTC) medications, vitamins or herbal supplements.**
- Place a warm washcloth, water bottle or heating pad (set on low) directly on the affected area.

Most swollen glands don't require any treatment because they are fighting an infection somewhere else in the body. An exception to this is when the gland itself develops a bacterial infection, making it red and tender. Sometimes a doctor will prescribe antibiotics to get rid of the bacteria causing the infection.

Decision *helper*   Swollen Glands
DO THESE APPLY:

- Swollen glands and signs of infection are present *(redness around the area or red streaks leading away from it; swelling; warmth or tenderness; pus; fever of 101° F [38.3° C] or higher; tender or swollen lymph nodes)*   **YES** ▶

Call Doctor Now

NO ↓

- You have swollen glands and a sore throat
- Swollen glands are present in multiple locations
- Swollen glands persist or have increased in size for two to three weeks
- Swollen glands follow a cat scratch or tick bite
- Swollen glands and a fever are present for two days or more
- You have enlarged glands just above the collar bone
- A gland is larger than one-half inch (1.0 cm) in diameter   **YES** ▶

Call Doctor

NO ↓

See *What You Can Do, Strep Throat,* p. 149.   ▶

Apply Self-Care

Different Symptoms?
See *Sore Throat and Laryngitis,* p. 150.

Ear Pain

When fluid accumulates in the *middle ear* (the part of the ear located behind the eardrum), pressure builds up and causes pain.

Middle Ear Infection

Middle ear infections (*otitis media*) usually occur as a complication of an upper respiratory infection (see index for specific topics), when the *eustachian tubes* located between the ear and the throat swell and close. Fluid and mucus gather in the blocked middle ear, allowing bacteria to breed.

The hallmark symptom of otitis media—persistent ear pain—may be accompanied by decreased hearing, a sense of fullness or ringing in the ear (see *Tinnitus*, p. 159), fever, headache, runny nose and dizziness.

Vertigo is the dizzy feeling of being off balance. More specifically, it's the sensation that the room or objects are moving around you. A middle ear infection can cause vertigo, as can toxic substances in the body or other types of infection.

WHAT YOU CAN DO ✓

Otitis media requires a visit to your doctor, who may prescribe watchful waiting or antibiotic treatment, and possibly a decongestant.

After the visit, try the following:

- Get plenty of rest.
- Increase the amount of clear fluids you drink, unless your fluid intake has been limited by your doctor.
- Place a warm washcloth, water bottle or heating pad (set on low) directly on the affected ear. (See *Heating Pad, First-Aid Supplies*, p. 336.)
- Blow your nose gently, with your mouth open.
- Use a cool-mist vaporizer to moisturize the air and help control levels of mucus.
- Take acetaminophen (Tylenol), ibuprofen (Advil, Motrin) or aspirin to relieve discomfort. Decongestants or nose drops may help decrease nasal secretions and shrink mucous membranes. **NEVER give aspirin to children/teenagers**

unless your health care provider orders it. It can cause Reye's syndrome, a rare but often fatal condition. CAUTION: Talk to your doctor or pharmacist before taking any other medications, including over-the-counter (OTC) medications, vitamins or herbal supplements.

Note: DO NOT insert any type of object in the ear to relieve itching or pain.

For symptoms of vertigo:

- Lie quietly in a darkened room.
- Avoid sudden movements.
- Focus on one object or keep your eyes closed to help ease spinning sensations.

See *Decision helper,* p. 157.

Fluid in Middle Ear

Serous otitis media results when fluid collects in the middle ear, either from a previous infection or ongoing irritations such as allergies. An infection is not necessarily associated with this condition but can occur if bacteria build up. Symptoms may include temporary hearing loss and a feeling of stuffiness or sensitivity in the ear.

WHAT YOU CAN DO ✓

Most cases of serous otitis media clear up over several weeks. Chewing gum or swallowing may help open the eustachian tube, and taking decongestants or pain relievers may provide additional relief. CAUTION: Talk to your doctor or pharmacist before taking any other medications, including over-the-counter (OTC) medications, vitamins or herbal supplements.

If the problem does not clear up with self-care, a doctor may prescribe a higher dose of decongestant or use a device to force air into the eustachian tube and middle ear. If a bacterial infection is involved, antibiotics may be prescribed.

See *Decision helper,* p. 157.

Ruptured Eardrum

If you've recently had a cold with ear pain and congestion, and then notice white to yellow or bloody ear discharge, contact your doctor. Infections, blows to the head or inserting sharp objects into the ear can rupture the eardrum.

See a doctor promptly; antibiotics may be prescribed to prevent or treat an infection in the middle ear.

A one-time rupture is not serious. The eardrum usually heals within two months. However, repeated eardrum ruptures may cause hearing loss.

WHAT YOU CAN DO ☑

Pain can be relieved by using over-the-counter (OTC) pain relievers and a heating pad set on low. **CAUTION: Talk to your doctor or pharmacist before taking any other medications, including over-the-counter (OTC) medications, vitamins or herbal supplements.** Hearing almost always returns to normal after the eardrum heals.

Barotitis

"Airplane ears" (*barotitis*) usually occurs as a result of air pressure changes— driving in the mountains, flying in an airplane—or having a cold or stuffy nose. This results in a blocked-up feeling in the ears.

WHAT YOU CAN DO ☑

Yawning, swallowing, chewing gum or gently blowing through your nose while holding your nose shut and closing your mouth to "pop" the ears, may solve the problem. Using an oral decongestant or decongestant nasal spray 30 minutes before an airplane descends can also help.

Decision Ear Pain
helper **DO THESE APPLY:**

- Ear pain is accompanied by a severe headache, a change in mental status or stiff neck (see **Meningitis,** p. 240)

[YES]→

H

Seek
Emergency
Care

[NO]

- The person looks very ill and there is swelling, redness and pain around the ear

[YES]→

Call Doctor
Now

[NO]

- Ear infection is suspected
- Ear pain occurs with the following:
  - Fever
  - Bloody or other discharge
  - Decreased hearing
  - Dizziness
  - Ringing or a sense of fullness in the ears
- Ear pain lasts more than an hour
- Any earache lasts longer than 12 to 24 hours
- Symptoms of barotitis do not improve after taking a decongestant for a day or two
- Symptoms increase—or fail to improve—after two or three days of antibiotic treatment
- Stuffy ears or hearing loss persists, without other symptoms, more than 10 days after a cold clears up

[YES]→

Call Doctor

[NO]

See **What You Can Do,** p. 154, 155, 156.

→

Apply
Self-Care

Hearing Loss

Twenty-five percent of people over age 65 experience some degree of hearing loss. It can affect a person's thinking and memory. Fortunately, there are steps you can take to prevent hearing loss or improve the situation if it already exists.

Presbycusis

The most common form of age-related hearing loss is *presbycusis,* the gradual loss of the ability to hear high-pitched sounds. People with presbycusis continue to hear midrange or lower-pitched tones, but have difficulty discriminating spoken words, which are usually composed of high-frequency tones. While it's progressive, presbycusis doesn't usually lead to deafness. Fortunately, it's the kind of hearing loss that can most easily be helped by a hearing aid.

WHAT YOU CAN DO ✓

- Be alert to changes in your hearing, particularly the inability to hear high-pitched sounds.
- Those around you will be the first to notice your hearing loss. Notice their reactions—are you missing parts of conversations? Do they claim you're shouting? Are you avoiding social situations that may call attention to your hearing loss?
- If so, see your doctor and arrange for a hearing evaluation.

Hearing Aids

A hearing aid amplifies those frequencies you hear least well. It consists of a small microphone, a battery-powered amplifier to make the sound louder, a volume control and a small speaker that transmits the amplified sound into your eardrum. An *audiologist* (hearing technician) can help you determine what kind of hearing aid will be best for you, fit the device to your ear and show you how to operate it.

Ear Wax

The purpose of ear wax is to protect the ear and keep it clean. The wax is normally in liquid form and drains by itself. Ear wax almost never causes problems unless you try to "clean" your ears using a cotton swab or some other instrument, which can pack the ear wax down tightly. If compacted ear wax builds up, it can block the ear canal, sometimes causing a stuffy feeling and hearing loss.

Ear wax usually doesn't cause pain or a fever. If you experience these symptoms, suspect an ear infection. (See *Middle Ear Infection,* p. 154.)

PREVENTION ☑

In most cases, taking warm showers or washing the outside of the ears with a washcloth and warm water provides enough vapor to prevent the buildup of wax.

The ears should be left alone unless the ear wax is causing some problem, like a ringing in the ears or hearing loss.

WHAT YOU CAN DO ☑

Normally, packed-down ear wax can be removed by gently flushing the ear with warm water using a bulb syringe (available at drugstores). Always use water that is as close to body temperature as possible. Using cold water can cause dizziness and vomiting.

Wax softeners such as hydrogen peroxide (3 percent), Debrox or Cerumenex, also can be used. Follow instructions carefully for commercial softening products.

Never put anything into the ear if you think the eardrum might be ruptured.

> See *Decision helper,* p. 160.

Tinnitus

Tinnitus is the persistent sensation of noise (ringing, buzzing, roaring, whistling or hissing) in the ear. It can be the symptom of almost any ear disorder as well as many diseases. Some common treatable causes include excess ear wax, ear infections, dental problems and certain medications (antibiotics and large amounts of aspirin).

Tinnitus can also be caused by prolonged exposure to loud noise that damages the hair cells of the *cochlea* (the winding, cone-shaped tube that forms part of the inner ear).

WHAT YOU CAN DO ☑

To protect your hearing, limit your exposure to loud noises such as power tools, industrial machinery and loud music (wear ear plugs when needed). If tinnitus persists, discuss possible causes with your doctor. If the cause is unclear, your treatment will probably involve ways to mask or reduce the sensation. You may find your symptoms are helped by reducing the amount of *sodium* (salt), caffeine and alcohol in your diet. (See *Eating Right*, p. 338.) Learning ways to eliminate and cope with stress may also make a difference. (See *Stress*, p. 313.)

Decision *helper* Hearing Loss
DO THESE APPLY:

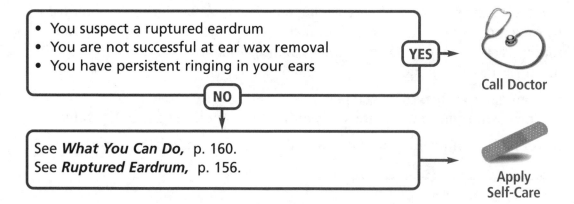

- You suspect a ruptured eardrum
- You are not successful at ear wax removal
- You have persistent ringing in your ears

YES → Call Doctor

NO

See **What You Can Do,** p. 160.
See **Ruptured Eardrum,** p. 156.

→ Apply Self-Care

Mouth Concerns

The aging process results in subtle changes within the mouth. Taste buds on the tongue decrease, so some foods may seem blander than they used to. However, the ability to sense bitter tastes does not decrease, and the combination of bland and bitter may result in an unpleasant, metallic taste.

As taste becomes a little "duller," many people resort to using more salt and sugar to enhance the flavor of foods. A healthier alternative is to add flavor with herbs and spices such as garlic, onion, oregano, thyme, and nutmeg.

Dry mouth is also common. Mouth tissues become thinner and hold less moisture, and certain medications may reduce the amount of saliva the glands produce. Dehydration caused by hot weather and drinking inadequate amounts of water can also contribute to a dry mouth. (See *Dehydration,* p. 203.)

A severely dry mouth (*xerostomia*) can affect chewing, swallowing and digestion. Sucking on lozenges or hard candy or taking frequent sips of water can help minimize symptoms. Talk to your doctor or dentist if symptoms persist.

Dental Care

Bacteria that are not removed from the teeth by brushing or flossing become a sticky, colorless film called *plaque.* Food particles, especially sugar, stick to plaque and produce acid, which damages tooth enamel. When this damage, or *decay,* spreads down the root canal to the nerve, it causes pain and inflammation—a *toothache.*

Another problem caused by an accumulation of plaque is gum disease, or *gingivitis,* an inflammation of the gums that can cause redness, discomfort, swelling, watery discharge and bleeding when you brush or chew. Gingivitis can also cause crevices between the gums and teeth, which can deepen into pockets. In severe cases, this can result in tooth loss.

Poorly fitting dentures also can cause difficulty chewing, pain, mouth sores and *leukoplakia,* damaged tissue that can develop into mouth cancer.

PREVENTION ☑

Most dental problems can be prevented by good self-care and regular visits to the dentist. Have your teeth professionally checked and cleaned every six to 12 months. If you wear dentures, take good care of them. Clean them regularly so you'll look your best and avoid bad breath. If your dentures don't fit well, ask your dentist to adjust them or ask about newer kinds of artificial teeth.

Brushing

Brush your teeth thoroughly twice a day, especially after eating. Try to remove plaque from all tooth surfaces. Use a soft-bristled toothbrush with rounded tips and replace it every three to four months. Also brush your tongue, which helps keep breath fresh.

Waterpiks and electric toothbrushes may help clean hard-to-reach areas. Check with your dentist about what's best for you.

The formation of *tartar,* mineral deposits that get trapped on the teeth by plaque, can be slowed by tartar-control toothpastes.

Flossing

Daily flossing is the best way to prevent gum disease between the teeth. Curve the floss around the tooth being cleaned and slide it under the gumline. With both fingers holding the floss against the tooth, move the floss up and down several times to scrape off the plaque.

WHAT YOU CAN DO ☑

If you have a toothache, aspirin, ibuprofen (Advil, Motrin) or acetaminophen (Tylenol) may lessen the pain until you see a dentist. **NEVER give aspirin to children/teenagers unless your health care provider orders it. It can cause Reye's syndrome, a rare but often fatal condition. CAUTION: Talk to your doctor or pharmacist before taking any other medications, including over-the-counter (OTC) medications, vitamins or herbal supplements.**

FINAL NOTES ☑

If you have tooth or gum pain, see your dentist or call your doctor.

Mouth Sores

Cold Sores

Oral herpes, which causes cold sores and fever blisters, is a common viral infection characterized by small, fluid-filled sores on the skin and mucous membranes of the mouth. This herpes simplex type 1 virus is not the same as—but is related to—herpes simplex type 2, which causes *genital herpes.*

About 90 percent of Americans are infected with oral herpes by the age of 5. Following the initial infection, the virus remains dormant with new episodes recurring at different frequencies for different people. New outbreaks can be triggered by a variety of factors including dental treatment, sunburn, food allergies, anxiety, menstruation, fever-producing illness or a suppressed immune system.

PREVENTION ✓

The virus is very contagious and can be transmitted through personal contact or contact with contaminated objects such as kitchen utensils, razors or towels. If you have an active infection, avoid close physical contact with others and do not share personal items.

WHAT YOU CAN DO ✓

- Salves can relieve pain, but are not effective in all cases. Try various methods, such as over-the-counter (OTC) oral and topical *analgesics* (pain relievers). Use what works best for you.
- Acyclovir (Zovirax) and other *antiviral* (virus-fighting) agents may speed healing if applied during the initial outbreak. Oral acyclovir is sometimes prescribed for frequent or severe outbreaks.

Attacks of oral herpes usually go away, with or without treatment, within seven to 10 days and have no lasting complications.

See *Decision helper,* p. 165.

Canker Sores

A *canker sore* is a painful ulcer that develops on the gums, tongue or inside the mouth. The cause is unknown but any of the following increase the likelihood of getting one: viruses, allergies, gastrointestinal disease, immune reactions, deficiencies of iron, B12 or folic acid, and stress or trauma to the inside of the mouth.

WHAT YOU CAN DO ✓

There's no known way to prevent canker sores, but nonprescription topical anesthetic gels or rinses will lessen the pain. A dental protective paste, such as Orabase, prevents irritation of the sores. Acetaminophen (Tylenol) and nonsteroidal anti-inflammatory drugs may help relieve discomfort, too.

Thrush

Thrush, or *oral candidiasis,* is a fungal yeast infection that causes painful, creamy-white sore patches in the mouth or throat. Eating or brushing your teeth can scrape off the patches, causing bleeding.

Some people develop thrush when they are on antibiotics. Conditions such as diabetes, AIDS or immunosuppressive therapy can make people more susceptible to the infection as well.

WHAT YOU CAN DO ✓

Although thrush often disappears on its own, an antifungal medication usually speeds healing. Nystatin, in liquid or tablets, may be recommended by your doctor. With treatment, symptoms usually disappear within seven to 10 days.

A diet of soft foods may lessen discomfort until the symptoms are gone.

> The goals for treatment of mouth sores are to relieve pain and maintain an adequate fluid intake, as mouth sores can often interfere with eating or drinking. Try drinks that soothe a tender mouth, such as cold liquids, Popsicles or frozen juices.

Mouth Sores

DO THESE APPLY:

- Fever and mouth sores appear after starting any medication   **YES** → Call Doctor Now

NO ↓

- An undiagnosed mouth sore persists for two weeks
- You suspect that medication may be causing mouth sores
- Painful ulcers occur on the gums, tongue or inside the mouth, especially with large or multiple lesions (suggestive of canker sores)
- You have frequent or severe cold sores
- Creamy-white sore patches appear inside the mouth, on the tongue or in the throat (suggestive of thrush)
- You are being treated for thrush and your symptoms persist for more than 10 days

YES → Call Doctor

NO ↓

See *What You Can Do, Cold Sores,* p. 163; *Canker Sores,* p. 164; *Thrush,* p. 164.

→ Apply Self-Care

Respiratory Concerns

Changes in the respiratory system occur gradually in older adults. Lungs become restricted by ribs that don't move quite as freely. As *vertebrae* (bones of the spine) compress with age, lung volume may diminish.

These changes typically don't cause problems in healthy adults—especially if you're getting regular exercise to strengthen and expand your chest muscles. However, you may find that strenuous activities more difficult than you did when you were younger and it may take longer to catch your breath afterward. This is common. Recovery from respiratory illness also may take longer.

Influenza

Influenza, also known as the *flu,* is a highly contagious respiratory infection caused by a virus. Symptoms are similar to those of a common cold, but are more severe; they include sudden onset of fever, chills, headache, sore throat, cough, stuffy nose, watery eyes, exhaustion and muscular aches.

Influenza often occurs in epidemics during the "flu season," which generally lasts from late fall to early spring. Flu is spread by inhaling virus-laden droplets when an infected person sneezes, coughs or even talks.

PREVENTION ☑

Getting vaccinated against influenza reduces the incidence of infection and is particularly important for adults over age 50 and people with chronic diseases or impaired immune systems. However, any person can benefit from flu vaccine, so call your doctor early in the fall to discuss preventive treatment.

WHAT YOU CAN DO ☑

- Take aspirin, acetaminophen (Tylenol) or ibuprofen (Advil, Motrin) to relieve aches and pains. **NEVER give aspirin to children/teenagers unless your health care provider orders it. It can cause Reye's syndrome, a rare but often fatal condition. CAUTION: Talk to your doctor or pharmacist before taking any other medications, including over-the-counter (OTC) medications, vitamins or herbal supplements.**
- Drink plenty of clear liquids—water, juice, ginger ale—to restore fluids, unless your fluid intake has been limited by your doctor.
- Drink salty liquids like chicken soup and bouillon to help combat dizziness and restore fluids.
- Gargle with warm salt water (one-fourth teaspoon [1.2 mL] of salt added to eight ounces [230 mL] of water), drink tea with honey or lemon, or use lozenges to soothe sore throat pain.
- Get plenty of rest.
- Try decongestants to help relieve runny nose and watery eyes.

FINAL NOTES ☑

A number of prescription medications are available to either prevent influenza or shorten its course, should you become infected.

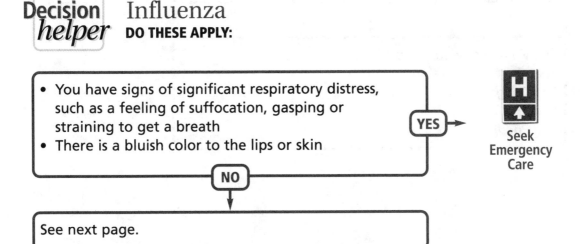

Decision helper Influenza **DO THESE APPLY:**

- You have signs of significant respiratory distress, such as a feeling of suffocation, gasping or straining to get a breath
- There is a bluish color to the lips or skin

YES → **H** ↑ Seek Emergency Care

NO ↓

See next page.

Do these apply: See previous page.

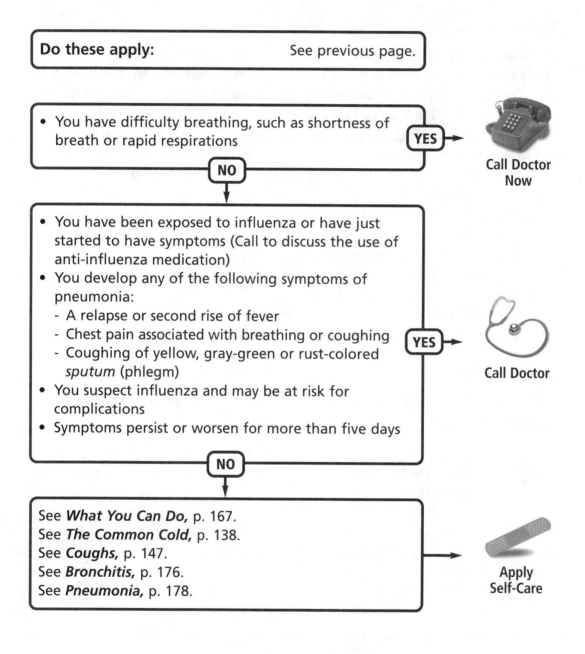

- You have difficulty breathing, such as shortness of breath or rapid respirations   **YES** ➡ **Call Doctor Now**

NO

- You have been exposed to influenza or have just started to have symptoms (Call to discuss the use of anti-influenza medication)
- You develop any of the following symptoms of pneumonia:
  - A relapse or second rise of fever
  - Chest pain associated with breathing or coughing
  - Coughing of yellow, gray-green or rust-colored *sputum* (phlegm)
- You suspect influenza and may be at risk for complications
- Symptoms persist or worsen for more than five days

YES ➡ **Call Doctor**

NO

See *What You Can Do,* p. 167.
See *The Common Cold,* p. 138.
See *Coughs,* p. 147.
See *Bronchitis,* p. 176.
See *Pneumonia,* p. 178.

➡ **Apply Self-Care**

Wheezing

The respiratory system resembles an upside-down tree with the "trunk" at the throat and the "limbs" (*bronchi*), smaller "branches" (*bronchioles*), and "leaves" (*alveoli* or air sacs) in the lungs. *Wheezing* is a high-pitched whistle caused by the obstruction of air passing through the bronchi and bronchioles. The restriction may be due to narrowing of the airway walls or a blockage in the passage and can be localized in a small area or spread throughout the lungs.

Wheezing can be heard in lung infections such as pneumonia or bronchitis, when an object or mucus blocks an airway. It is the most prominent symptom of asthma (see *Asthma*, p. 173) and is also common in allergic reactions and *chronic obstructive pulmonary disease* (a severe lung disease). Wheezing needs professional evaluation when it first occurs.

Chronic Obstructive Pulmonary Disease (COPD)

Emphysema and *chronic bronchitis* are diseases that cause permanent lung damage. They share symptoms such as cough, *sputum* (phlegm) production, shortness of breath, limited airflow and poor oxygen exchange in the lungs.

Emphysema involves damage to the air sacs, which become brittle and enlarged, decreasing their ability to exchange oxygen and carbon dioxide. Chronic bronchitis is an inflammation of the lower breathing passages (*bronchi*). These diseases commonly occur together and are almost always the result of smoking.

Unfortunately, there is no cure for COPD. The goal of treatment is to enhance breathing capacity and ease the struggle to breathe.

Allergic Reaction

Allergic reactions occur when the body's immune system reacts and goes on the defensive against an element that usually is harmless. Allergens trigger your body's *antibodies* (protective agents) to counterattack and release chemicals, called *histamines,* directly into various body tissues. Your symptoms are the result of tissues reacting to these chemicals. Allergic wheezing is common in people who have asthma.

Wheezing can be created by spasms in bronchial and bronchiolar walls, swelling in the wall lining and production of excess mucus. *This can be a serious allergic reaction which can quickly become life-threatening.*

PREVENTION ✓

- If you smoke, start taking steps to kick the habit. (See *Smoking Cessation,* p. 346.)
- Avoid respiratory irritants such as secondary smoke or exposure to fumes.
- Avoid anything that has triggered an allergic attack in the past. (See *Allergic Reaction,* p. 123.)
- Wear or carry medical-alert identification related to your allergies and any chronic disease.
- Inform all doctors, dentists and pharmacists about your allergies.
- Ask your doctor about pneumonia and flu vaccinations.
- Exercise regularly. (See *Staying Active,* p. 343.) Swimming and water aerobics are especially good for building up your respiratory strength.
- Learn stress-management techniques if stress is a factor in your wheezing. (See *Stress,* p. 313.)
- Maintain normal weight to prevent additional stress on your respiratory system.
- Contact your doctor for information about further prevention and treatment of your specific wheezing problems.

WHAT YOU CAN DO ✓

- Drink at least two quarts (1.9 L) of water daily to thin bronchial mucus.
- Maintain a humid environment with a cool-mist vaporizer.
- Learn and use relaxation techniques. (See *Stress,* p. 313.) Anxiety and panic increase breathing distress and waste energy.
- If you have asthma, use your peak-flow meter, bronchodilators and other medications, as directed by your doctor. Do not wait for early symptoms to go away on their own.

 Wheezing
DO THESE APPLY:

- You have symptoms of significant respiratory distress, such as a feeling of suffocation, gasping or straining to get a breath
- There is a bluish color to the lips or skin
- You have signs of a severe allergic reaction with the sudden onset of any of the following:
  - Loss of consciousness, confusion or agitation
  - Tightness in the chest, wheezing, hives or itching
  - Swelling of the lips, tongue, mouth or throat

YES →

Seek
Emergency
Care

NO

- You have difficulty breathing, such as shortness of breath or rapid respirations
- An acute episode of wheezing occurs for the first time
- Wheezing is more severe or not responding to usual treatment
- Wheezing is accompanied by a chronic health problem such as heart disease
- Wheezing begins soon after a dose of new medication (Discontinue use.)
- Chest pain is associated with breathing or coughing
- *Sputum* (phlegm) is yellow, gray-green or rust-colored

YES →

Call Doctor
Now

NO

See next page.

Do these apply: See previous page.

- Wheezing requires additional medication and treatment to control or prevent
- You need more information and education to understand and control wheezing

YES ➞

Call Doctor

NO

See **What You Can Do,** p. 170. See **Asthma,** p. 173.
See **Hay Fever,** p. 141. See **Chest Wall Pain,** p. 185.
See **Bronchitis,** p. 176. See **Pneumonia,** p. 178.

Apply
Self-Care

Asthma

Asthma is a chronic lung disease that inflames, swells and constricts lung airways and causes coughing, wheezing, chest pain and an increased production of mucus. Frequently, an asthma attack involves a feeling of suffocation or even panic.

If you have allergies, you're particularly susceptible to asthma. Many people with asthma are sensitive to dust, animal dander, pollen, mold and other common allergens. If you're like most people with asthma, appropriate care and drug therapy can help you lead a normal, active life. There is no routine screening to detect the likelihood of developing asthma.

PREVENTION ✓

If you have asthma, these are some steps you can take to reduce the number and severity of attacks:

- If your doctor has given you an acute-care regimen and you begin to have an attack, implement the measures immediately. The key to managing an asthma attack is to prevent it from getting out of control.
- Eliminate or reduce exposure to "triggers" that cause attacks, such as cigarette smoke, pollen, dust and other irritants.
- If pollen triggers attacks, stay inside as much as possible during periods of high pollen count—preferably an inside environment with filtered air.
- Remove the carpets in your home, and at work if possible, to decrease attacks. Dust mites, which often trigger attacks, thrive in carpeting.
- Enclose your mattress and pillow in plastic zipper bags to reduce your exposure to potential allergens.
- Drink plenty of fluids (unless your fluid intake has been limited by your doctor), which may loosen mucus in your lungs and make breathing easier.
- Keep a record of daily treatment, acute-care measures, and pertinent information about symptoms, treatment and your response to treatment.

WHAT YOU CAN DO ✓

Self-evaluation and self-care are the most important things you can do to control asthma attacks. Discuss a self-care plan with your doctor that includes:

- Daily or routine drug therapy
- A symptom diary
- What medications to take when an attack begins
- When to seek medical or emergency care
- Use of a portable peak flow meter to help you monitor your asthma status

FINAL NOTES ✓

Your doctor will diagnose asthma by taking your medical history and performing a physical examination. In some cases, tests of lung function and chest x-rays also may be used to confirm the diagnosis.

Asthma drugs are often administered using a *metered dose inhaler* (MDI). This "tubular" (tube-shaped) device propels small particles of drug through the mouth into the lungs. If you have difficulty using an MDI, your doctor may recommend modifications for proper drug treatment.

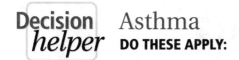

Asthma

DO THESE APPLY:

- You have symptoms of significant respiratory distress, such as a feeling of suffocation, gasping or straining to get a breath
- There is a bluish color to the lips or skin
- You are confused, lethargic or extremely anxious
- You have sharp chest pains
- An asthma attack is out of control

YES →

Seek Emergency Care

NO

- You have difficulty breathing, such as shortness of breath or rapid respirations
- Your prescribed regimen for acute attacks provides little relief
- An asthma attack seems to be getting out of control

YES →

Call Doctor Now

NO

- You have asthma and do not have a self-care plan that includes what to do when an attack begins
- You have not been diagnosed with asthma but have noticed:
  - A dry cough when you exercise and/or at night
  - Difficulty breathing, tight chest, wheezing

YES →

Call Doctor

NO

See *What You Can Do,* p. 174.

→

Apply Self-Care

Bronchitis

Acute bronchitis is an inflammation of the airways that results from irritation or infection. It frequently follows a bout with the flu or a cold and may last up to two weeks.

Bronchitis is usually characterized by a cough accompanied by soreness and tightness in the chest. The cough is often dry at first, but becomes productive after a few days. The presence of yellow, gray-green or rust-colored *sputum* (phlegm) may indicate a bacterial infection.

Chronic bronchitis is a more serious condition that involves a permanent thickening of the passageways to the lungs. In both types, the cells lining the inside of the breathing passages that normally sweep away mucus and debris stop working. The cough response is the body's way of ridding itself of these irritants. (See *COPD, Wheezing*, p. 169.)

WHAT YOU CAN DO ✓

- If you smoke, start taking steps to kick the habit. (See *Smoking Cessation*, p. 346.)
- Drink plenty of liquids—about six to eight glasses per day (unless your fluid intake has been limited by your doctor).
- Use a cool-mist vaporizer to help keep your secretions thin.
- Avoid respiratory irritants. If you must work around them, use a respirator or other protective gear.
- Get plenty of rest to enable your lungs to heal.
- Unless your doctor instructs otherwise, avoid around-the-clock usage of cough suppressants containing dextromethorphan (DM) or codeine. Coughing can actually help eliminate secretions from your airways. Cough syrups only temporarily relieve a cough; they won't cure it. Old-fashioned home remedies (tea with honey) may provide similar relief.

Decision *helper* Bronchitis
DO THESE APPLY:

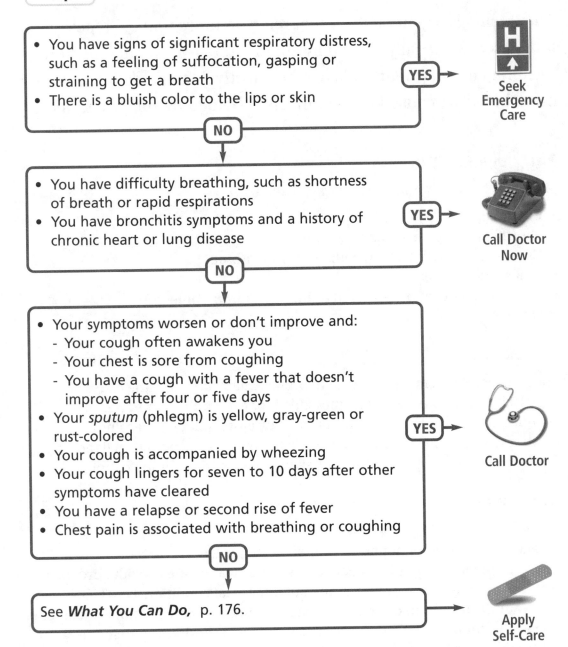

- You have signs of significant respiratory distress, such as a feeling of suffocation, gasping or straining to get a breath
- There is a bluish color to the lips or skin

YES → Seek Emergency Care

NO

- You have difficulty breathing, such as shortness of breath or rapid respirations
- You have bronchitis symptoms and a history of chronic heart or lung disease

YES → Call Doctor Now

NO

- Your symptoms worsen or don't improve and:
  - Your cough often awakens you
  - Your chest is sore from coughing
  - You have a cough with a fever that doesn't improve after four or five days
- Your *sputum* (phlegm) is yellow, gray-green or rust-colored
- Your cough is accompanied by wheezing
- Your cough lingers for seven to 10 days after other symptoms have cleared
- You have a relapse or second rise of fever
- Chest pain is associated with breathing or coughing

YES → Call Doctor

NO

See *What You Can Do,* p. 176.

→ Apply Self-Care

Pneumonia

Pneumonia is a general term that refers to more than 50 types of lung diseases, usually caused by either viral or bacterial infection. Bacteria-caused pneumonia can be effectively treated with antibiotics, but virus-caused pneumonia isn't helped by such treatment.

NOTE YOUR SYMPTOMS ☑

Most forms of pneumonia are characterized by:

- Coughing
- Shortness of breath and labored breathing
- Chest pain associated with coughing or breathing
- Chills and/or fever
- Yellow, gray-green, rust-colored or bloody *sputum* (phlegm)
- Fatigue

PREVENTION ☑

Pneumococcal vaccine is available to protect against the leading cause of bacterial pneumonia and is recommended for everyone older than age 65, or anyone without a spleen or with a chronic disease. Influenza vaccine can prevent viral pneumonia and is available to anyone over the age of 6 months. Contact your doctor or local public health department for information.

WHAT YOU CAN DO ☑

- Get plenty of rest.
- Take aspirin, acetaminophen (Tylenol) or ibuprofen (Advil, Motrin). **NEVER give aspirin to children/teenagers unless your health care provider orders it. It can cause Reye's syndrome, a rare but often fatal condition. CAUTION: Talk to your doctor or pharmacist before taking any other medications, including over-the-counter (OTC) medications, vitamins or herbal supplements.**
- Drink plenty of clear liquids unless you're on a fluid-restricted diet.

- Drink chicken soup, bouillon and other salty liquids to restore fluids and minimize dizziness when you stand.

Decision *helper* Pneumonia
DO THESE APPLY:

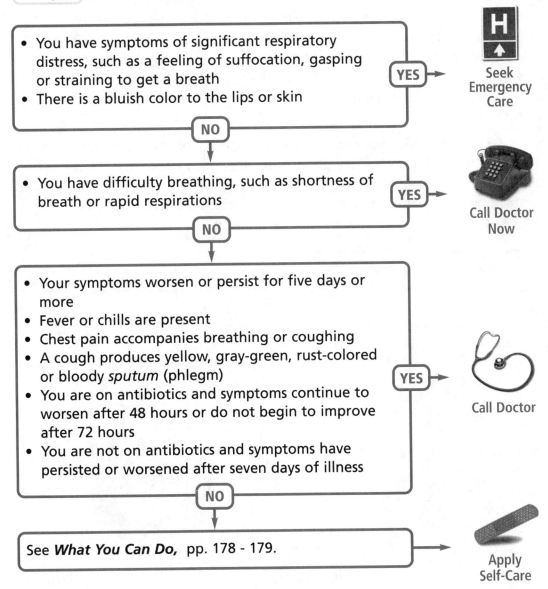

- You have symptoms of significant respiratory distress, such as a feeling of suffocation, gasping or straining to get a breath
- There is a bluish color to the lips or skin

YES → **H** ↑ Seek Emergency Care

NO

- You have difficulty breathing, such as shortness of breath or rapid respirations

YES → Call Doctor Now

NO

- Your symptoms worsen or persist for five days or more
- Fever or chills are present
- Chest pain accompanies breathing or coughing
- A cough produces yellow, gray-green, rust-colored or bloody *sputum* (phlegm)
- You are on antibiotics and symptoms continue to worsen after 48 hours or do not begin to improve after 72 hours
- You are not on antibiotics and symptoms have persisted or worsened after seven days of illness

YES → Call Doctor

NO

See *What You Can Do,* pp. 178 - 179.

→ Apply Self-Care

Heart Concerns

The heart is a tough and remarkable organ. It beats thousands of times each day, carrying blood and oxygen throughout the body.

After years of constant work, it's not surprising that the heart begins to weaken somewhat. The aging heart takes longer to speed up in response to a stimulus or activity. For example, upon standing, more blood needs to be pumped to the brain and throughout the body to maintain blood pressure. In order to do this, the heart beats faster. Because this response becomes slower with age, older adults may occasionally feel lightheaded (indicating a drop in blood pressure) when standing up. Over time, the heart's pumping action may become less efficient as well. This can make you tire more quickly during strenuous activities.

Some factors that affect your risk of developing heart problems are beyond your control—such as family history, gender and age. However, a number of lifestyle changes—such as not smoking, eating a nutritious diet, exercising regularly, controlling chronic diseases like hypertension and diabetes, and managing stress—can dramatically lower your risk of heart disease.

For more details on preventing heart disease, see Prevention, *Chest Pain*, p. 185.

CORONARY ARTERIES

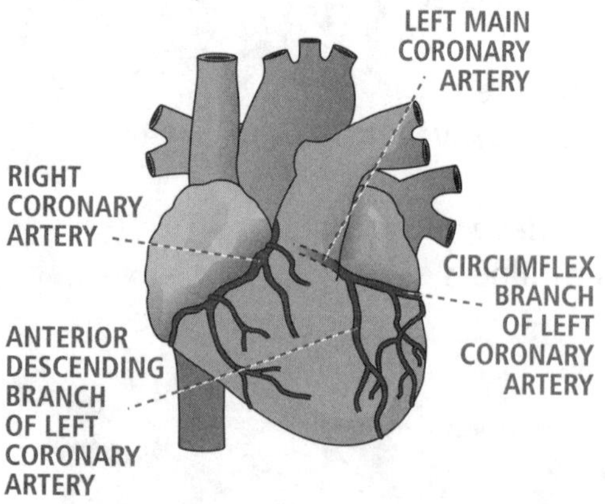

LEFT MAIN CORONARY ARTERY

RIGHT CORONARY ARTERY

ANTERIOR DESCENDING BRANCH OF LEFT CORONARY ARTERY

CIRCUMFLEX BRANCH OF LEFT CORONARY ARTERY

Figure 15

BLOOD FLOW THROUGH THE HEART

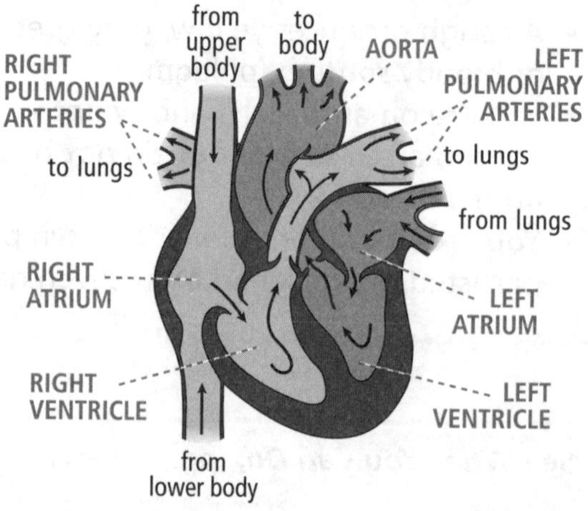

from upper body

to body

AORTA

RIGHT PULMONARY ARTERIES

LEFT PULMONARY ARTERIES

to lungs

to lungs

from lungs

RIGHT ATRIUM

LEFT ATRIUM

RIGHT VENTRICLE

LEFT VENTRICLE

from lower body

Figure 16

Heart Disease

Because more older adults die from heart disease than any other cause, it's important to prevent problems when possible, be familiar with symptoms of common heart conditions, and be ready to take appropriate action if serious symptoms occur.

Coronary Artery Disease (CAD)

Fatty deposits (*plaque*) can form in the arteries, causing a condition known as *atherosclerosis,* or "narrowing" of the arteries. (See Figures 17 and 18.) Plaque makes the insides of the arteries less slippery, causing *platelets* (the sticky blood cells that help stop bleeding) to stick there. This reduces blood flow to the heart over time and increases the risk of blood clots. The diminished flow also results in *ischemia* (lack of oxygen) to the heart, which causes *angina* (chest pain). If the heart is deprived of oxygen for very long, a *myocardial infarction* (heart attack, or death of part of the heart muscle) occurs. (See *Heart Attack* and *Heart Pain,* p. 184.) This group of conditions affecting circulation to the heart is called *coronary artery disease* (CAD).

Nitroglycerin, one of the primary drugs used to treat CAD, helps open the coronary arteries to increase blood flow to the heart muscle. If your doctor recommends nitroglycerin for occasional chest pain, make sure the two of you discuss the type of symptoms you might expect, and what you should do if the symptoms or pain change in any way while using this medication.

ARTERY WITH NORMAL BLOOD FLOW

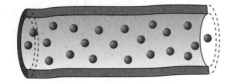

Figure 17

ARTERY WITH REDUCED BLOOD FLOW

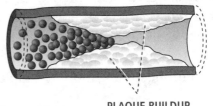

PLAQUE BUILDUP

Figure 18

Many other medications and treatment options are also used to treat CAD, including *angioplasty* (a procedure that re-opens clogged arteries by inflating a tiny balloon inside the artery), *stents* to keep the artery open, and bypass surgery.

WHAT YOU CAN DO ✓

Regardless of age, lifestyle changes that affect how you nourish and maintain your body can have a dramatic impact on reducing or preventing CAD. Research shows that controlling your intake of saturated fats is important since high levels in the blood contribute to atherosclerosis.

To learn more, see the *Prevention* section of this book, p. 337.

Heart Failure

The heart pumps and distributes blood throughout the body, carrying oxygen and nutrients to the tissues. (See Figures 15 and 16, p. 180.) When the heart is weakened and can no longer pump efficiently, blood begins to back up in the lungs and pools in the extremities and other organs. Breathing becomes difficult when you lie down. This condition is known as *heart failure,* and a number of treatments are available for it, including medications and diet restrictions.

TREATMENT OPTIONS ✓

Heart failure is treated with medications to reduce the workload of the heart or improve its pumping action. *Diuretics* (medications known as water pills that increase fluid loss) remove water from the blood and prompt the body to produce more urine. This lightens the heart's workload since there is less fluid to continuously pump throughout the body. *Cardiac glycosides,* such as digoxin (Lanoxin) help improve the *contractile force* (pumping action) of the heart muscle. *ACE inhibitors* such as enalapril (Vasotec) and captopril (Capoten) and *beta-blockers* such as atenolol (Tenormin) and propranolol (Inderal) relax artery walls, allowing the heart to work better without working harder. They are used to improve symptoms of heart failure and reduce mortality rates and the need for hospitalization in people with heart failure.

To minimize the amount of fluid your body retains, your doctor may recommend other options, including limited amounts of fluid and salt in your diet. In some cases, surgery may be needed to repair a faulty heart valve.

Regular exercise is now considered an important part of the treatment plan. Your doctor can help design an appropriate exercise program for you.

Peripheral Vascular Disease (PVD)

Some degree of *arteriosclerosis* (hardening of the arteries) and *atherosclerosis* (buildup of plaque deposits in the blood vessels) occurs as part of the natural aging process and contributes to poor circulation. Many older adults find that even mildly cold temperatures make their hands and feet cold, from the narrowing of blood vessels and restricted blood flow to the fingers and toes. This interference with circulation in the extremities is called *peripheral vascular disease* (PVD).

WHAT YOU CAN DO ✓

Getting regular exercise, giving up smoking and cutting back on caffeine can help prevent or minimize PVD. To relieve uncomfortable symptoms, try wearing warm socks or gloves, walking, or moving your arms in circles to force more blood into the fingers and toes. Soaking your hands and feet in warm water before bedtime and wearing socks to bed may also bring relief.

Sometimes medications are used to *dilate*, or widen, the arteries to improve circulation.

Chest Pain

Chest pain is often associated with the heart and can be a frightening symptom. Although this discomfort may be a warning from your heart and must be handled correctly, there are many other causes of chest pain that are less serious and easier to treat. Knowing the different types of chest pain can help you make the right decisions about what to do for it. **All chest pain should be taken seriously.**

Heart Pain

Angina pectoris is a warning that the heart muscle is not getting enough oxygen. Anginal pain is a tightness, squeezing or feeling of pressure over the front of the chest. It may also be felt in the throat and jaw or down one or both arms. It usually comes on with exertion, stress or overeating and lasts less than 15 minutes. **Any angina means that the heart is in trouble; the pain does not have to be severe to be serious.**

Sharp heart pain may be caused by an infection in the heart's outer lining (*pericarditis*), or inner lining (*endocarditis*). This sometimes follows an infection in another part of the body. *Palpitations* (irregular heartbeats) can cause sudden, brief jabs of pain, usually in the left side of the chest. (See *Palpitations*, p. 188.)

Heart Attack

Chest pain that is crushing, squeezing or increasing in pressure may be a warning of heart attack, known as *myocardial infarction.* The pain is like angina, and may not be severe, but it continues for more than 15 minutes and is not eased with rest. It is often accompanied by nausea, sweating, dizziness, shortness of breath and a feeling of doom or danger. The symptoms are caused by a completely blocked coronary artery which stops blood flow to a part of the heart muscle.

Chest Wall Pain

The chest wall contains skin, muscles, ligaments, ribs and rib cartilage. Pain can be caused by infection, inflammation, bruises, strains, sprains or broken ribs. Chest wall pain is usually sharp or knife-like and limited to a small area. It often comes and goes for days; touching, bending, stretching, coughing or taking a deep breath may cause or increase pain.

Other Non-Heart Pain

Anxiety is a common cause of chest pain. It may be a sharp jab or dull pressure and is often located in the left chest area. Pain from *hyperventilation* (excessive rapid breathing) often causes or comes with anxiety. (See *Hyperventilation Syndrome*, p. 317.)

Chest pain can come from the lungs, *pleura* (the thin membranes that cover the lungs), esophagus, diaphragm or several of the organs in the upper abdomen. Pain from the lungs and pleura is similar to chest wall pain and frequently follows a cold or flu-like illness. Lung problems like pneumonia, blood clots and asthma may produce chest pain.

If the discomfort is caused by the esophagus or the stomach, there may be an acid taste in the mouth and a burning feeling in the chest that improves after eating.

PREVENTION ✓

There are many causes of chest pain, and prevention is not possible for all of them. However, good health habits decrease your risk of illness and improve your chances of a quick, full recovery.

- Maintain a normal body weight. (See *Eating Right*, p. 338.)
- Follow a low-fat, well-balanced diet. (See *Eating Right*, p. 338.)
- Exercise regularly. (See *Staying Active*, p. 343.)
- If you smoke, start taking steps to kick the habit. (See *Smoking Cessation*, p. 346.)
- Have regular checkups to help detect any health problems early. (See *Catching Problems Early*, p. 351.)
- Learn about any chronic illnesses you have and follow your doctor's advice. (See *Steps to Self-Management*, p. 370.)
- Learn about stress and stress management. (See *Stress*, p. 313.)

WHAT YOU CAN DO ✓

- Learn CPR (see *CPR*, p. 20) and know what to do for emergencies. (See *Emergencies Introduction*, p. 18.)
- Try to identify what may be causing your pain; avoid activities or foods that cause discomfort.
- If chest wall pain is caused by injury, treat with the RICE process (see *Strains and Sprains*, p. 62) and take aspirin or ibuprofen (Advil, Motrin) for pain and inflammation. **NEVER give aspirin to children/teenagers unless your health care provider orders it. It can cause Reye's syndrome, a rare but often fatal condition. CAUTION: Talk to your doctor or pharmacist before taking any other medications, including over-the-counter (OTC) medications, vitamins or herbal supplements.**
- If pain is from stress or hyperventilation, follow stress-reduction methods. (See *Stress*, p. 313.)
- To relieve pain from problems with the stomach or esophagus:
  - Eat smaller meals.
  - Don't smoke.
  - Avoid foods and drugs that seem to trigger pain.
  - Raise the head of your bed on 4- to 6-inch (10 to 15 cm) blocks and don't eat for at least three hours before bedtime.
  - Take antacids. (Follow directions on the package.)

Decision *helper* Chest Pain
DO THESE APPLY:

- There is crushing, squeezing or increasing pressure in the chest
- Chest, jaw, neck, shoulder or arm discomfort occurs with:
  - Shortness of breath
  - Confusion, dizziness, weakness or a faint feeling
  - Sweating
  - Nausea or vomiting
  - Rapid or irregular pulse
- Chronic heart disease exists and chest pain is not relieved with nitroglycerin medication

Rest quietly with your head elevated on pillows; stay warm.

Wait for emergency transport or advice from the emergency system. Chew an aspirin while you wait.

YES

Seek
Emergency
Care

Apply
Emergency
First Aid

NO

- Chest wall pain occurs with fever
- Chronic heart disease and chest pain is more frequent, more intense or present during times of rest

YES

Call Doctor
Now

NO

- There is chest pain and cough with yellow, gray-green or rust-colored *sputum* (phlegm)
- There is no diagnosis of angina and you have episodes of chest pain with exertion, heavy eating or stress, that subside within 15 minutes
- Your symptoms worsen or have not improved after 48 hours of self-care

YES

Call Doctor

NO

See *What You Can Do,* p. 186.

Apply
Self-Care

Palpitations

Everyone feels a skip, flutter, flip-flop, thump or pounding in their chest at times. These feelings are *palpitations* and are caused by a change in your normal heart rhythm; they can be very strong, rapid or irregular beats.

Causes of palpitations include *hyperventilation* (excessive rapid breathing), anxiety, fever, overactive thyroid, stimulants such as caffeine and nicotine, alcohol and many drugs and medicines. Palpitations, or *arrhythmias,* can occur in some types of heart disease. In most cases, palpitations are brief, harmless and go away without treatment.

PREVENTION ✓

- Exercise regularly. (See *Staying Active,* p. 343.)
- If you smoke, start taking steps to kick the habit. (See *Smoking Cessation,* p. 346.)
- Limit the amount of alcohol (see *Alcohol Use,* p. 349) and caffeine you drink.
- Read warnings on packages and labels of all the drugs you take.
- Do what you can to control your stress. (See *Stress,* p. 313.)
- Have regular checkups to help detect and treat health problems early. (See *Catching Problems Early,* p. 351.)

WHAT YOU CAN DO ✓

- Look for the cause of your palpitations. Do they come after consuming certain foods or beverages? At a specific time of day? During or following a certain activity? Eliminate the possible cause and see if it takes care of the problem.
- Ask your doctor or pharmacist about possible medication side effects.
- Follow the prevention guidelines listed above.
- Relax and remember that most palpitations are harmless.

Palpitations
DO THESE APPLY:

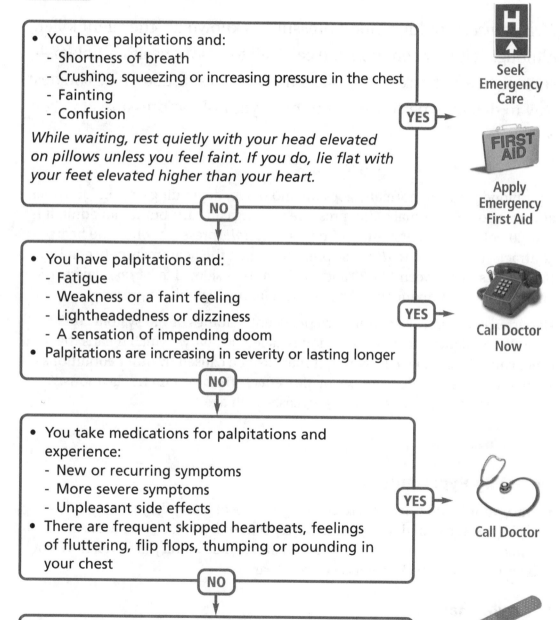

- You have palpitations and:
  - Shortness of breath
  - Crushing, squeezing or increasing pressure in the chest
  - Fainting
  - Confusion

While waiting, rest quietly with your head elevated on pillows unless you feel faint. If you do, lie flat with your feet elevated higher than your heart.

YES →

H ↑

Seek
Emergency
Care

FIRST AID

Apply
Emergency
First Aid

NO

- You have palpitations and:
  - Fatigue
  - Weakness or a faint feeling
  - Lightheadedness or dizziness
  - A sensation of impending doom
- Palpitations are increasing in severity or lasting longer

YES →

Call Doctor
Now

NO

- You take medications for palpitations and experience:
  - New or recurring symptoms
  - More severe symptoms
  - Unpleasant side effects
- There are frequent skipped heartbeats, feelings of fluttering, flip flops, thumping or pounding in your chest

YES →

Call Doctor

NO

See *What You Can Do,* p. 188.

Apply
Self-Care

Hypertension

Hypertension, or high blood pressure, is known as "the silent killer." Although it is very common and can lead to serious health problems—such as heart attack and stroke—it often goes undetected. The best way to detect hypertension is to have your blood pressure checked regularly.

Your blood pressure normally goes up and down, depending on your activities and emotions. A normal blood pressure reading can vary, but for an adult, it is 120/80 or lower. The first number refers to *systolic* pressure, when the heart contracts; the second to *diastolic* pressure, when the heart rests between beats. Blood pressure between 120/80 and 140/90 are considered to be *pre-hypertension* and may indicate an increased risk of developing high blood pressure.

Hypertension is usually defined as consistent readings of 140 systolic, or 90 diastolic, or higher. Most hypertension is called "primary," which means that the exact cause is unknown. However, it may also be caused by other conditions—such as diabetes, kidney disease, or side effects from certain medications. A person's risk of hypertension also increases with age.

WHAT YOU CAN DO ✓

Detecting Hypertension

- Have your blood pressure checked regularly—at least every two years.
- If you are at risk of developing hypertension or heart disease because of high cholesterol, obesity, diabetes, family history, or sedentary lifestyle, have your blood pressure checked at least once a year.

Lifestyle Changes

Lifestyle changes are key to reducing high blood pressure:

- Get regular exercise. (See *Staying Active,* p. 343.) Check with your doctor before beginning an exercise program.
- Lose weight if you are overweight.
- If you smoke, start taking steps to kick the habit. (See *Smoking Cessation,* p. 346.)
- Restrict dietary sodium intake to no more than 2,400 mg (about one teaspoon of salt [5 mL]) per day and reduce dietary fats, especially saturated fats. (See *Eating Right,* p. 338.)
- Eliminate or restrict alcohol consumption. (See *Alcohol Use,* p. 349.)

The National Heart, Lung and Blood Institute (NHLBI) recommends the Dietary Approaches to Stop Hypertension or "DASH" diet:

- Eat 7 to 8 servings of grains and grain products (whole wheat bread and pastas, brown rice, etc.) each day.
- Eat 8 to 10 servings of fruits and vegetables per day. One serving is equal to 1 medium apple, 1/2 cup (115 mL) of fruit, 3/4 cup (173 mL) of juice, 1 cup (230 mL) of leafy vegetables or 1/2 cup (115 mL) of other vegetables.
- Get adequate potassium each day (3.5 mg). Good sources are orange juice, bananas, potatoes and winter squash.
- Get 2 1/2 to 3 servings of low-fat or nonfat dairy products daily. One serving is 1 cup (230 mL) of milk or yogurt, 1 to 1 1/2 ounces (30 to 45 grams) of low-fat cheese, or 2 ounces (60 grams) of processed cheese.

Medications

If you are diagnosed with high blood pressure, your doctor may combine lifestyle modifications with a "stepped approach" to medication treatment, often beginning with *diuretics* (medications known as water pills that increase fluid loss) and progressing to drugs that act directly on the blood vessels, heart and blood chemistry.

The goal of medical treatment is to control hypertension while creating as few side effects as possible.

FINAL NOTES ✓

It's crucial that you comply with the treatment program your doctor prescribes if you are diagnosed with hypertension. If you have problems with any part of the program, talk to your doctor. Your doctor will decide how often to have follow-up visits, based on the severity of your hypertension, treatment response and other factors.

 Hypertension
DO THESE APPLY:

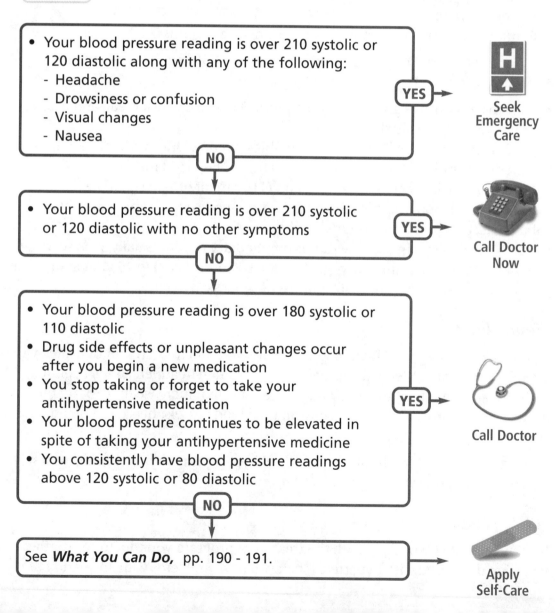

- Your blood pressure reading is over 210 systolic or 120 diastolic along with any of the following:
  - Headache
  - Drowsiness or confusion
  - Visual changes
  - Nausea

YES → Seek Emergency Care

NO

- Your blood pressure reading is over 210 systolic or 120 diastolic with no other symptoms

YES → Call Doctor Now

NO

- Your blood pressure reading is over 180 systolic or 110 diastolic
- Drug side effects or unpleasant changes occur after you begin a new medication
- You stop taking or forget to take your antihypertensive medication
- Your blood pressure continues to be elevated in spite of taking your antihypertensive medicine
- You consistently have blood pressure readings above 120 systolic or 80 diastolic

YES → Call Doctor

NO

See *What You Can Do,* pp. 190 - 191.

→ Apply Self-Care

Abdominal/GI

Aging brings normal changes in the way your body processes food. Food may take longer to travel down the *esophagus* (the food pipe to your stomach) because of decreased *peristalsis* (muscular contractions) within the esophagus and digestive system. Secretions that aid digestion may also lessen and—along with decreased muscle contractions—cause food to move more slowly through the stomach and intestines. The result may be more frequent constipation.

In addition, you may experience *reflux* (flowing back) of gastric fluids from the stomach into the lower end of the esophagus. This occurs because the *lower esophageal sphincter* (a muscular band at the junction of the esophagus and stomach) weakens as you age, causing the symptoms of gastric reflux—commonly called *heartburn.*

Your sense of taste and smell may become duller as you get older, causing food to taste flat or unappealing. To compensate for this, many individuals add extra salt to their food. This can lead to problems such as fluid retention, which puts added strain on the heart. (For tips on alternatives to salt, see *Mouth Concerns,* p. 161; *Fiber and Salt,* p. 341.)

While these physiological changes are a normal part of aging, there are a number of simple ways you can take charge of the situation—including adapting your diet and activity levels—to decrease or even eliminate symptoms. The following chapters will help you understand when these problems can be managed through self-care and when it is appropriate to see your doctor.

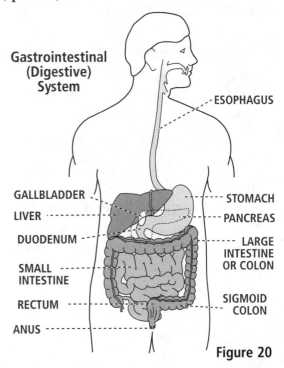

Gastrointestinal (Digestive) System

ESOPHAGUS

GALLBLADDER

LIVER

DUODENUM

SMALL INTESTINE

RECTUM

ANUS

STOMACH

PANCREAS

LARGE INTESTINE OR COLON

SIGMOID COLON

Figure 20

Nausea and Vomiting

Nausea is most often traced to a viral infection or "stomach flu" that produces a queasy stomach. When nausea intensifies, you may vomit. The condition can also be caused by medications, stress, food poisoning or a head injury. Because nausea and vomiting can be connected with so many medical problems—some of them serious—it's important to watch your symptoms closely.

NOTE YOUR SYMPTOMS ✓

The most dangerous threat posed by vomiting is dehydration (see *Dehydration*, p. 203), which can occur quickly, particularly in older adults. Severe dehydration can be life-threatening and symptoms should be carefully monitored.

Signs of dehydration include:

- Unusual thirst
- Sunken-looking eyes
- Dry mouth and cracked lips
- Infrequent urination or dark yellow urine
- Skin that is no longer elastic

Nausea and vomiting may indicate serious medical conditions if:

- You vomit bright red blood or what looks like coffee grounds (see *Peptic Ulcer*, p. 212)
- You have abdominal pain that is severe or localized in one area (see *Abdominal Pain*, p. 218)
- Vomiting is accompanied by a headache and a stiff neck (see *Meningitis*, p. 240)

Some nausea and vomiting can be traced to food poisoning. (See *Stomach Flu and Food Poisoning,* p. 197.) The cause is organisms that inflame the intestines, found in certain foods that are not stored or handled properly.

Suspect food poisoning if:

- Your symptoms are shared by others who ate the same food
- Nausea and vomiting begin six to 48 hours after eating food that may not have been stored correctly

WHAT YOU CAN DO ✓

Give Your Stomach a Break

- Avoid solid foods.
- For 12 to 24 hours after symptoms begin, slowly sip any of the following:
  - Non-prescription *electrolyte* (minerals such as sodium and potassium) supplements such as Pedialyte, RiceLyte or Rehydralyte (found in the infant formula section of most groceries)
  - Clear liquids such as water and diluted bouillon (unless your doctor has restricted your sodium intake)
- As your symptoms improve, try unbuttered rice, potatoes or noodles; crackers or toast; unsweetened hot or cold cereals; soups with rice and meat; and yogurt, bananas and applesauce.
- Do not take aspirin or other pain relievers.
- Increase liquids gradually; start drinking a few sips at a time. Do this even if you can't keep anything down for long.
- Suck ice chips if no other liquids stay down.

FINAL NOTES ✓

While patience and self-care normally do the trick for an upset stomach, it's important to be alert to serious and sudden complications.

See *Decision helper,* p. 196.

Decision *helper* Nausea and Vomiting
DO THESE APPLY:

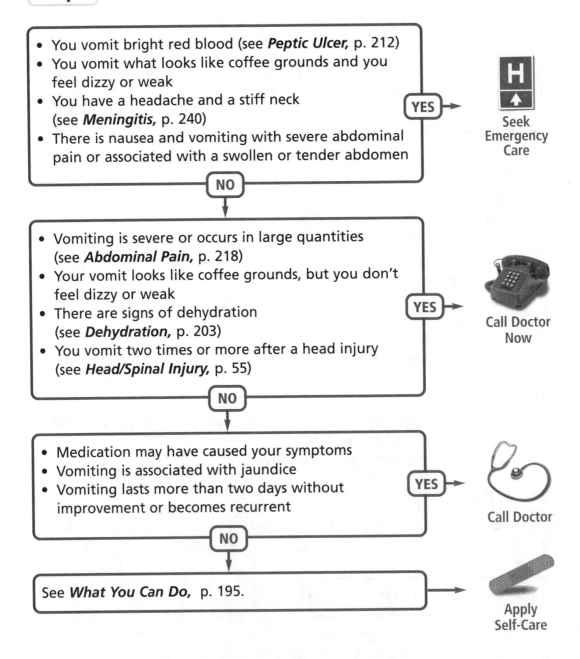

- You vomit bright red blood (see **Peptic Ulcer,** p. 212)
- You vomit what looks like coffee grounds and you feel dizzy or weak
- You have a headache and a stiff neck (see **Meningitis,** p. 240)
- There is nausea and vomiting with severe abdominal pain or associated with a swollen or tender abdomen

YES → Seek Emergency Care

NO

- Vomiting is severe or occurs in large quantities (see **Abdominal Pain,** p. 218)
- Your vomit looks like coffee grounds, but you don't feel dizzy or weak
- There are signs of dehydration (see **Dehydration,** p. 203)
- You vomit two times or more after a head injury (see **Head/Spinal Injury,** p. 55)

YES → Call Doctor Now

NO

- Medication may have caused your symptoms
- Vomiting is associated with jaundice
- Vomiting lasts more than two days without improvement or becomes recurrent

YES → Call Doctor

NO

See **What You Can Do,** p. 195.

→ Apply Self-Care

Stomach Flu and Food Poisoning

Stomach flu and food poisoning have different causes but many of the same symptoms. However, they both fall under the general category of *gastroenteritis*, which is commonly caused by food-borne bacteria, or by viruses spread—hand-to-mouth—by contaminated objects.

Symptoms—vomiting, diarrhea, abdominal cramping and fever—usually take three to 36 hours to develop, with the resulting illness lasting 12 hours to several days.

PREVENTION ✓

Stomach Flu

- Maximize your resistance to infection with a healthy diet, plenty of rest and regular exercise.
- Wash your hands frequently.
- Keep your hands away from your nose, eyes and mouth.

Food Poisoning

- Carefully refrigerate (between 34° F [1° C] and 40° F [4° C]) all foods—especially poultry, fish, meats and eggs. Don't eat anything that has been kept between 40° F (4° C) and 140° F (60° C) for more than two hours.
- Defrost foods in the microwave or refrigerator—not on the kitchen counter.
- Avoid foods made with raw eggs, as well as rare or uncooked meats.
- Be especially careful with large, cooked meats like whole turkeys. Refrigerate leftovers as soon as dinner is over. Remove thick bones and cut meat into portions less than three inches (8 cm) thick to speed cooling.
- Thoroughly reheat leftover meats to at least 165° F (74° C) before serving them to destroy any bacteria.

- Wash all utensils, counter tops and cutting boards that have touched raw meat in hot, soapy water before reusing them. Wash your hands frequently.
- Follow home-canning and freezing instructions carefully. Throw out any cans or jars that have leaks or bulging lids. Do not touch the contents and wash your hands after handling the container.

WHAT YOU CAN DO ✓

- Do not eat solid foods while vomiting persists.
- Slowly sip any of the following:
  - Non-prescription *electrolyte* (minerals such as sodium and potassium) supplements such as Pedialyte, RiceLyte or Rehydralyte (found in the infant formula section of most groceries)
  - Clear liquids such as water and diluted bouillon (unless your doctor has restricted your sodium intake)
- As your symptoms improve, try unbuttered rice, potatoes or noodles; crackers or toast; unsweetened hot or cold cereals; soups with rice and meat; and yogurt, bananas and applesauce.
- Do not take aspirin or other pain relievers.
- If you suspect food poisoning, check with anyone else who may have eaten the same food. When possible, save a sample of the suspected food in case analysis becomes necessary.

For additional self-care, see *Nausea and Vomiting* (p. 194); *Diarrhea* (p. 200); *Dehydration* (p. 203).

> Many forms of bacteria can cause food poisoning, including *salmonella* (typically found in dairy products, eggs, poultry, red meat and seafood) and *E. coli* (most commonly found in improperly cooked ground meats). A rare but fatal form of food poisoning called *botulism* is usually caused by eating foods with a low-acidity content—such as corn and beans—that have been improperly home-canned.

Decision *helper* Stomach Flu and Food Poisoning

DO THESE APPLY:

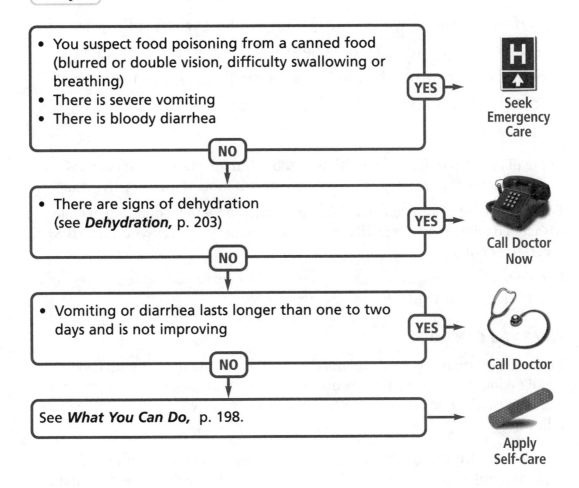

- You suspect food poisoning from a canned food (blurred or double vision, difficulty swallowing or breathing)
- There is severe vomiting
- There is bloody diarrhea

YES → Seek Emergency Care

NO

- There are signs of dehydration (see *Dehydration,* p. 203)

YES → Call Doctor Now

NO

- Vomiting or diarrhea lasts longer than one to two days and is not improving

YES → Call Doctor

NO

See *What You Can Do,* p. 198. → Apply Self-Care

Diarrhea

Diarrhea (frequent, watery stools) takes place when solid waste is pushed through the intestines before the water in the waste has time to be reabsorbed by the body. In most cases, diarrhea is *acute* (short-lived), and responds well to self-care measures.

Acute diarrhea is most commonly caused by viral infections. Other causes include bacterial infections, food allergies or irritation of the digestive tract.

For some people, however, diarrhea is a *chronic* (ongoing) condition, usually associated with an intestinal disorder such as irritable bowel syndrome (IBS) or ulcerative colitis.

For older adults, the greatest risk of diarrhea is *dehydration,* which occurs if water is lost faster than the body can replace it.

WHAT YOU CAN DO ☑

Although antidiarrheal medications such as Kaopectate or Imodium can help, avoid taking them for the first six hours after symptoms occur, since diarrhea can help rid the body of the harmful organisms. While you are waiting, try the following:

- Slowly sip drinks containing *electrolytes* (minerals such as sodium and potassium), such as Pedialyte, RiceLyte or Rehydralyte (found in the infant formula section of most groceries). These solutions may be consumed full-strength or diluted with water. However, be sure to check with your doctor first, since the high salt in these drinks can be dangerous for people with conditions like high blood pressure, heart disease, diabetes, glaucoma or a history of stroke.
- Drink clear liquids, such as water or bouillon (unless your health care provider has restricted your sodium intake), or suck on ice chips. Note: Avoid juices and sodas, which can increase diarrhea.

- As your symptoms improve, eat bland, easily digested foods such as unbuttered rice, potatoes or noodles; crackers or toast; unsweetened hot or cold cereals; soups with rice and meat; yogurt; bananas or applesauce.
- For several days, avoid spicy foods, alcohol and foods high in fat, which are all difficult to digest.

To relieve chafed skin related to diarrhea:

- Gently cleanse yourself after bowel movements with pre-moistened towels or baby wipes, which are less irritating than toilet paper; wash your hands thoroughly afterward.
- Bathe and change your underclothing daily.
- Try over-the-counter (OTC) medicated pads to relieve pain and itching, such as Preparation H, Tucks or Fleet wipes.
- Apply 1 percent hydrocortisone cream to inflamed or itchy areas, but ONLY if sores or infection are not present.

Dehydration

Diarrhea can quickly lead to dehydration, a serious complication that can be life-threatening if it isn't stopped. Dehydration depletes cells of the fluid and electrolytes they need to function properly. If water and electrolyte levels remain low for an extended period, blood pressure can drop to dangerously low levels as well. This can lead to shock or severe damage to internal organs such as the kidneys, brain or liver. (See *Dehydration*, p. 203.)

Diarrhea
DO THESE APPLY:

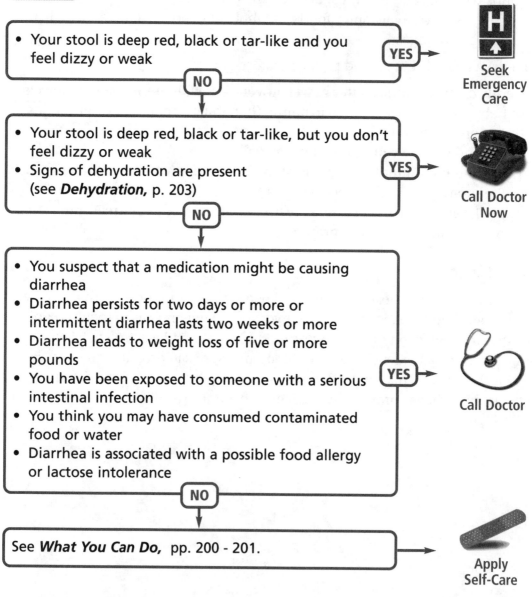

- Your stool is deep red, black or tar-like and you feel dizzy or weak **[YES]** → Seek Emergency Care

[NO]

- Your stool is deep red, black or tar-like, but you don't feel dizzy or weak
- Signs of dehydration are present (see *Dehydration,* p. 203) **[YES]** → Call Doctor Now

[NO]

- You suspect that a medication might be causing diarrhea
- Diarrhea persists for two days or more or intermittent diarrhea lasts two weeks or more
- Diarrhea leads to weight loss of five or more pounds
- You have been exposed to someone with a serious intestinal infection
- You think you may have consumed contaminated food or water
- Diarrhea is associated with a possible food allergy or lactose intolerance **[YES]** → Call Doctor

[NO]

See *What You Can Do,* pp. 200 - 201. → Apply Self-Care

Dehydration

Dehydration is the excessive loss of water in the body and is a dangerous risk of vomiting (see *Nausea and Vomiting,* p. 194), diarrhea (see *Diarrhea,* p. 200) and heat exhaustion/sun stroke (see *Heat Exhaustion,* p. 32). It can occur quickly in older adults. Dehydration also depletes the body of two essential minerals, sodium and potassium, which are *electrolytes.* Severe dehydration can be life-threatening, and symptoms should be carefully monitored.

Signs of dehydration include:

- Unusual thirst
- Sunken-looking eyes
- Dry mouth and cracked lips
- Infrequent urination or dark yellow urine
- Skin that is no longer elastic

WHAT YOU CAN DO ☑

To prevent dehydration or keep it from getting worse:

- At the first sign of illness, increase your fluid intake to eight to 10 large glasses of water a day until it stops.
- Drink a rehydration fluid like Pedialyte, RiceLyte or Rehydralyte (found in the infant formula section of most groceries) to replace lost electrolytes. (Because of the sodium content, consult your doctor first if you have high blood pressure, heart disease, diabetes, glaucoma or a history of stroke.) These formulas may be consumed full-strength or diluted with water.
- After vomiting is under control, drink clear liquids like water and bouillon. (See *Nausea and Vomiting,* p. 194.)

See *Decision helper,* p. 204.

Decision *helper*   Dehydration
DO THESE APPLY:

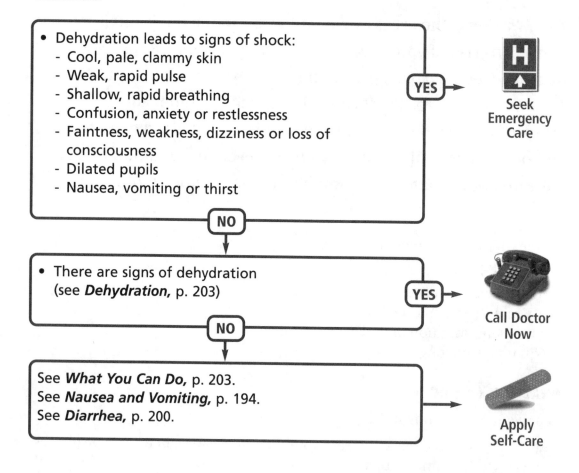

- Dehydration leads to signs of shock:
  - Cool, pale, clammy skin
  - Weak, rapid pulse
  - Shallow, rapid breathing
  - Confusion, anxiety or restlessness
  - Faintness, weakness, dizziness or loss of consciousness
  - Dilated pupils
  - Nausea, vomiting or thirst

YES → **H ↑**
Seek
Emergency
Care

NO

- There are signs of dehydration
  (see *Dehydration*, p. 203)

YES → Call Doctor Now

NO

See *What You Can Do,* p. 203.
See *Nausea and Vomiting,* p. 194.
See *Diarrhea,* p. 200.

→ Apply
Self-Care

Constipation

Constipation is a decreased frequency of bowel movements accompanied by hard, dry stools. However, there is no standard for what constitutes normal bowel movements. Normal for you may be two bowel movements a day or one every three days.

Other symptoms of constipation include difficulty passing stools, abdominal pain and fullness, a feeling of incomplete bowel movements, bloating and gas.

Changes in stools (color, consistency, texture and bulk) generally are not serious. Chronic constipation occurs more frequently in older adults, whose diet and fluid consumption patterns may be inadequate.

WHAT YOU CAN DO ✓

Constipation often can be successfully treated through self-care:

- If your eating habits have changed (other than for medical reasons), go back to the diet you had before the problems began.
- Improve your diet by adding more high-fiber foods, such as whole grains, bran, beans, leafy and raw vegetables, and fruits—especially dried fruits.
- Drink plenty of fluids, especially water.
- Increase your daily exercise, especially if you sit all day at work.
- Investigate ALL medications you take to see if they cause constipation. (However, DO NOT stop taking a prescribed medication without consulting your doctor).

If these steps don't work, consider over-the-counter (OTC) remedies such as bulk laxatives containing methylcellulose or psyllium, which draw water into the stool; Milk of Magnesia (not for individuals with kidney problems); or stool softeners. **CAUTION: Talk to your doctor or pharmacist before taking any other medications, including over-the-counter (OTC) medications, vitamins or herbal supplements.**

A reduction in the frequency of bowel movements with no other symptoms does not necessarily require treatment.

Hemorrhoids

Hemorrhoids are swollen, inflamed tissues located around the outside or inside of the anus. They are extremely common and can be caused or aggravated by constipation, straining to move the bowels, obesity or a sedentary lifestyle.

Symptoms may include pain, itching, burning, swelling, bleeding and a sense of incomplete emptying of the rectum. Frequently, hemorrhoidal bleeding is indicated by bright red blood on the toilet paper or in the toilet bowl after bowel movements.

WHAT YOU CAN DO ✓

Simple self-care is usually the key to initial treatment:

- Keep the anal area clean with pre-moistened towels or "baby wipes."
- Soak in a warm *sitz bath* (hip-high water), which usually proves soothing.
- Avoid sitting for long periods of time, if possible, or sit on a rubber doughnut. Stretch frequently.
- Try over-the-counter (OTC) hydrocortisone creams to reduce swelling and inflammation. Avoid creams with topical *anesthetics* (pain relievers), since they may slow healing. **CAUTION: Talk to your doctor or pharmacist before taking any other medications, including over-the-counter (OTC) medications, vitamins or herbal supplements.**
- Take steps to avoid constipation and straining to move the bowels. Eat high-fiber foods or take over-the-counter (OTC) fiber supplements. Drink plenty of fluids and exercise regularly. (See *Getting and Staying Healthy,* p. 338.) The occasional use of a mild laxative might be of value, but a better choice is a simple stool softener. Ask your doctor if any medications you take might cause constipation (iron is notorious for this); a stool softener may decrease this side effect.

Decision *helper* Constipation/Hemorrhoids
DO THESE APPLY:

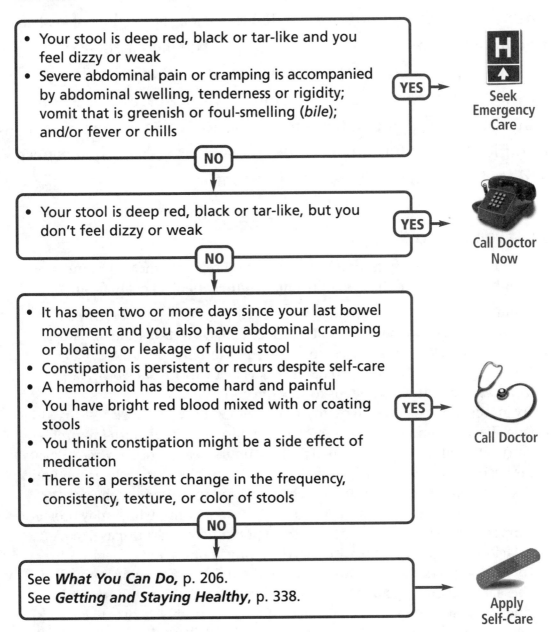

- Your stool is deep red, black or tar-like and you feel dizzy or weak
- Severe abdominal pain or cramping is accompanied by abdominal swelling, tenderness or rigidity; vomit that is greenish or foul-smelling (*bile*); and/or fever or chills

YES → Seek Emergency Care

NO

- Your stool is deep red, black or tar-like, but you don't feel dizzy or weak

YES → Call Doctor Now

NO

- It has been two or more days since your last bowel movement and you also have abdominal cramping or bloating or leakage of liquid stool
- Constipation is persistent or recurs despite self-care
- A hemorrhoid has become hard and painful
- You have bright red blood mixed with or coating stools
- You think constipation might be a side effect of medication
- There is a persistent change in the frequency, consistency, texture, or color of stools

YES → Call Doctor

NO

See *What You Can Do,* p. 206.
See *Getting and Staying Healthy*, p. 338.

→ Apply Self-Care

GERD and Heartburn

Gastroesophageal reflux disease (GERD) is caused by the flow of gastric acid from the stomach into the esophagus. The pain associated with GERD is called *heartburn* (a burning sensation), which typically spreads from the upper abdomen into the lower breastbone. Sour material may be regurgitated into the mouth, and swallowing may be difficult or painful. Other symptoms, such as asthma, hoarseness and sore throat may also be associated with GERD.

WHAT YOU CAN DO ✔

Heartburn will generally respond to a number of self-care measures. **But remember, any chest pain, even burning, requires medical evaluation.**

- Avoid irritants such as alcohol, aspirin and ibuprofen (Advil, Motrin).
- Avoid fatty or spicy foods, chocolate, peppermint, citrus fruits and tomatoes, and beverages like citrus juices, coffee, tea and carbonated drinks.
- Avoid large meals. Eat small frequent meals instead and eat slowly.
- If you smoke, start taking steps to kick the habit.
- Try to reduce stress if it seems to make your symptoms worse. (See *Stress*, p. 313.)
- Don't lie down immediately after eating. If nighttime heartburn is a problem, don't eat anything for at least two to three hours before going to bed. Elevate the head of the bed with 4- to 6-inch (10 to 15 cm) blocks to incline your body.
- Don't wear tight-fitting clothing such as girdles, tight-fitting pants or belts.
- Take antacids such as Maalox, Mylanta, Gelusil or Tums, which may provide temporary relief. (If you have high blood pressure or heart disease, don't use antacids with sodium salts without consulting your doctor.)
- Try *acid reducers*, medications that decrease the production of stomach acid. These medications include famotidine (Pepcid), ranitidine (Zantac), nizatidine (Axid) and cimetidine (Tagamet). If symptoms persist after two weeks, consult your doctor before continuing use. **CAUTION: Talk to your doctor or pharmacist before taking any other medications, including over-the-counter (OTC) medications, vitamins or herbal supplements.**

FINAL NOTES ☑

People who are prone to GERD may suffer repeated attacks of heartburn. Chronic severe symptoms may lead to complications, including certain pre-cancerous conditions. However, with self-care you can control the symptoms of simple heartburn with no lasting ill effects.

Decision *helper* Heartburn
DO THESE APPLY:

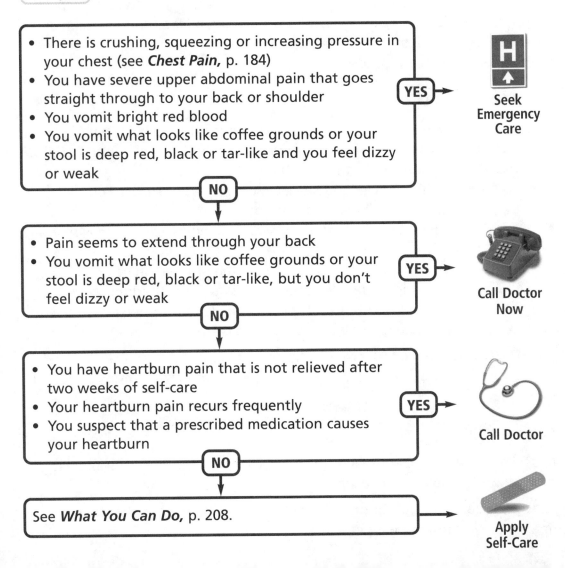

- There is crushing, squeezing or increasing pressure in your chest (see *Chest Pain,* p. 184)
- You have severe upper abdominal pain that goes straight through to your back or shoulder
- You vomit bright red blood
- You vomit what looks like coffee grounds or your stool is deep red, black or tar-like and you feel dizzy or weak

YES → **H** ↑ Seek Emergency Care

NO

- Pain seems to extend through your back
- You vomit what looks like coffee grounds or your stool is deep red, black or tar-like, but you don't feel dizzy or weak

YES → Call Doctor Now

NO

- You have heartburn pain that is not relieved after two weeks of self-care
- Your heartburn pain recurs frequently
- You suspect that a prescribed medication causes your heartburn

YES → Call Doctor

NO

See *What You Can Do,* p. 208. → Apply Self-Care

Gastritis

Gastritis is a painful inflammation of the lining of the stomach. This may occur more frequently with advancing age.

Causes include bacterial infection (often with H. pylori), acute stress, alcohol abuse, or nonsteroidal anti-inflammatory drugs (NSAIDs), such as aspirin or ibuprofen (Advil, Motrin). Symptoms may include upper abdominal pain or bloating, diarrhea, nausea and vomiting, sometimes with bright red blood or what looks like coffee grounds.

WHAT YOU CAN DO ✓

- Take over-the-counter (OTC) antacids to provide possible pain relief.*
- Don't use tobacco and moderate your use of alcohol and caffeinated drinks. (See *Getting and Staying Healthy,* p. 338.)
- Avoid foods that may trigger gastritis, such as pickles or spices. Food sensitivities can vary from person to person.
- Avoid NSAIDs and other drugs that cause or worsen gastritis. (See *Home Pharmacy,* p. 331.)
- Try acid reducers, medications that decrease the production of stomach acid. These medications include famotidine (Pepcid), ranitidine (Zantac), nizatidine (Axid) and cimetidine (Tagamet).* If symptoms persist after two weeks, consult your doctor before continuing use.

* **CAUTION: Talk to your doctor or pharmacist before taking any other medications, including over-the-counter (OTC) medications, vitamins or herbal supplements.**

FINAL NOTES ✓

If OTC medications do not relieve the pain, your doctor may recommend a more powerful prescription drug.

Gastritis is generally not serious. In most cases, the pain stops spontaneously or after minor lifestyle changes.

Decision *helper* Gastritis
DO THESE APPLY:

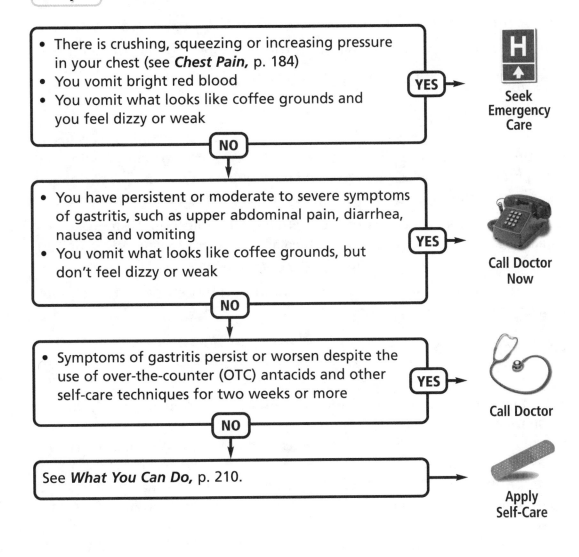

- There is crushing, squeezing or increasing pressure in your chest (see **Chest Pain,** p. 184)
- You vomit bright red blood
- You vomit what looks like coffee grounds and you feel dizzy or weak

YES → Seek Emergency Care

NO

- You have persistent or moderate to severe symptoms of gastritis, such as upper abdominal pain, diarrhea, nausea and vomiting
- You vomit what looks like coffee grounds, but don't feel dizzy or weak

YES → Call Doctor Now

NO

- Symptoms of gastritis persist or worsen despite the use of over-the-counter (OTC) antacids and other self-care techniques for two weeks or more

YES → Call Doctor

NO

See **What You Can Do,** p. 210.

→ Apply Self-Care

Peptic Ulcer

Peptic ulcers are craters or eroded areas in the protective lining of the stomach or intestine that are almost always caused by bacterial infection with Helicobacter pylori (H. pylori).

The most common type of peptic ulcer is called a *duodenal ulcer,* which occurs in the upper part of the small intestine. Severe ulcers can lead to pain, bleeding and even perforations—holes—in the wall of the stomach or intestine. **A perforated ulcer is a life-threatening emergency and needs immediate surgical repair.**

Although ulcers are usually associated with H. pylori infection, cigarette smoking and the use of certain drugs such as aspirin, ibuprofen (Advil, Motrin) and corticosteroids may also cause them in some people.

Thanks to significant advances in treatment, with early detection, most people recover from ulcers within four to six weeks.

WHAT YOU CAN DO ☑

To speed the healing process if you have a peptic ulcer:

- Start taking steps to kick the habit if you smoke; also avoid coffee, alcohol, aspirin and ibuprofen (Advil, Motrin).
- Avoid hot or spicy foods if they cause discomfort; for the most part you can eat a normal diet, however.
- Don't drink large amounts of milk. Calcium may stimulate acid production.
- For temporary relief from ulcer pain, take over-the-counter (OTC) antacids such as Maalox or Mylanta.*
- Try acid reducers, medications that decrease the production of stomach acid. These medications include famotidine (Pepcid), ranitidine (Zantac), nizatidine (Axid) and cimetidine (Tagamet).* If symptoms persist after two weeks, consult your doctor before continuing to use them.

* **CAUTION: Talk to your doctor or pharmacist before taking any other medications, including over-the-counter (OTC) medications, vitamins or herbal supplements.**

Tell your doctor if you have a history of ulcers. Common medications taken for other ailments can increase your risk of ulcer recurrences.

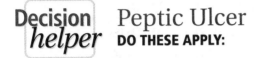

Decision Peptic Ulcer
helper **DO THESE APPLY:**

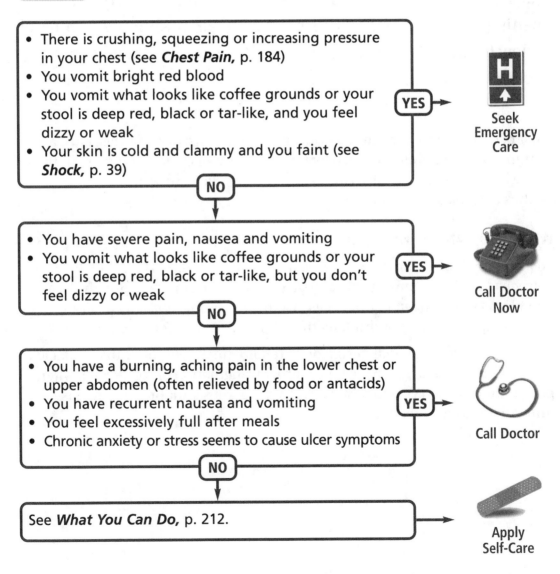

- There is crushing, squeezing or increasing pressure in your chest (see *Chest Pain,* p. 184)
- You vomit bright red blood
- You vomit what looks like coffee grounds or your stool is deep red, black or tar-like, and you feel dizzy or weak
- Your skin is cold and clammy and you faint (see *Shock,* p. 39)

YES → Seek Emergency Care

NO

- You have severe pain, nausea and vomiting
- You vomit what looks like coffee grounds or your stool is deep red, black or tar-like, but you don't feel dizzy or weak

YES → Call Doctor Now

NO

- You have a burning, aching pain in the lower chest or upper abdomen (often relieved by food or antacids)
- You have recurrent nausea and vomiting
- You feel excessively full after meals
- Chronic anxiety or stress seems to cause ulcer symptoms

YES → Call Doctor

NO

See *What You Can Do,* p. 212. → Apply Self-Care

Hiatal Hernia

Hiatal (abdominal) hernia occurs when part of the stomach protrudes above an opening in the *diaphragm*—the muscle wall that separates the chest cavity from the abdominal cavity. The opening is called a *hiatus*. This protrusion allows stomach contents to flow backward (*reflux*) into the *esophagus* (the tube that connects the throat and stomach).

Most people with a hiatal hernia don't have symptoms; others experience a burning pain (heartburn) caused by reflux. Symptoms tend to be more noticeable when a sufferer reclines. Obesity, a low-fiber diet and wearing tight clothes may make reflux worse.

WHAT YOU CAN DO ✓

To prevent reflux, eat small meals and avoid acidic foods and alcohol. Elevate your head while sleeping by using extra pillows or putting 4- to 6-inch (10 to 15 cm) blocks under the upper bed legs. Avoid tight-fitting clothing, reclining after eating, and eating or drinking three hours or less before bedtime.

Most cases of abdominal hernia don't require treatment other than antacids or other medications to relieve heartburn. **Strangulation of the hernia, when part of the stomach gets pinched off, is a dangerous situation that needs immediate surgical repair.**

Decision *helper* — Hiatal Hernia

DO THESE APPLY:

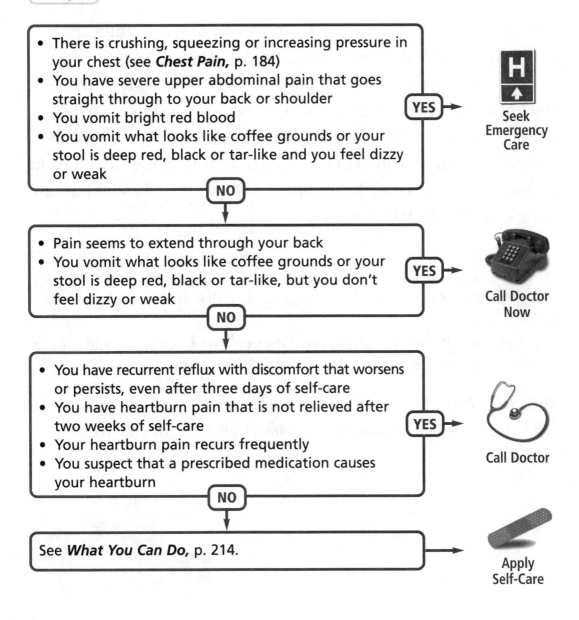

- There is crushing, squeezing or increasing pressure in your chest (see *Chest Pain,* p. 184)
- You have severe upper abdominal pain that goes straight through to your back or shoulder
- You vomit bright red blood
- You vomit what looks like coffee grounds or your stool is deep red, black or tar-like and you feel dizzy or weak

YES → **H ↑** Seek Emergency Care

NO

- Pain seems to extend through your back
- You vomit what looks like coffee grounds or your stool is deep red, black or tar-like, but you don't feel dizzy or weak

YES → Call Doctor Now

NO

- You have recurrent reflux with discomfort that worsens or persists, even after three days of self-care
- You have heartburn pain that is not relieved after two weeks of self-care
- Your heartburn pain recurs frequently
- You suspect that a prescribed medication causes your heartburn

YES → Call Doctor

NO

See **What You Can Do,** p. 214.

→ Apply Self-Care

Inguinal Hernia

An *inguinal hernia* occurs when a section of the small intestine protrudes through the abdominal muscles, causing a lump in the groin. In men, the hernia often protrudes into the *scrotum,* the sac that holds the testes. An inguinal hernia usually results from weak abdominal muscles and increased pressure in the abdomen. This combination forces a loop of intestine out through the weak area in the muscle wall. Obesity, heavy lifting and prolonged coughing can cause a hernia or make it worse.

Symptoms can include swelling in the groin that goes away when you lie down or when gentle pressure is applied, and groin pain that occurs when you bend or lift.

Strangulation of the hernia, when part of the intestine gets trapped and cannot be reduced, is an emergency and needs immediate surgical repair.

WHAT YOU CAN DO ✓

Surgery is the only cure for this type of hernia. Until the hernia is repaired, avoid heavy lifting.

Decision *helper* Inguinal Hernia
DO THESE APPLY:

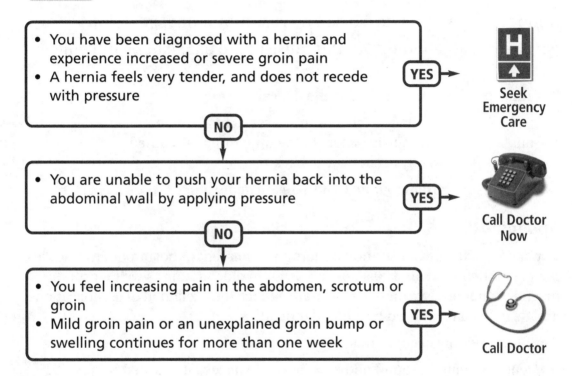

- You have been diagnosed with a hernia and experience increased or severe groin pain
- A hernia feels very tender, and does not recede with pressure

YES → **Seek Emergency Care**

NO

- You are unable to push your hernia back into the abdominal wall by applying pressure

YES → **Call Doctor Now**

NO

- You feel increasing pain in the abdomen, scrotum or groin
- Mild groin pain or an unexplained groin bump or swelling continues for more than one week

YES → **Call Doctor**

Abdominal Pain

Abdominal pain can be caused by very minor or very serious conditions, and finding out the cause of the pain can be difficult.

Locating the pain can help determine the cause:

- Appendix—pain usually occurs in the lower right abdomen
- Gallbladder—pain usually occurs in the upper right abdomen
- Kidney—pain usually occurs in the back

However, it's important to note that there are many other causes as well.

Appendicitis

Appendicitis, the most common abdominal emergency, most frequently strikes people in their teens and 20s, but can occur in older adults as well. Accurate diagnosis and rapid treatment can greatly reduce the likelihood of complications and death, usually caused by a burst appendix.

Symptoms usually occur in this order:

- Vague discomfort around and just above the navel; later, a sharper pain or tenderness in the lower right quarter of the abdomen that is worse with movement
- Possible nausea, vomiting and loss of appetite
- Fever from 99° F (37.2° C) to 101° F (38.3° C)
- Constipation or, less commonly, diarrhea

Once appendicitis is confirmed, the appendix is usually removed. This surgery, called an *appendectomy*, is relatively low-risk.

WHAT YOU CAN DO ☑

If you suspect appendicitis, seek medical attention right away. Do not use laxatives or apply heat to the area. Both can make the appendix rupture more quickly.

See *Decision helper*, p. 222.

Gallbladder Disease

The gallbladder stores bile that is made in the liver, then passes the bile on to the intestines to help digest fats. If there is a large amount of fat and cholesterol in the system, some of the bile may turn into *gallstones.* As the bile flows from the gallbladder to the intestines through the bile ducts, these gallstones can block the ducts, causing severe pain, local inflammation or *jaundice* (yellow skin). If the stones stay in the gall-bladder, they cause no discomfort.

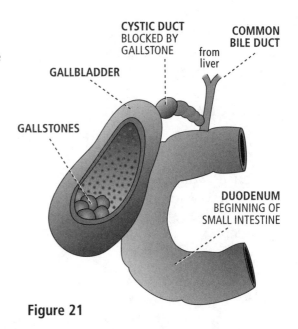

Figure 21

The pain usually occurs in the pit of the stomach or the upper right side of the abdomen and radiates to the upper right side of the back. It usually begins one to three hours after a large or fatty meal and persists for several hours. It may be accompanied by nausea and vomiting.

WHAT YOU CAN DO ✓

The greatest risk factors for gallbladder disease are eating a high-calorie, high-fat diet (which increases bile production), obesity and extreme dieting. Avoid fatty foods and overeating to help prevent a gallbladder attack. If you need to lose weight, aim for a moderate loss of one pound per week.

See *Decision helper,* p. 222.

Kidney Stones

Kidney stones are most common in adults between the ages of 30 and 40, but can occur in older adults as well. They vary in size from microscopic to several centimeters in diameter and are usually made of calcium. They recur in about half of all people who get them.

Certain *diuretics* (water pills) and calcium-based antacids may increase the risk of kidney stones, as they increase the amount of calcium in the urine. High calcium levels in the urine can lead to calcium crystal formation in the kidneys or urinary tract.

NOTE YOUR SYMPTOMS ✓

- Severe pain in the *flank* (the area between the last rib and the hip) and/or pubic region
- Nausea, vomiting (usually with severe pain) or abdominal bloating
- Pain traveling along the urinary tract and into the genitals, as the stone passes out of the body
- Chills, fever, and frequent or difficult urination
- Bloody urine

WHAT YOU CAN DO ✓

Kidney stones cannot be "cured" by self-care, but increasing fluids (especially water) to three to four quarts (2.8 to 3.7 liters) per day and making some dietary modifications (ask your doctor for recommendations) can reduce recurrences in many people. In some cases, prescription medication helps ease symptoms.

FINAL NOTES ✓

Most kidney stones pass spontaneously, requiring only fluids and a pain reliever, with no further treatment. Medication may be prescribed to help dissolve existing stones and prevent new ones. For a small percentage of kidney stones, additional medical treatment may be required.

See *Decision helper,* p. 222.

Gas

Everyone produces intestinal *flatus* (gas), which is a normal by-product of the digestive process. Gas may be expelled during a bowel movement or passed throughout the day. In most cases, excess gas is not the result of disease and is not a serious condition. It can, however, be bothersome and embarrassing.

Excessive gas may be caused by certain foods, medications, a lack of certain digestive enzymes, *malabsorption* (a group of digestive impairments caused by a variety of factors) or, rarely, infection.

Some people are sensitive to gas in the bowel and experience abdominal pain or cramping as a result.

WHAT YOU CAN DO ✓

- Limit foods that may cause excess gas, such as beans and other legumes, wheat and wheat bran, oats, Brussels sprouts, sauerkraut, cabbage, corn, rutabagas, apricots, bananas and prunes. (To minimize gas in beans, soak dry beans overnight, then use fresh water to cook them.) If dairy products give you gas, try cultured milk products such as yogurt and buttermilk, or milk products with added *lactase,* which breaks down lactose so it can be more easily digested.
- Consume a high-fiber diet and, unless your fluid intake has been limited by your doctor, drink plenty of water to avoid constipation.
- Add an anti-gas product such as Beano to high-fiber foods.
- Cut back on fried foods, fatty meats, cream sauces and gravies, which can increase gas and bloating.
- Limit use of fructose and sorbitol, two sugar substitutes that can contribute to gas.
- Eat slowly and chew thoroughly. Large pieces of food are harder to digest.

See *Decision helper,* p. 222.

Decision *helper*   Abdominal Pain
DO THESE APPLY:

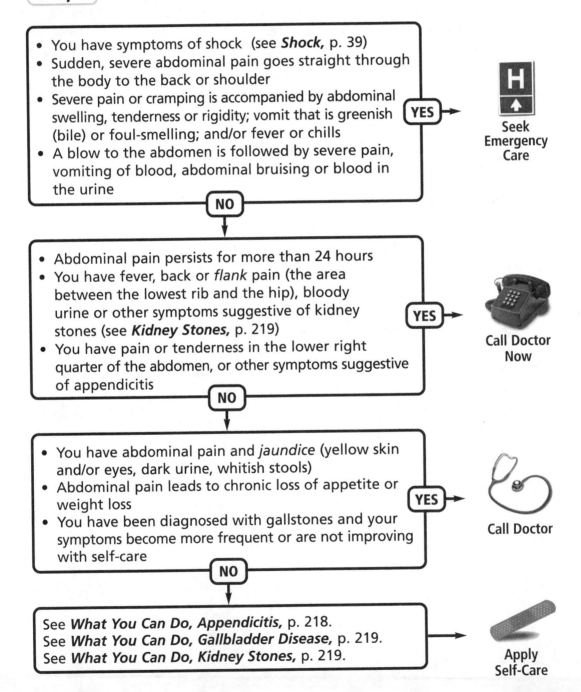

- You have symptoms of shock (see **Shock,** p. 39)
- Sudden, severe abdominal pain goes straight through the body to the back or shoulder
- Severe pain or cramping is accompanied by abdominal swelling, tenderness or rigidity; vomit that is greenish (bile) or foul-smelling; and/or fever or chills
- A blow to the abdomen is followed by severe pain, vomiting of blood, abdominal bruising or blood in the urine

YES → **Seek Emergency Care**

NO ↓

- Abdominal pain persists for more than 24 hours
- You have fever, back or *flank* pain (the area between the lowest rib and the hip), bloody urine or other symptoms suggestive of kidney stones (see **Kidney Stones,** p. 219)
- You have pain or tenderness in the lower right quarter of the abdomen, or other symptoms suggestive of appendicitis

YES → **Call Doctor Now**

NO ↓

- You have abdominal pain and *jaundice* (yellow skin and/or eyes, dark urine, whitish stools)
- Abdominal pain leads to chronic loss of appetite or weight loss
- You have been diagnosed with gallstones and your symptoms become more frequent or are not improving with self-care

YES → **Call Doctor**

NO ↓

See **What You Can Do, Appendicitis,** p. 218.
See **What You Can Do, Gallbladder Disease,** p. 219.
See **What You Can Do, Kidney Stones,** p. 219.

→ Apply Self-Care

Diverticulosis and Colon Cancer

Digestion is completed in the *colon,* or large intestine, where water is removed from the digested food and the remaining waste is formed into *feces* (stool). The final two sections of the colon are called the *sigmoid colon* and the *rectum* (see Figure 20, p. 193). During digestion the muscles in the intestinal wall tighten, causing pressure inside the colon to move the stool into the rectum toward the *anus* (rectal opening). The stool is expelled when the *anal sphincter,* a ring of muscle at the end of the rectum, relaxes during a bowel movement.

Diverticulosis

Small sac-like pouches called *diverticula* often develop in the wall of the colon. The condition of having these diverticula is called *diverticulosis,* and its cause is unknown. This condition is usually not serious, and often there are no symptoms. Constipation or heavy straining with a bowel movement can increase the pressure in your colon, causing the pouches to become stretched or filled with stool. This may result in mild cramping and pain, especially in the lower left side of your *abdomen,* or belly.

If the diverticula become infected or inflamed, the condition is called *diverticulitis.* This can become a very

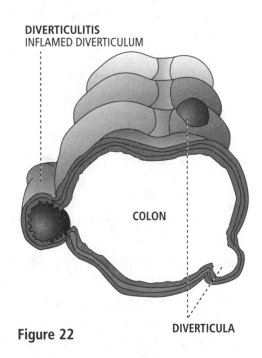

DIVERTICULITIS
INFLAMED DIVERTICULUM

COLON

DIVERTICULA

Figure 22

serious illness. Symptoms of diverticulitis may be only mild cramping at first. The cramping may slowly increase over a few days to become severe abdominal pains with fever and nausea. The colon can become completely blocked, and the infection may spread throughout the abdominal cavity.

NOTE YOUR SYMPTOMS ✓

- Symptoms may indicate diverticulitis; diverticulosis often has no symptoms
- Abdominal cramping; pain may be mild at first and slowly become severe
- Pain may be more severe on lower left side of abdomen
- Fever or chills
- Nausea or vomiting
- Intermittent pain or pain relieved by a bowel movement
- Tender, full, tight abdomen
- Constipation

WHAT YOU CAN DO ✓

- Treatment of diverticulosis is primarily directed at preventing constipation:
  - Eat a diet high in fiber. (See *Eating Right,* p. 338.)
  - Unless your fluid intake has been limited by your doctor, drink eight glasses of water daily.
  - Use fiber or bulk laxatives regularly to prevent chronic constipation. **CAUTION: Talk to your doctor or pharmacist before taking any other medications, including over-the-counter (OTC) medications, vitamins or herbal supplements.**
  - Avoid straining with bowel movements.
- **If you suspect diverticulitis: DO NOT eat solid foods. Call your doctor.**

Colon Cancer

Colorectal (colon-rectum) cancer, also called colon cancer, is a common form of cancer in older adults. The cause of colorectal cancer is not known, but there is a large incidence in countries where diets are high in animal fat and low in fiber. Your risk is increased if you have a family history of colorectal cancer, previous history of colon *polyps* (protruding growths or tumors) or current *ulcerative colitis* (an inflammatory bowel disease). Colorectal cancers are curable when detected and treated early. (See *Catching Problems Early,* p. 351.)

PREVENTION ✓

- Eat a high-fiber, low-fat diet.
- Exercise regularly and drink plenty of water (unless your fluid intake has been limited by your doctor) to keep the bowels functioning appropriately.
- Get regular screening tests for colorectal cancer (testing for blood in the stool) every year, with a sigmoidoscopy and/or a colonoscopy, as advised by your doctor (usually every five to 10 years).
- Report any change in bowel patterns or any rectal bleeding to your doctor.

Decision *helper* Diverticulosis and Colon Cancer
DO THESE APPLY:

- You have deep red, maroon, black, or tar-like stool along with dizziness or weakness

YES →

H ↑
Seek Emergency Care

NO ↓

- You have deep red, maroon, black, or tar-like stool without dizziness or weakness
- You have been diagnosed with diverticulosis and experience increasing abdominal pain, tenderness or guarding, vomiting, fever, or rectal bleeding

YES →

Call Doctor Now

NO ↓

- You are on antibiotics and symptoms have worsened after 48 hours, or failed to improve after 72 hours of treatment
- You have any of the following:
  - Mild abdominal tenderness
  - Cramping
  - Increasing discomfort

YES →

Call Doctor

Diabetes and Thyroid Concerns

The *endocrine* system produces and secretes hormones, which serve as a sort of chemical messenger system that coordinates many of the body's functions. Changes in this complex system are natural as we age. Glucose metabolism may slow, for example, causing unusual fatigue, weight loss or gain, or other symptoms. It's important to note changes such as these and to report anything that seems significant to your health care provider.

Diabetes

The sugars and starches you eat (carbohydrates) are converted by the body into *glucose,* a sugar used by the cells for energy. The hormone *insulin,* normally created by special cells in the pancreas, plays a key role in glucose metabolism. Without it, glucose cannot pass through cell membranes.

In people with diabetes, insulin is either not produced in sufficient amounts or something prevents it from working properly, a condition called *insulin resistance.* The result in both cases is too little glucose in the cells and too much in the blood. This can damage the heart, blood vessels, eyes, kidneys, nerves and other organs. The exact cause of diabetes is still unknown. Genetics and autoimmune diseases may play a part in type 1 diabetes. Weight gain, lack of exercise and a family history of diabetes are all contributing factors to type 2 diabetes.

Type 1 and Type 2 Diabetes

There are two types of diabetes, although they have similar symptoms and treatments. With *type 1 diabetes,* the immune system destroys the beta cells of the pancreas, which produce insulin. Without insulin, glucose cannot pass into cells for use and blood sugar rises rapidly. Looking for a new energy source, the cells draw on fat instead. When fat is broken down in this manner, serious medical problems arise. Type 1 diabetes is most common in children, but it can develop at any age.

The majority of diabetics have *type 2 diabetes*. The condition is most common among overweight adults, although the rate is rising in children and adolescents. Approximately 18 percent of people over age 65 and a quarter of those over age 85 have diabetes. Nearly a third of diabetics have a family history of the disease. In type 2 diabetes, insulin production is reduced, and that which is produced is not properly used or absorbed. Blood sugar levels rise gradually, often making symptoms difficult to detect at first. The consistently elevated levels of blood sugar are damaging, however, and can lead to a number of severe problems.

NOTE YOUR SYMPTOMS ☑

Both types of diabetes have similar symptoms. However, symptoms develop rapidly in type 1 diabetes and gradually in type 2 diabetes; it may take years to notice symptoms of type 2 diabetes.

Almost half of older adults with diabetes don't know they have it. Be alert to the following symptoms:

- Frequent urination
- Bladder and/or urinary tract infections
- Increased thirst, overeating
- Fatigue, low energy
- Nausea, vomiting
- High blood pressure
- Weight loss (most typical in children and young adults)
- Tingling in the hands and feet
- Blurred vision
- Lowered resistance to infection
- Cuts, sores or blisters on the feet that are slow to heal
- Impotence (occasionally)

WHAT YOU CAN DO ☑

Either type of diabetes can be managed, but it's crucial to follow your health care provider's treatment plan, which will include proper nutrition, an exercise plan and, often, medications. In general, the diabetic diet is based on the Food Guide Pyramid (see page 339), but because diabetic nutrition issues are complex, it is recommended that a registered dietitian be consulted for specific recommendations. While some individuals with type 2 diabetes can control their disease with diet and exercise alone, others require the addition of oral diabetic medications and/or insulin. Those with type 1 diabetes always require insulin. The treatment goal is to maintain normal levels of blood glucose in the body throughout the day.

With exercise, the right foods, and, when necessary, weight loss, the body has a remarkable tendency to normalize glucose levels.

If you need to lose weight, the goal is to limit calories with a nutritionally balanced food selection and to increase exercise. A reasonable guideline is to lose one pound a week, which typically means reducing calorie intake or increasing energy expenditure by 500 calories per day.

Exercise plays a key role in managing diabetes, normalizing blood sugar levels and assisting the body in combating insulin resistance. It also burns calories and reduces appetite (helping you normalize your weight) and improves strength, stamina and energy levels. More important, exercise significantly reduces a diabetic's risk of heart disease. However, people with advanced diabetes may have associated problems that make some forms of exercise more appropriate than others. Consult your doctor prior to modifying your diet and exercise routines.

Foot care is also important. Keep your feet clean and warm, and your toenails trimmed. Wear socks and well-fitting, supportive shoes to help prevent injuries. Check your feet daily and report any unhealing sores to your doctor.

See *Decision helper,* p. 233.

Diabetic Retinopathy

Vision loss is a serious complication of diabetes, as high levels of blood glucose may break the blood vessels in the eyes, making vision blur. Untreated diabetes can also lead to the growth of abnormal blood vessels in the eyes, further impairing vision. Consistent management of blood sugar and regular visits (at least yearly) to an *ophthalmologist* (eye specialist) can help minimize or prevent eye damage or blindness.

Hypoglycemia

Monitoring and controlling blood glucose is crucial to the successful management of diabetes. When glucose drops too low, *hypoglycemia* occurs. Symptoms include hunger, weakness, dizziness, headache, shakiness and confusion. Hypoglycemia can be triggered by taking too much insulin, exercising too strenuously or getting off schedule on a meal plan.

WHAT YOU CAN DO ☑

If you have symptoms of hypoglycemia, take a quick-acting sugar right away. Hard candy, orange juice or sugar cubes are good sources. **If symptoms don't go away, seek immediate care.**

See *Decision helper,* p. 233.

Thyroid Problems

The *thyroid* is a small, butterfly-shaped gland located in the neck. You could call it a "chemical commander" that sends activity messages to the brain, heart, liver, kidney and bones. The thyroid also controls how the body burns fuel to produce energy. Increased amounts of thyroid hormones can speed the body's chemical reactions. Lowered amounts can slow body processes. Either way, mental and physical ability can be affected.

Thyroid problems are common among older adults, yet these problems sometimes go undetected. Symptoms such as hair loss, dry skin, fatigue and weakness can develop slowly and some people dismiss them as part of the aging process. Thyroid problems are not a stage of life. They can and should be treated.

Hypothyroidism

With *hypothyroidism*, the thyroid gland produces too little thyroid hormone. Hypothyroidism occurs more often in women than men, most frequently in people between the ages of 35 and 60. In the United States, the most common cause of hypothyroidism is *Hashimoto's disease*, a condition in which the immune system produces antibodies that attack the thyroid gland. Worldwide, the most common cause is the lack of iodine in the diet. Medical or surgical therapy for hyperthyroidism may also cause hypothyroidism.

NOTE YOUR SYMPTOMS ☑

The symptoms of hypothyroidism can develop slowly over months, which is why some of the following symptoms may go unnoticed:

- Fatigue and lack of energy
- Difficulty in performing mental tasks
- Slowed heart rate
- Constipation

- Weight gain in spite of less food
- Dry, lifeless hair
- Increased susceptibility to cold temperatures
- Numbness or tingling in the hands
- Poor memory, reduction in mental prowess
- Muscle cramps
- Poor hearing, hoarse voice, speech problems
- Heavy and/or prolonged menstrual periods
- Impotence

WHAT YOU CAN DO ☑

Everybody feels "slowed down" at times. However, if you experience one or more of the above symptoms consistently, check with your doctor. Hypothyroidism can be treated with medication. Long-term follow-up care is important, and annual checkups are a must. If you change doctors, be sure to notify your new doctor of this condition.

See *Decision helper,* p. 233.

Hyperthyroidism

Hyperthyroidism, or too much thyroid hormone, is most commonly caused by an autoimmune condition called *Graves' disease.* No one knows what triggers this condition, which is more common in women than in men. Thyroid problems are common later in life. The danger is ignoring the symptoms because you think they are a common consequence of growing older.

NOTE YOUR SYMPTOMS ☑

Too much thyroid hormone, or a hyperthyroid gland, can result in one or more of the following symptoms:

- Feelings of anxiety, inability to sit still
- Difficulty in relaxing or getting to sleep
- Shaky hands
- Reduced sensitivity to cold temperatures

- Increased sweating
- Irregular, faster heartbeats
- Shortness of breath after mild exertion
- Diarrhea
- Itchy eyes
- Unexpected weight loss
- Extreme weakness
- Swelling of the thyroid gland (*goiter*)
- In premenopausal women, few or no menstrual periods

Less common symptoms include a gritty feeling in the eyes or eyes that appear to bulge, as well as blurred vision.

WHAT YOU CAN DO ☑

It is possible to recover completely from hyperthyroidism with treatment. The most common treatment for this disorder is radioactive iodine. It is consumed in the form of a clear, salty drink and acts upon the thyroid gland to slow it down. Surgery may also be required to remove part or all of the overactive thyroid. Whichever treatment is recommended, the chances of reversing the problem are excellent.

See *Decision helper,* p. 233.

FINAL NOTES ☑

Both hypo- and hyperthyroidism are treatable. Diagnosis in the early stages is important. Warning signs of these problems can be missed, ignored or misdiagnosed. Staying tuned in to your own body and its signals will help you and your doctor develop the best care regimen.

Decision *helper* Diabetes/Thyroid Concerns
DO THESE APPLY:

- A person with diabetes loses consciousness
- A person with diabetes develops symptoms of *hyperglycemia* (high blood sugar):
  - Sudden and severe increase in thirst or urination
  - Sweet or fruity-smelling breath
  - Weakness or drowsiness
  - Nausea, vomiting or diarrhea
- A person with diabetes shows signs of *hypoglycemia* (low blood sugar), even after eating something containing sugar. Symptoms of hypoglycemia:
  - Weakness, drowsiness or hunger
  - Trembling or nervousness
  - Dizziness
  - Cold sweat or pallor
  - Blurred vision
  - A tingling sensation in the hands or feet

YES →

Seek
Emergency
Care

NO

- A person with diabetes has symptoms of an illness that are affecting blood sugar levels

YES →

Call Doctor
Now

NO

- You think you have symptoms suggestive of diabetes
- You have diabetes and your glucose levels are consistently elevated
- You have diabetes and are having difficulty complying with your treatment plan or you need additional information about medication or diet
- You think you have symptoms of hypo- or hyperthyroidism

YES →

Call Doctor

Muscles/Bones/Joints

It is normal to experience some loss of strength, endurance and flexibility as you age. Muscle mass decreases, bones weaken and joints stiffen. However, it's possible to significantly *slow* these effects of aging—and the development of chronic conditions such as arthritis and osteoporosis (see *Osteoporosis,* p. 238)— by maintaining a healthy diet (see *Eating Right,* p. 338) and a physically active lifestyle that keeps your body strong and vital. (See *Staying Active,* p. 343.)

Getting regular exercise such as walking, swimming, golfing, aerobic dancing or riding a bicycle can help you minimize pain and maximize movement. For details on preventing and self-managing chronic illness, see *Managing Illness,* p. 361.

Arthritis

Arthritis (joint inflammation) refers to several diseases that cause joint pain, swelling and stiffness. There are more than 100 different types of arthritis, but the majority of them fall into one of four categories. (See *Major Types of Arthritis,* p. 235.)

Osteoarthritis (also called degenerative joint disease) is common among older adults. The *cartilage* (a material that cushions bones at the joints) begins to wear out and bone rubs against bone. Pain is the first symptom and is often worsened by exercise. Osteoarthritis starts slowly and usually begins on one side of the body. Morning stiffness may follow periods of inactivity, and joint discomfort often occurs before a change in the weather. As the disease progresses, the joints become swollen and inflexible, and a grating sensation may accompany movement. Over time the inflammation may deform joints; this is especially noticeable in the hands, where knuckles become enlarged.

Rheumatoid arthritis is an immune disorder in which the body attacks the lining of the joints, causing painful inflammation. It can affect as many as 15 or 20 joints at a time, as well as the lungs, spleen, skin and brain. Tenderness in all active joints is one of the earliest recognizable signs. Unlike osteoarthritis, rheumatoid arthritis frequently affects both sides of the body, such as both feet or both hands. The affected joints are painful and warm to the touch. Small lumps called *nodules*—ranging in size from a pea to a walnut—may occur under the skin near the elbows, nose, scalp or knees, or under the toes, although they are not usually painful. Other symptoms may include fatigue and weight loss.

Most arthritic conditions cannot be cured, but their detrimental effects can be limited with consistent self-care and medical support.

Major Types of Arthritis

Cause	Symptoms	Commonly Affects
Osteoarthritis		
Cartilage in joints wears out (*degenerates*)	Pain, stiffness, swelling in joints, especially fingers; may improve with rest; bony growth spurs can occur	Men and women, worsens with age
Rheumatoid Arthritis		
Membrane lining of joint is inflamed; your immune system attacks your own tissues; causes unclear	Pain, stiffness, swelling in joints, with low-grade fever; doesn't subside with rest	Middle-aged women
Gout		
Build-up of uric acid crystals in joint fluid	Pain, stiffness, swelling, especially in big toe, ankle or knee	Men more often; aggravated by foods high in purines (such as organ meats) or alcoholic beverages
Ankylosing Spondylitis		
Inflammation in spine, other joints; thought to be genetically linked	Pain, stiffness in back, neck and other torso joints such as hips	Men and women before age 35

PREVENTION ✓

While you can't prevent arthritis, it is possible to delay its onset and slow the degenerative process.

- Avoid trauma, overuse and repetitive or jarring activities. Vary your exercise and activity schedule to allow changes in the pressure and stress on joints.
- Exercise regularly. Aerobic exercise increases blood flow to nourish joint tissues. Exercising with weights strengthens muscles that support and protect joints. Stretching and range-of-motion exercises help maintain joint flexibility. (See *Staying Active,* p. 343.)
- Control your weight. Excess pounds place stress on weight-bearing joints such as knees. (See *Eating Right,* p. 338.)

WHAT YOU CAN DO ✓

After arthritis has developed in a joint, self-care can help you maintain joint function and decrease pain, swelling and inflammation.

- Take aspirin or ibuprofen (Advil, Motrin) to relieve pain and inflammation. (Follow directions and warnings on package.) **NEVER give aspirin to children/ teenagers unless your health care provider orders it. It can cause Reye's syndrome, a rare but often fatal condition. CAUTION: Talk to your doctor or pharmacist before taking any other medications, including over-the-counter (OTC) medications, vitamins or herbal supplements.**
- Rest sore joints. If you must continue to put weight or stress on the joint, take breaks and rest.
- For inflamed, swollen joints, apply ice for 15 to 20 minutes at a time, more frequently initially, then three to four times a day for up to 48 hours. Leave ice off for at least 15 minutes between applications. For protection, place a washcloth between bare skin and ice and change the cloth if it becomes wet.
- If the joint is not swollen, apply warm, moist heat for 20 minutes, three or four times a day. Follow heat with gentle full-range-of-motion exercises and gentle massage.
- When joint pain and inflammation subside, continue the prevention measures listed above.
- Become informed about your type of arthritis. Ask your doctor for self-care treatments, and about resources in your community such as support groups, physical therapy, occupational therapy and stores that carry medical supplies.

For information about Lyme disease as a cause of arthritis, see *Tick Bites,* p. 126.

Arthritis is a slowly progressive disease that can be managed well with a combination of self-care and medical treatment. However, seek prompt medical treatment if you have an infection near a joint, a broken bone near an arthritic joint, or nerve damage.

Decision *helper* Arthritis
DO THESE APPLY:

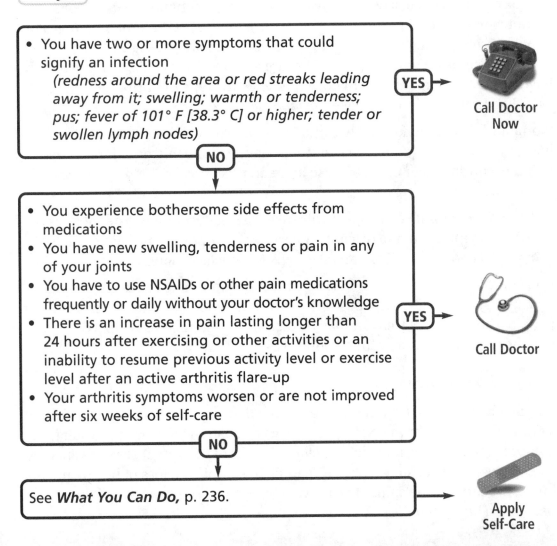

• You have two or more symptoms that could signify an infection
(redness around the area or red streaks leading away from it; swelling; warmth or tenderness; pus; fever of 101° F [38.3° C] or higher; tender or swollen lymph nodes)

YES → Call Doctor Now

NO

• You experience bothersome side effects from medications
• You have new swelling, tenderness or pain in any of your joints
• You have to use NSAIDs or other pain medications frequently or daily without your doctor's knowledge
• There is an increase in pain lasting longer than 24 hours after exercising or other activities or an inability to resume previous activity level or exercise level after an active arthritis flare-up
• Your arthritis symptoms worsen or are not improved after six weeks of self-care

YES → Call Doctor

NO

See *What You Can Do,* p. 236.

→ Apply Self-Care

Osteoporosis

Osteoporosis is a gradual, progressive loss of bone mass that over time causes bones to become weaker and more susceptible to *fractures* (breaks). With proper early treatment the continuous "thinning" of the bones can usually be stopped.

This disease occurs most commonly in women after menopause and affects one in four women over the age of 60. This is because the production of *estrogen* (a female hormone that contributes to bone thickness and strength) declines and eventually stops after menopause. Men are at lower risk because they generally have greater bone mass and do not experience the type of hormonal changes associated with menopause. (See *Menopause,* p. 281.)

Women who are the most likely candidates for osteoporosis are Asian or white, have a slender body frame, are inactive or have a family history of the disease. Women who smoke or drink are also at greater risk—as are long-term users of corticosteroids.

Talk to your doctor if you suspect you are at risk of developing osteoporosis or have any symptoms of the disease. The earlier osteoporosis is diagnosed, the sooner you and your doctor can take steps to slow its progress.

Bone density can be measured using x-ray procedures such as bone mineral density tests and CT scans. These are not recommended as routine screening for people without symptoms but may be recommended to assist with a decision whether to start treatment for osteoporosis.

NOTE YOUR SYMPTOMS ✓

A bone breaking with little cause is often the first sign of osteoporosis. Other symptoms include chronic pain, especially back pain. The pain may result from compression fractures in which *vertebrae* (bones of the spine) are weakened by osteoporosis and partially collapse, leading to stooping, a loss of height and an increased curve in the spine. The curve may become so pronounced that it becomes a hump (*gibbus*).

WHAT YOU CAN DO ✓

Taking steps to slow bone loss prior to menopause is the most effective way of preventing or reducing the effects of osteoporosis—especially if you are at high risk. However, you can realize benefits whenever you begin.

- Get plenty of weight-bearing exercise—walking, running, jumping, aerobic dancing, climbing stairs, lifting weights, yoga—to keep your bones strong. (Swimming is an excellent aerobic exercise, but it's not particularly helpful in strengthening weight-bearing bones.)
- Make sure your diet includes plenty of calcium to help reduce bone loss. Women who are premenopausal or who are on estrogen need 1,000 mg daily, while postmenopausal women who are not on estrogen, and all women over age 65, need 1,500 mg. Low-fat dairy products or calcium supplements are good sources. The antacid Tums is an inexpensive and easy way to get calcium.*
- Vitamin D helps your bones absorb calcium. Get out in the sun regularly; it's a good source of vitamin D. Vitamin D fortified milk and cereals are other good sources. Postmenopausal women need 400-600 IU per day of vitamin D.*
- If you smoke, start taking steps to kick the habit.
- Keep alcohol consumption to a minimum.
- If you are menopausal, discuss whether hormone replacement therapy (HRT) or other medications may help.
- Take special care to avoid sudden movements or falls that can cause fractures. (See *Safety*, p. 355; *Hip Pain*, p. 260.)

* **CAUTION: Talk to your doctor or pharmacist before taking any other medications, including over-the-counter (OTC) medications, vitamins or herbal supplements.**

FINAL NOTE ✓

A number of medications such as the drug alendronate (Fosamax), risedronate (Actonel) and calcitonin (Miacalcin) are approved for treatment of osteoporosis in postmenopausal women. Hormone replacement therapy may be appropriate for some women, as is testosterone for some men. Ask your doctor if drug therapy is a treatment option for you.

Neck Pain

Most neck pain is caused by straining the muscles or tendons in the neck and generally can be treated at home. But there are many reasons for neck pain.

Neck pain caused by an accident or injury, such as whiplash from a car accident, can indicate a serious or even life-threatening injury to the spinal cord. (See *Head/Spinal Injury,* p. 55.) Chronic neck pain can be the indirect result of the aging process, resulting in *degenerative* (wear and tear) disk disease. Other possible causes of neck pain are arthritis (see *Arthritis,* p. 234), meningitis or a pinched nerve.

Meningitis

Meningitis is an infectious disease that can be life-threatening. The classic symptoms are fever, headache and an extremely stiff neck—so stiff that you can't touch your chin to your chest. It can also cause intense muscle spasms in the neck. (See *Decision helper,* p. 242.)

Pinched Nerve

A pinched nerve can be caused by arthritis or a neck injury. The pain may extend down the arm or cause numbness or tingling in the arm or hand. **If you suspect a pinched nerve, call your doctor.**

WHAT YOU CAN DO ☑

Environmental factors—your surroundings—can contribute to or cause neck pain. An uncomfortable mattress, a pillow that's too high, or an ill-fitting desk chair or work area all take their toll on the neck muscles.

If your neck hurts more in the morning:

- Try a firmer mattress on your bed, or use a bed board under your mattress to firm up a softer mattress.
- Use a pillow designed to protect your neck, or no pillow at all.

- Fold a bath towel lengthwise into a four-inch (10 cm) strip and wrap it around your neck; secure it with a safety pin while you sleep.

If your neck hurts more at night:

- Consider whether poor posture may be contributing to your pain. Walk, stand and sit with your ears, shoulders and hips in a straight line.
- Make any necessary adjustments to your office chair or work area.
- Keep your elbows at a 90-degree angle for typing.
- Consider trying some of the following neck exercises every two hours:
    - Sit or stand with an extremely erect posture to stretch the muscles in the back of your neck. Do it gently, repeating six times.
    - Squeeze your shoulder blades together gently six times.
    - Starting from an extremely erect posture, gently drop your head backward. Repeat six times.
    - Gently drop your head backward, forward and side to side with gentle pressure from your hands. Repeat six times.

If your neck hurts anytime:

- Try aspirin or ibuprofen (Advil, Motrin) to help relieve pain and inflammation. **NEVER give aspirin to children/teenagers unless your health care provider orders it. It can cause Reye's syndrome, a rare but often fatal condition. CAUTION: Talk to your doctor or pharmacist before taking any other medications, including over-the-counter (OTC) medications, vitamins or herbal supplements.**
- Apply ice for 15 to 20 minutes at a time, more frequently initially, then three to four times a day for up to 48 hours. Leave ice off for at least 15 minutes between applications. For protection, place a washcloth between bare skin and ice and change the cloth if it becomes wet.
- Use heat from a heating pad (on the low setting) or try taking a shower (if muscle swelling is not a problem). Limit the use of heat to 20-minute sessions.

See *Decision helper,* p. 242.
See *Headaches,* p. 81.

 Neck Pain
DO THESE APPLY:

- Neck pain is associated with fever, headache and a stiff neck (see **Meningitis,** p. 240)
- Neck pain and/or arm pain occurs with any of the following:
  - Chest pressure
  - Shortness of breath
  - Dizziness
  - Sweating
  - Nausea or vomiting
  - Rapid or irregular pulse
- Any of the following occur after an injury:
  - Weakness or paralysis of the arms or legs
  - Irregular or slowed pulse or respirations
  - Loss of bowel or bladder control
  - Unrelenting neck pain
  - New numbness or tingling
- Neck pain follows an accident that occurs while under the influence of alcohol or drugs
- You have difficulty moving your jaw or swallowing or your neck swells progressively

YES →

Seek
Emergency
Care

NO

- Neck pain travels down one arm, or an arm is numb and tingles
- There is no improvement with self-care after 24 hours

YES →

Call Doctor

NO

See **What You Can Do,** pp. 240 - 241.

Apply
Self-Care

Back Pain

Four out of five adults have back pain severe enough to interrupt their daily routines at least once in their lives. A common and frustrating problem to treat, there is no quick, easy cure; recovery is slow; the pain often recurs; and prevention and treatment require life-long commitment.

Self-care is the major factor in preventing and treating back pain. Understanding the anatomy of the back and the most common injuries may help you decrease your risk of back pain.

Your backbone is a gently curving stack of round, donut-shaped bones called *vertebrae* that form a protective tunnel for your *spinal cord.* (See Figures 23 and 24.) The spaces between the vertebrae are filled by *disks,* packets of tough cartilage with a jelly-like filling, that cushion and absorb impact. Your spinal

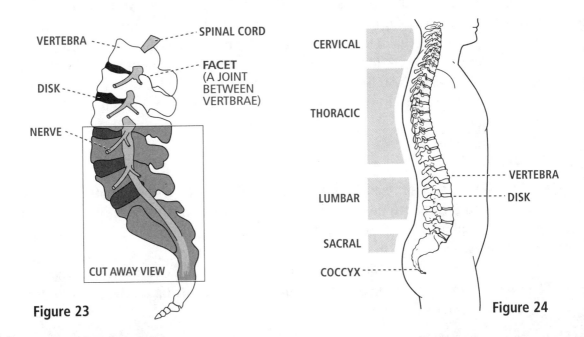

Figure 23

VERTEBRA

SPINAL CORD

FACET
(A JOINT
BETWEEN
VERTBRAE)

DISK

NERVE

CUT AWAY VIEW

CERVICAL

THORACIC

LUMBAR

SACRAL

COCCYX

VERTEBRA

DISK

Figure 24

cord, a bundle of major nerves, leaves your brain through the *vertebral tunnel* and sends branches around the disks out to the rest of your body. Large muscles and ligaments support the spine as it twists, bends, stretches, turns and sustains an upright posture.

Causes

There are many causes of back pain: muscles can be strained, torn or go into spasm; ligaments and tendons may be overstretched and sprained; disks become worn down (*degenerative disk disease*), move out of alignment (*slipped disk*) or rupture (*herniated disk*); and bones wear down or change, as in arthritis or a fracture. (See *Osteoporosis*, p. 238.) Occasionally, infection and tumors can cause back pain. In addition, back pain may not originate from the back itself but may be *referred pain* from problems in the prostate in men or reproductive organs in women, or from kidney infections or disorders in the stomach and intestines. (See *Kidney Stones*, p. 219.)

Pain from strains, sprains and minor disk damage is usually sudden, sharp and eases over two to three days with self-care. The sharp pain from a herniated disk or fractured vertebra usually lasts several weeks and requires medical care. A steady ache is often a sign of disease, such as arthritis or referred pain.

Any back problem that causes swelling or a shifting in the alignment of the spine can put pressure on a nerve. Numbness, weakness or tingling are signs of nerve irritation. Nerves in the neck produce symptoms in the arms and upper body, while spinal nerves in the middle and lower back affect the back, buttocks, legs and feet. Pressure on the *sciatic nerve* causes sharp, shooting pains down the back of the leg into the foot. Back pain can be constant or occur during movement.

PREVENTION ☑

- Maintain good posture and keep the right amount of curve in your lower back:
  - Stand tall with your ear, shoulder, hip and ankle in a line. Do not lock your knees. Balance weight evenly on your feet.
  - Avoid wearing high heels.
  - Sit tall with your shoulders back and your lower back supported. Keep knees even with or higher than your hips. Avoid sitting in one position for longer than one hour.

- Use correct posture when lifting:
  - Bend your knees and lift with your leg muscles. Keep your back straight.
  - Never bend forward to lift. Keep the load close to your body.
  - Avoid turning or twisting while holding a heavy object.
  - Avoid lifting heavy loads above your waist.
- Sleep on a firm surface. Provide support for your lower back and under your knees if it feels more comfortable.
- Rise up from a prone position correctly. Rising is actually lifting your body's weight; roll to your side and use your arms and legs to lift up.
- Maintain correct body weight. Obesity or a large abdomen can pull your lower back out of alignment.
- Exercise to maintain good muscle tone in your back and abdomen. Walking, swimming and biking are all good activities.
- Learn stress management and muscle-relaxation techniques such as stretching. (See *Stress,* p. 313.)

Choosing an Exercise Program for Your Back

By maintaining good muscle tone in your back and abdomen, you significantly reduce your chances of suffering a new back injury, or aggravating an old one. A daily routine focused on strengthening and stretching will go far in helping you stay active and pain-free.

Performing back-saving exercises (described on the following pages) for about 30 minutes a day will produce the greatest benefits. Sporadic, intense bouts of exercise may do more harm than good. Set aside 15 minutes in the morning and 15 minutes at night for best results.

If you find that an exercise causes more back pain or aggravates an injury, stop and reevaluate your back pain and exercise techniques with your doctor or physical therapist. Of course, you should always check with your doctor before starting any exercise program, especially if you are recovering from a back problem. Most therapeutic exercise programs are graduated, and your doctor will likely want to alter the exercises as you progress.

See *Decision helper,* p. 251.

Exercises for Your Back

A. Knee-to-chest raise, to help loosen a tense back or hips: Lie on your back on the floor and bring your right knee to your chest. Clasp your hands over your shin, hold the position and count to five. Repeat with the left leg, then both legs.

B. Pelvic tilt, to reduce a swayed back by strengthening the abdominal and back muscles: Lie on your back on the floor. Press your lower back to the floor and simultaneously tighten your abdominal muscles and buttocks. This movement should be very small. Hold the position and count to five, then release. Repeat five times.

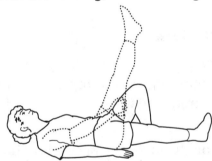

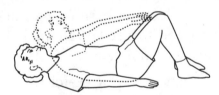

C. Hamstring stretch, to help stretch and loosen the muscles on the back of the thigh: Lie on your back on the floor. Slowly raise your right leg in a straight position, supporting it with your hands until you feel a stretch. Stop before you feel any pain or discomfort. Hold the position and count to five. Slowly lower the leg to the floor and repeat the exercise five times. Repeat with the left leg. **Caution: Be sure to use your hands to guide your outstretched leg toward you.**

D. Half sit-ups, to help strengthen abdominal muscles: Lie on your back, knees bent, feet flat on the floor. Reach forward toward your knees slowly raising your head and neck until your shoulders barely lift off the floor. Hold and count to five. Slowly lower yourself to the starting position and repeat five times. **Caution: Keep your head in line with your shoulders.**

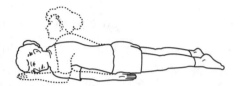

E. Lower back rotation, to limber and strengthen back muscles: Lie on your back with both feet on the floor. Rotate your head to one side while dropping your knees to the opposite side. Hold and count to five. Slowly return to the starting position. Then, alternating sides, repeat 10 times.

F. Elbow props, to strengthen low back muscles and help maintain the normal lumbar curve: Lie on your stomach, turn your head to one side and relax your arms at your sides. Stay in this relaxed position for three to five minutes. Then, prop yourself up on your elbows and hold for two to three minutes. Lie back down in the starting position for one minute. Repeat five times. **Caution: Keep your lower back completely relaxed.**

Advanced Exercises

If you have a back injury, check with your doctor or physical therapist before doing these exercises.

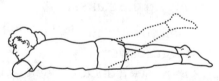

G. Hip hyperextension, to strengthen and limber hip, buttock and back muscles: Lie on your stomach with your arms folded under your chin in front of you. Straighten and tighten your left leg, then slowly raise it from your hip. Return the leg to the floor and repeat five times with the same leg. Switch legs and repeat on the right side. **Caution: Don't lift the pelvis to raise the leg. Keep each leg straight and stiff.**

H. Press-ups, to strengthen lower back muscles and help maintain the normal lumbar curve: Lie on your stomach with your hands placed on the floor, as pictured. Do a partial push-up while keeping your pelvis on the floor. Hold this raised position and count to five. Slowly lower yourself to the starting position. Repeat five times. **Caution: Relax your lower back and legs.**

Exercises to Avoid

Some common, but potentially harmful exercises are:

- Leg lifts (extending both legs and lifting them simultaneously while lying on your back)
- Heavy weightlifting with the upper body
- Sit-ups done with straight legs
- Knee-to-chest exercises and/or bent-knee sit-ups done during severe back pain
- Any stretching done sitting with your legs in a V position (frequently part of aerobic class routines)

NOTE YOUR SYMPTOMS ✓

If you have injured your back and are unsure whether to see your doctor or treat the pain at home, take a moment to answer the following questions:

- Did the back pain follow an impact (forceful contact or collision) injury or accident?
- Have you had pain for more than a few days?
- Is your pain worse after a few days of rest?
- Does your back pain interfere with sleep, work or any other daily activity?
- Do you have shooting pains, tingling, numbness or weakness in your legs?
- Do you have trouble raising your feet while going up the stairs?

If you answered "no" to each of these questions, then you are an ideal candidate for resolving your back problems on your own. If you answered "yes" to one or more questions, self-care may still help, but you should see a doctor to determine the most appropriate treatment plan for your injury. Even with a doctor's help, a self-care program is important to your recovery.

See *Decision helper,* p. 251.

WHAT YOU CAN DO ✓

- Avoid bed rest unless it is ordered by your doctor. Resume normal activity as soon as possible. Avoid any activity that puts stress on your back. Immediately stop any activity that causes or increases pain. Complete recovery may take up to six weeks.
- Apply ice for 15 to 20 minutes at a time, more frequently initially, then three to four times a day for up to 48 hours. Leave ice off for at least 15 minutes between applications. For protection, place a washcloth between bare skin and ice and change the cloth if it becomes wet.
- Once pain has lessened, take warm showers with water directed at the painful area.
- Take aspirin or ibuprofen (Advil, Motrin) to ease pain and inflammation. **NEVER give aspirin to children/teenagers unless your health care provider orders it. It can cause Reye's syndrome, a rare but often fatal condition. CAUTION: Talk to your doctor or pharmacist before taking any other medications, including over-the-counter (OTC) medications, vitamins or herbal supplements.**
- Sleep on a firm surface. If possible, place a piece of plywood between the mattress and box springs.
- Support your back while sleeping. Place a pillow under your knees or lie on your side, knees bent, with a pillow between them.
- If back pain starts with no known cause, look for signs of a problem in another area of your body that may be causing referred pain.
- For minor muscle soreness in your back, apply heat for 20 minutes at a time. Place a warm washcloth, warm water bottle or heating pad (always on low) directly on the affected area.

If you have back pain, try doing the exercises shown on the following page. If you can successfully complete all three, then you can probably cautiously resume your normal activities. Be sure to maintain good posture and avoid any exaggerated movements. As long as it does not increase your pain, repeat all three exercises two to three times throughout the day. If one exercise in particular aggravates your pain, skip it and focus on the other two.

First Aid for Back Pain

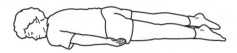

J. Lie flat on your stomach with your arms placed at your sides. Turn your head to one side and relax as much as possible.

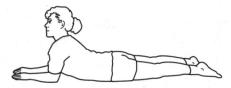

I. Stand with your hands on your hips and lean backward, gently stretching your back. If you are prone to dizziness, make sure you are supported when doing this exercise.

K. After one or two minutes flat on your stomach, prop yourself up on your elbows, arching your back. Hold for two to five minutes. Stop if you feel pain.

Decision *helper* Back Pain

DO THESE APPLY:

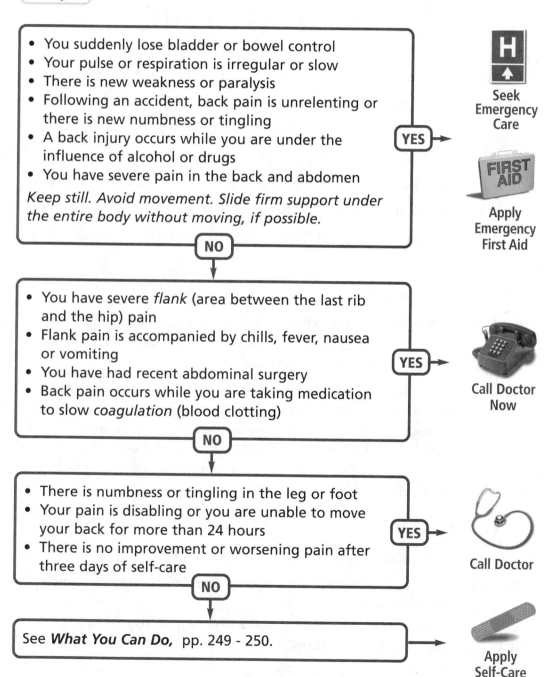

- You suddenly lose bladder or bowel control
- Your pulse or respiration is irregular or slow
- There is new weakness or paralysis
- Following an accident, back pain is unrelenting or there is new numbness or tingling
- A back injury occurs while you are under the influence of alcohol or drugs
- You have severe pain in the back and abdomen

Keep still. Avoid movement. Slide firm support under the entire body without moving, if possible.

YES →

Seek Emergency Care

Apply Emergency First Aid

NO

- You have severe *flank* (area between the last rib and the hip) pain
- Flank pain is accompanied by chills, fever, nausea or vomiting
- You have had recent abdominal surgery
- Back pain occurs while you are taking medication to slow *coagulation* (blood clotting)

YES →

Call Doctor Now

NO

- There is numbness or tingling in the leg or foot
- Your pain is disabling or you are unable to move your back for more than 24 hours
- There is no improvement or worsening pain after three days of self-care

YES →

Call Doctor

NO

See ***What You Can Do,*** pp. 249 - 250. →

Apply Self-Care

Shoulder/Elbow/ Wrist/Arm Pain

Arm pain usually involves the shoulder, elbow or wrist joints and is often caused by repetitive movements that stress the soft tissues near these joints: the muscles, tendons and *bursae* (little fluid filled sacs at the joints that help muscles slide over the muscles or bones). If the bursae are involved, the injury is called *bursitis*, while injury to a tendon is called *tendonitis*. Both cause similar symptoms of pain, limitation of movement, inflammation and sometimes swelling.

Bursitis and Tendonitis

In the shoulder, bursitis can start with a nagging ache that develops into severe pain, while tendonitis of the shoulder (rotator cuff tendonitis) is sometimes only felt when the arm is in certain positions.

Tennis elbow, which can be either bursitis or tendonitis, refers to any pain on the outside of the elbow and upper forearm. It is sometimes the result of play-ing tennis, but is more often caused by any repeated "twisting" motion of the forearm, wrist and hand. Similarly, *golfer's elbow* occurs in the inner part of the elbow and with bending the fingers or wrists, and may be related to playing golf or similar movements.

WHAT YOU CAN DO ☑

If you experience bursitis or tendonitis, you may get relief from:

- Resting the part of the arm that hurts, and avoiding the motion or activity that causes the condition
- Putting ice or cold packs on the area. At the first sign of trouble, apply ice for 15 to 20 minutes at a time, more frequently initially, then three to four

times a day for up to 48 hours. Leave ice off for at least 15 minutes between applications. For protection, place a washcloth between bare skin and ice and change the cloth if it becomes wet.

- Taking ibuprofen (Advil, Motrin) or aspirin. **NEVER give aspirin to children/teenagers unless your health care provider orders it. It can cause Reye's syndrome, a rare but often fatal condition. CAUTION: Talk to your doctor or pharmacist before taking any other medications, including over-the-counter (OTC) medications, vitamins or herbal supplements.**
- Maintaining strength and motion by gently moving the affected part through its full range of motion. The goal is not to let your arm get stiff.

See *Decision helper,* p. 255.

Carpal Tunnel Syndrome

Carpal tunnel syndrome results from compression of the *median nerve* (the major nerve) of the wrist. It is usually caused by continuous activities that involve repetitive use of the wrists and hands, such as computer keyboard use or exposure to vibration (using a hand-held sander, for example). The condition also can be the result of a wrist injury.

Hobbies that often cause symptoms include knitting, gardening, weightlifting, painting and playing certain musical instruments. Medical conditions that result in swelling of the wrist—diabetes, certain thyroid conditions, arthritis and excessive alcohol consumption—also may cause carpal tunnel syndrome.

Neglecting this condition can lead to permanent nerve damage and subsequent loss of hand function.

NOTE YOUR SYMPTOMS ✓

The pain associated with carpal tunnel syndrome is often described as burning, and can be accompanied by tingling, numbness or weakness of the hand, as well as shooting pain (particularly in the thumb and first two fingers). The pain is frequently worse at night and in the early morning. Unless an injury has occurred, the pain usually increases gradually.

WHAT YOU CAN DO ✓

If you suspect you have carpal tunnel syndrome, the first step is to identify the activity causing the symptoms.

If you discover that the cause is related to certain tasks:

- Try modifying your project or workspace. Adjust your worktable, desk, chair or keyboard height, or use a wrist pad.
- Avoid repetitive hand motions with your wrist bent (the way you hold scissors, for example).
- Take periodic breaks and stretch your hands and fingers.

For Relief:

- Apply ice for 15 to 20 minutes at a time, more frequently initially, then three to four times a day for up to 48 hours. Leave ice off for at least 15 minutes between applications. For protection, place a washcloth between bare skin and ice and change the cloth if it becomes wet.
- Rest and elevate the hand and forearm above the level of the heart.
- Splint the wrist in a neutral position to immobilize it. The splint can be worn 24 hours a day if necessary, or in bed.
- Hang your arm over the bed if problems occur while you sleep.
- Limit your salt intake.
- Try using over-the-counter (OTC) anti-inflammatory medication, such as ibuprofen (Advil, Motrin) or aspirin. **NEVER give aspirin to children/teenagers unless your health care provider orders it. It can cause Reye's syndrome, a rare but often fatal condition. CAUTION: Talk to your doctor or pharmacist before taking any other medications, including over-the-counter (OTC) medications, vitamins or herbal supplements.**

Decision *helper*   Shoulder/Elbow/Wrist/Arm Pain
DO THESE APPLY:

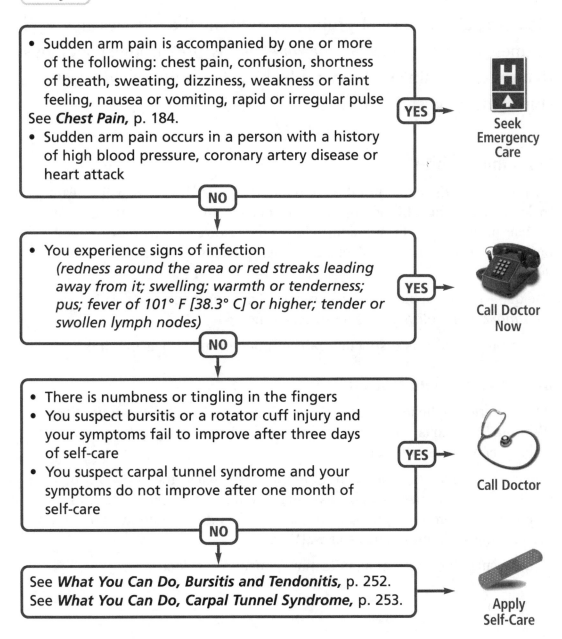

- Sudden arm pain is accompanied by one or more of the following: chest pain, confusion, shortness of breath, sweating, dizziness, weakness or faint feeling, nausea or vomiting, rapid or irregular pulse See *Chest Pain*, p. 184.
- Sudden arm pain occurs in a person with a history of high blood pressure, coronary artery disease or heart attack

YES → Seek Emergency Care

NO

- You experience signs of infection
  (redness around the area or red streaks leading away from it; swelling; warmth or tenderness; pus; fever of 101° F [38.3° C] or higher; tender or swollen lymph nodes)

YES → Call Doctor Now

NO

- There is numbness or tingling in the fingers
- You suspect bursitis or a rotator cuff injury and your symptoms fail to improve after three days of self-care
- You suspect carpal tunnel syndrome and your symptoms do not improve after one month of self-care

YES → Call Doctor

NO

See *What You Can Do, Bursitis and Tendonitis*, p. 252.
See *What You Can Do, Carpal Tunnel Syndrome*, p. 253.

→ Apply Self-Care

Leg Pain

Most leg pain is caused by injury or straining the muscles and ligaments of the leg. (See *Strains and Sprains,* p. 62.) Other conditions that cause leg pain are thrombophlebitis, intermittent claudication, shin splints and varicose veins.

Thrombophlebitis

Thrombophlebitis is inflammation and blood clots in the veins, which usually make the legs ache. This aching generally occurs after a period of inactivity, such as prolonged bed rest, taking a long plane ride or sitting for extended periods. Calf veins may feel firm and tender. Swelling may be difficult to detect.

The danger is that a blood clot can break off and go to the lungs. This is called a *pulmonary embolism* and is life-threatening.

If thrombophlebitis is suspected, call your doctor as soon as possible.

Intermittent Claudication

When arteries in the legs narrow, the resulting pain is called *intermittent claudication.* The pain is "intermittent" because it's brought on by exercise and stops after a few minutes of rest.

When arteries narrow, blood cannot reach the muscles efficiently. During increased activity, such as vigorous walking, pain occurs. Older adults and heavy smokers are susceptible to this condition and are sometimes bothered even during such mild exercise as walking.

If you suspect intermittent claudication, consult your doctor.

Varicose Veins

Varicose veins are a common condition in which bluish, swollen and twisted veins develop in the legs. They usually begin to appear on the back of the calves or the insides of the legs when a person is between the ages of 20 and 40. They are almost always more unsightly than they are painful. While they can't be cured, they can be treated.

Varicose veins are caused by long-term swelling of the leg veins near the skin's surface. This happens when valves in the leg veins fail and the pumping action of the vein isn't sufficient to return all of the blood to the heart. Blood pools and the veins then become distorted and swollen, particularly during prolonged standing. Feet and ankles may swell and the calves and other affected areas may ache or feel heavy.

In severe cases, the skin around the veins may become dry, itchy, scaly or *ulcerated* (open sores).

Varicose veins tend to run in families. They can be aggravated by prolonged standing or sitting, by being overweight or by numerous pregnancies.

WHAT YOU CAN DO ✓

Varicose veins are common and usually mild enough for people to treat on their own. To lessen swelling and discomfort and prevent the condition from worsening:

- Walk regularly.
- Wear elastic support panty hose or hose that reach all the way to the knee; put them on after elevating your legs for 10 to 15 minutes or as soon as you get out of bed in the morning.
- Wear shoes that support your feet well.
- Lose weight if you are overweight.
- Avoid standing or sitting for prolonged periods. If this can't be avoided, develop a habit of contracting and relaxing your calf and leg muscles, knees and ankles several times a day.
- Avoid crossing your legs, wearing tight clothing or doing anything that inhibits the flow of blood from the legs to the heart.
- Never scratch an itchy varicose vein, since an ulcer can develop.

- If symptoms are bothersome, elevate your legs above chest level at least twice a day for 30 minutes each time. Put pillows under your calves (not knees) so your ankles are higher than your heart.

> See your doctor if, despite self-care measures, varicose veins develop ulcers, worsen or interfere with normal activities. Severe pain, tenderness and warmth in the area may indicate a blood clot. If you suspect a blood clot, avoid massaging or rubbing the leg and avoid unnecessary walking. Call your doctor **immediately** and elevate the leg until it can be examined.

Shin Splints

Shin splints is a general term used to describe leg pain on the front of the lower leg caused by overuse. It typically develops after a person who is sedentary overexerts. Pain and tenderness normally occur on the front or the inside of the shin bone about halfway between the knee and ankle, caused by repeated stress and inflammation.

WHAT YOU CAN DO ✓

For pain from overuse:

- Rest your legs for at least one week after overexertion.
- Apply ice for 15 to 20 minutes at a time, more frequently initially, then three to four times a day for up to 48 hours. Leave ice off for at least 15 minutes between applications. For protection, place a washcloth between bare skin and ice and change the cloth if it becomes wet.
- Take aspirin or ibuprofen (Advil, Motrin). **NEVER give aspirin to children/ teenagers unless your health care provider orders it. It can cause Reye's syndrome, a rare but often fatal condition. CAUTION: Talk to your doctor or pharmacist before taking any other medications, including over-the-counter (OTC) medications, vitamins or herbal supplements.**
- When the pain is gone, do exercises to gently stretch the calf muscles.
- Wear properly fitting, supportive shoes.

If symptoms persist, call your doctor.

Decision *helper* Leg Pain
DO THESE APPLY:

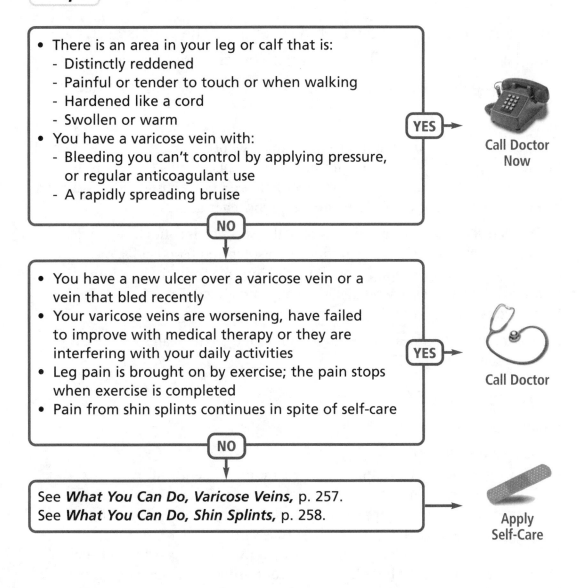

- There is an area in your leg or calf that is:
  - Distinctly reddened
  - Painful or tender to touch or when walking
  - Hardened like a cord
  - Swollen or warm
- You have a varicose vein with:
  - Bleeding you can't control by applying pressure, or regular anticoagulant use
  - A rapidly spreading bruise

YES → Call Doctor Now

NO ↓

- You have a new ulcer over a varicose vein or a vein that bled recently
- Your varicose veins are worsening, have failed to improve with medical therapy or they are interfering with your daily activities
- Leg pain is brought on by exercise; the pain stops when exercise is completed
- Pain from shin splints continues in spite of self-care

YES → Call Doctor

NO ↓

See *What You Can Do, Varicose Veins,* p. 257.
See *What You Can Do, Shin Splints,* p. 258.

→ Apply Self-Care

Hip Pain

Common causes of hip pain include overuse of the joint (starting a new exercise program or walking a long distance, for example), arthritis in the hip (see *Arthritis,* p. 234), infections in the joint or fractures.

Hip fractures are common among older adults whose bones are weakened and brittle, and even more common among people who have osteoporosis, which weakens the bones further. (See *Osteoporosis,* p. 238.) Fractures can result from a fall, or even from a sudden contraction of the leg muscles.

A hip fracture used to mean months of bed rest—which could lead to weakness and complications such as pneumonia, bed sores and blood clots. A surgical procedure called *ORIF* (open reduction and internal fixation) has dramatically improved the chances of a relatively speedy and effective recovery—but the best policy is to prevent a fracture in the first place.

For tips on ways to prevent falls and other accidents that can result in a hip fracture, see *Safety,* p. 355.

WHAT YOU CAN DO ✓

If pain is due to overuse:

- Take it easy and rest.
- Apply ice for 15 to 20 minutes at a time, more frequently initially, then three to four times a day for up to 48 hours. Leave ice off for at least 15 minutes between applications. For protection, place a washcloth between bare skin and ice and change the cloth if it becomes wet.
- Take aspirin or ibuprofen (Advil, Motrin). **NEVER give aspirin to children/ teenagers unless your health care provider orders it. It can cause Reye's syndrome, a rare but often fatal condition. CAUTION: Talk to your doctor or pharmacist before taking any other medications, including over-the-counter (OTC) medications, vitamins or herbal supplements.**
- If symptoms persist, call your doctor.

Decision *helper* Hip Pain
DO THESE APPLY:

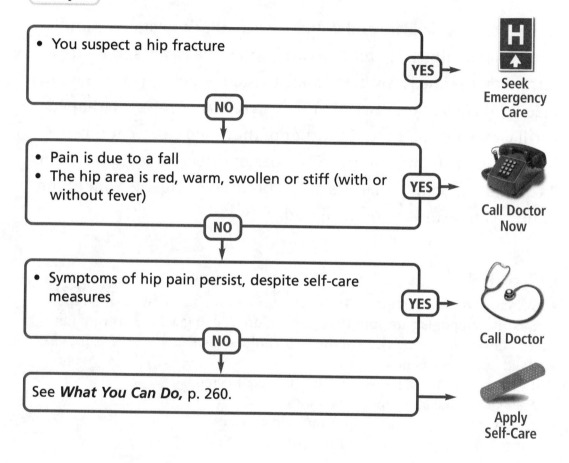

- You suspect a hip fracture

YES → **Seek Emergency Care**

NO ↓

- Pain is due to a fall
- The hip area is red, warm, swollen or stiff (with or without fever)

YES → **Call Doctor Now**

NO ↓

- Symptoms of hip pain persist, despite self-care measures

YES → **Call Doctor**

NO ↓

See *What You Can Do,* p. 260.

→ **Apply Self-Care**

Knee Pain

Knees are very delicate and vulnerable to injury. Ligaments and tendons that attach leg muscles and bones are easily sprained or torn when the knee is overextended, twisted or pushed from the side. (See *Strains and Sprains*, p. 62.) The *meniscus* (a crescent-shaped cartilage that is the shock absorber of the knee) can wear down, become too soft and tear from overuse or disease. (See *Arthritis*, p. 234.) The kneecap (*patella*) is a thin bone covering the front of the joint; it can be broken or displaced.

PREVENTION ✓

- Exercises that strengthen and stretch muscles and ligaments around the knee and upper leg are your best prevention. Walking, with warm-up and cool-down exercises, is one of the best choices. (See *Staying Active*, p. 343.)
- Avoid deep knee bends.
- If you have arthritis, take your medicine as directed.
- Wear stabilizing and supportive shoes.
- Avoid repeated, jarring motions on hard surfaces.
- Control your weight. (See *Eating Right*, p. 338.)

WHAT YOU CAN DO ✓

- If knee pain occurs after an injury, rest and immobilize your knee. Start RICE treatment immediately. (See *Strains and Sprains*, p. 62.)
- Pay attention to the pain and avoid any activity that may cause or increase it.
- Use a cane to take weight off the sore knee.
- DO NOT put a pillow under only your knee at night; this may stiffen the joint. Elevate the entire leg.
- If pain is caused by arthritis, see *Arthritis*, p. 234.

- Take aspirin or ibuprofen (Advil, Motrin) to ease pain and inflammation. **NEVER give aspirin to children/ teenagers unless your health care provider orders it. It can cause Reye's syndrome, a rare but often fatal condition. CAUTION: Talk to your doctor or pharmacist before taking any other medications, including over-the-counter (OTC) medications, vitamins or herbal supplements.**

Decision helper Knee Pain

DO THESE APPLY:

- Severe pain follows an injury
- The knee is deformed or bent in an abnormal way
- The bone protrudes or can be seen through the skin

Immobilize the knee. Elevate the leg if possible.
Apply a sterile bandage if the wound is open.
Apply ice. For protection, place a washcloth between bare skin and ice.

See **Broken Bones,** p. 65.

YES →

H ↑

Seek Emergency Care

FIRST AID

Apply Emergency First Aid

NO ↓

- You are unable to bear any weight on the knee
- Your knee is unstable, wobbly or very weak
- A popping sound, snapping or locking sensation occurs during or after a knee injury
- There is knee pain with swelling or pain in the calf
- The knee is red, painful and feels hot when touched
- There is knee pain with fever from no other apparent cause
- Severe knee pain is present even when you're not standing or putting weight on it

YES →

Call Doctor Now

NO ↓

See next page.

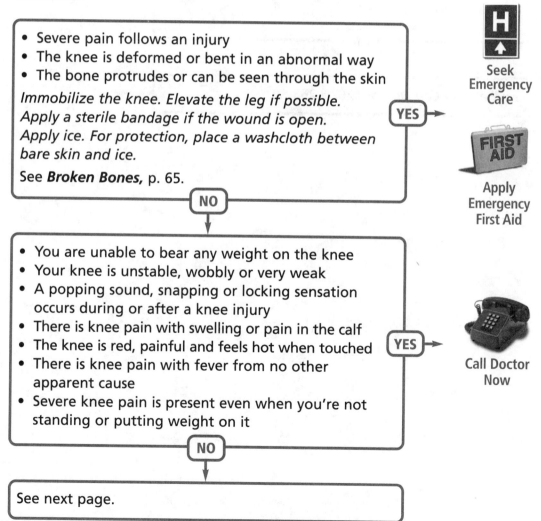

Do these apply: See previous page.

- Moderate knee pain is not improved by two or three days of self-care
- Knee pain improves but continues after six weeks of self-care
- You have been diagnosed with arthritis and new knee pain occurs (see *Arthritis,* p. 234)

YES →

Call Doctor

NO

See *What You Can Do,* pp. 262 - 263. →

**Apply
Self-Care**

Ankle Pain

Your ankle is a very complex, versatile joint. It is designed to keep your foot aimed in one direction while supporting the total weight of your body when you take a step. When it is not under pressure, the ankle allows the foot to flex and rotate. Problems develop when the ankle rotates under pressure, as in twisting your ankle stepping off a curb. The joint can also be injured by standing for extended periods on hard surfaces or supporting excess body weight.

Ankle pain may be due to a sprain in one or more ligaments (see *Strains and Sprains*, p. 62), inflammation in a tendon (see *Achilles Tendonitis*, p. 271), a fracture in the ankle bone (see *Broken Bones*, p. 65), or damage to the sliding surfaces in the joint (see *Arthritis*, p. 234). Whatever the cause of your ankle pain, it is a message to relieve the pressure, rest the joint and provide support. Continuing to walk on a painful ankle without treatment may increase damage and delay recovery.

Ankle Swelling

There is frequently swelling with pain in an ankle injury due to damaged muscles and ligaments. Ankle swelling without pain or injury is often from the accumulation of fluid that has leaked out of the *circulatory* (blood and lymph) *system*. Fluid retention (*edema*) is caused by the buildup of excess pressure in the veins that forces the fluid out into the surrounding tissue.

Anything that interferes with the flow of blood from the legs back to the heart can result in ankle swelling. Some causes—including prolonged standing or sitting with pressure on the back of your legs, constrictive clothing such as garters or knee-high stockings, varicose veins (see *Varicose Veins*, p. 257), or a diet high in salt or sodium—can be helped with self-care. When ankle swelling is a sign of a more serious health problem—such as a blood clot (see *Thrombophlebitis*, p. 256), heart failure, liver or kidney disease—treatment requires medical attention with individualized self-care.

PREVENTION ✓

- Wear shoes and clothing that fit well and provide adequate support.
- Avoid trauma, overuse or jarring activities.
- Exercise regularly. Always do warm-up and cool-down exercises.
- Walk or do leg exercises a few minutes every hour when standing or sitting for long periods.
- Avoid wearing clothing that restricts blood flow.
- Wear support stockings.
- Control your weight and limit sodium in your diet if it seems to be a factor.
- Take all medications as directed. Check with your doctor before decreasing or stopping any prescription drugs. (See *Using Medications,* p. 326.)

WHAT YOU CAN DO ✓

- If ankle pain follows an injury, start RICE immediately. (See *Strains and Sprains,* p. 62.)
- Use a cane or crutches to take pressure off the ankle, if necessary.
- Support an unstable ankle with high-topped shoes or elastic wrap. Wrap the ankle firmly, not tightly, with an elastic bandage. Start just above the toes, wrapping around the foot and then around the ankle in a figure-eight turn. Repeat figure-eight turns until the foot, ankle and lower leg (not the toes) are bandaged. Do not wrap too tightly or obstruct the blood flow. Loosen and rewrap the ankle if there is any tingling, numbness, change of color in the toes or increased swelling.
- Do not wrap a child's foot; the risk of cutting off circulation is too high.
- Take aspirin or ibuprofen (Advil, Motrin) to ease pain and inflammation. **NEVER give aspirin to children/teenagers unless your health care provider orders it. It can cause Reye's syndrome, a rare but often fatal condition. CAUTION: Talk to your doctor or pharmacist before taking any other medications, including over-the-counter (OTC) medications, vitamins or herbal supplements.**
- Elevate swollen ankles as often as possible with the feet above heart level.
- When pain decreases, exercise the ankle a few times a day:
  - Sit with the leg hanging freely; gently rotate the foot and ankle.
  - As the ankle becomes stronger, support it with elastic wrap and walk on tiptoes, then on your heels, to stretch and strengthen the joint.
  - Gradually increase the duration and frequency of exercise periods.

Decision *helper*   Ankle Pain
DO THESE APPLY:

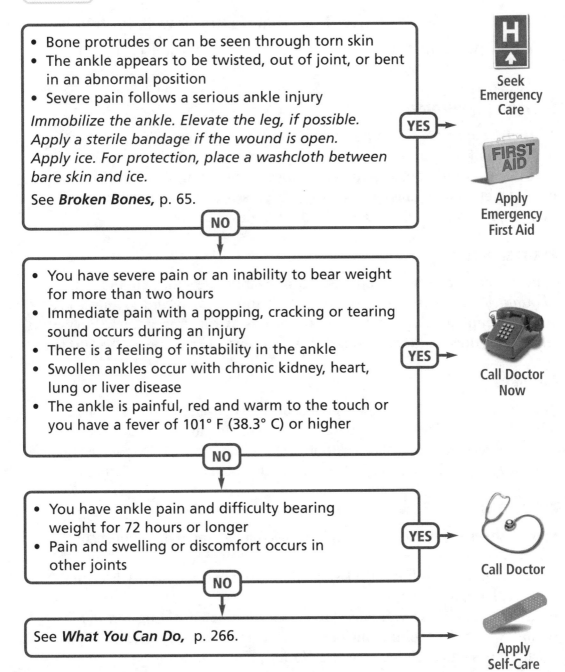

- Bone protrudes or can be seen through torn skin
- The ankle appears to be twisted, out of joint, or bent in an abnormal position
- Severe pain follows a serious ankle injury

Immobilize the ankle. Elevate the leg, if possible. Apply a sterile bandage if the wound is open. Apply ice. For protection, place a washcloth between bare skin and ice.

See **Broken Bones,** p. 65.

YES → **Seek Emergency Care**

Apply Emergency First Aid

NO ↓

- You have severe pain or an inability to bear weight for more than two hours
- Immediate pain with a popping, cracking or tearing sound occurs during an injury
- There is a feeling of instability in the ankle
- Swollen ankles occur with chronic kidney, heart, lung or liver disease
- The ankle is painful, red and warm to the touch or you have a fever of 101° F (38.3° C) or higher

YES → **Call Doctor Now**

NO ↓

- You have ankle pain and difficulty bearing weight for 72 hours or longer
- Pain and swelling or discomfort occurs in other joints

YES → **Call Doctor**

NO ↓

See **What You Can Do,** p. 266.

→ **Apply Self-Care**

Foot Pain

Most foot pain is caused by shoes that do not fit well. Problems can be easily prevented and usually respond well to self-care.

Morton's Neuroma

Morton's neuroma is swelling in one of the nerves that supplies sensation to the front half of your foot and toes. These nerves run parallel along the five long bones in your foot and end in the toes. Tight-fitting shoes squeeze the bones together and pinch the nerves. This pressure can cause swelling with intense pain in the ball of the foot and numbness between the toes.

Plantar Warts

Warts are caused by a virus and usually appear on the surface of the skin. A *plantar wart* appears on the ball of the foot and grows inward so it feels like you are stepping on a pebble. These warts look like an area of thick skin with small black dots scattered throughout and a center core beneath the surface.

Calluses

Calluses are hard, thickened layers of dead skin caused by friction. They often follow blisters and are a result of the skin thickening to protect an area against ongoing pressure. The ball of the foot is a very common site for calluses, especially if you wear high heels. Calluses can also occur anywhere friction occurs.

PREVENTION ✓

- Wear shoes that fit correctly. Avoid shoes that are too tight or loose, or that rub or slip.
- Wear high heels as little as possible. If unavoidable, alternate with pairs of shoes that have lower heels.
- Ease pressure areas with moleskin patches (available at drugstores).
- Limit your risk of contracting or spreading a foot virus by wearing slippers or bath shoes and avoiding going barefoot.

WHAT YOU CAN DO ✓

- Take aspirin or ibuprofen (Advil, Motrin) to ease pain and inflammation. **NEVER give aspirin to children/teenagers unless your health care provider orders it. It can cause Reye's syndrome, a rare but often fatal condition. CAUTION: Talk to your doctor or pharmacist before taking any other medications, including over-the-counter (OTC) medications, vitamins or herbal supplements.**
- For calluses, soak your feet in warm water for 15 minutes, then rub the area with a pumice stone to remove thickened skin. Follow this treatment by applying moisturizing lotion. Repeat the process daily until calluses disappear.
- Warts can be removed with salicylic acid plasters. Follow package directions.

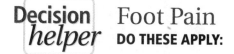

Decision *helper* Foot Pain
DO THESE APPLY:

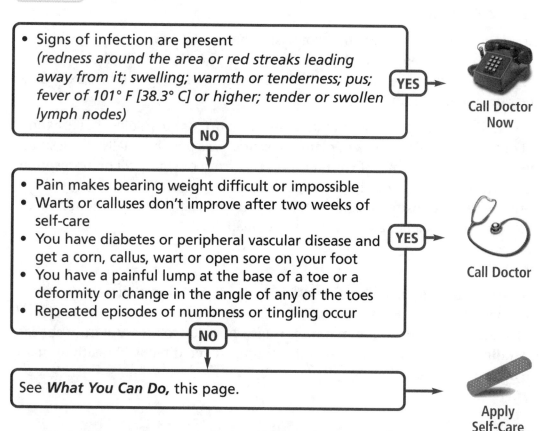

- Signs of infection are present
  (redness around the area or red streaks leading away from it; swelling; warmth or tenderness; pus; fever of 101° F [38.3° C] or higher; tender or swollen lymph nodes)

YES →

Call Doctor Now

NO

- Pain makes bearing weight difficult or impossible
- Warts or calluses don't improve after two weeks of self-care
- You have diabetes or peripheral vascular disease and get a corn, callus, wart or open sore on your foot
- You have a painful lump at the base of a toe or a deformity or change in the angle of any of the toes
- Repeated episodes of numbness or tingling occur

YES →

Call Doctor

NO

See *What You Can Do,* this page. →

Apply Self-Care

Heel Pain

Most heel pain is due to injury from repeated stress and trauma to the tissues that connect the bones of the feet and lower leg. These tissues bear your total body weight; are pulled in steps, twists and turns; are pounded in activities such as running and jogging; and often are stuffed into poorly fitting shoes with inadequate support. Is it any wonder that they sometimes hurt?

There are three primary causes of heel pain:

Plantar Fasciitis

The *plantar fascia* is a tough band of tissue that stretches from your heel bone to the ball of your foot. It can become inflamed when it is overstretched or torn by feet that flatten or roll inward with walking; feet with high arches; excessive stress or sudden turning.

Shoes that fit improperly, offer inadequate support, or have soles that are too stiff or thin increase your risk of plantar fasciitis. This pain is usually felt in small spots just behind the ball of your foot, right in front of your heel or along either side of the sole. There may be some swelling in the painful areas. Repeated plantar fasciitis or extreme overstretching can lead to the development of *bone spurs* (growths on a bone's surface) in the area.

Bursitis

Bursae (*bursa* for one) are little fluid-filled sacs at the joints that help muscles slide over other muscles or bones. The *calcaneal bursae* surround the back and underside of the heel. Inflammation is most often due to pressure from shoes or landing hard on the heel. Pain and swelling are felt directly beneath or on the back of the heel.

Achilles Tendonitis

The *Achilles tendon* is an elastic, fibrous band that attaches the muscles in the calf of your leg to your heel bone. A small stretch injury can make the tendon painful, swollen and less flexible—a condition called *Achilles tendonitis*.

Causes can include wearing shoes with inadequate support, insufficient warm-up prior to exercising, repeated pounding of the foot on hard surfaces, or turning the foot as it strikes the ground. The pain of Achilles tendonitis can be a sharp, burning sensation or a dull ache in the lower back of the leg and heel.

PREVENTION ✓

- Wear shoes that fit properly and have adequate arch support, are flexible and have sufficient padding in the heel cup.
- Ease pressure areas with moleskin patches.
- Remember to stretch and warm up before exercising, including prolonged walking on hard surfaces. (See *Staying Active*, p. 343.)
- Maintain a normal weight. (See *Eating Right*, p. 338.)

WHAT YOU CAN DO ✓

- Rest the area. Stop or decrease any activity that causes heel pain.
- Apply ice for 15 to 20 minutes at a time, more frequently initially, then three to four times a day for up to 48 hours. Leave ice off for at least 15 minutes between applications. For protection, place a washcloth between bare skin and ice and change the cloth if it becomes wet.
- Take aspirin or ibuprofen (Advil, Motrin) to ease pain and inflammation. **NEVER give aspirin to children/teenagers unless your health care provider orders it. It can cause Reye's syndrome, a rare but often fatal condition. CAUTION: Talk to your doctor or pharmacist before taking any other medications, including over-the-counter (OTC) medications, vitamins or herbal supplements.**
- Wear extra padding in shoes to protect and support the tender area.
- Try slow, gentle stretching of the back of the leg for Achilles tendonitis; stop if the pain starts or increases.

See *Decision helper*, p. 272.

Decision *helper* Heel Pain
DO THESE APPLY:

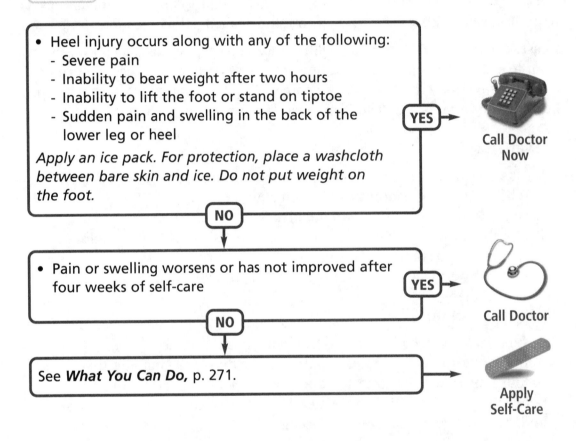

- Heel injury occurs along with any of the following:
  - Severe pain
  - Inability to bear weight after two hours
  - Inability to lift the foot or stand on tiptoe
  - Sudden pain and swelling in the back of the lower leg or heel

Apply an ice pack. For protection, place a washcloth between bare skin and ice. Do not put weight on the foot.

YES → Call Doctor Now

NO

- Pain or swelling worsens or has not improved after four weeks of self-care

YES → Call Doctor

NO

See *What You Can Do,* p. 271.

→ Apply Self-Care

Toe Pain

Although toes are small, they contain many bones, ligaments, tendons and joints. In addition to being susceptible to all the diseases and injuries that occur in larger joints and bones, toes are often pinched, stubbed and jammed, and have things dropped on them. What's more, they usually receive very little attention and care until they hurt.

Bunions

A *bunion* is swelling of the joint at the base of the big toe. The toe turns inward toward the other toes and may even overlap. This forces the joint outward, making it rub against shoes. Thick skin forms in the pressure area and, if the pressure is not relieved, a bony spur develops. The deformed joint often becomes inflamed and very painful.

Corns

Corns are hard, thickened areas of skin caused by pressure or friction. Corns usually occur at the top of the toes where the tissue is squeezed between the bones in the toe and tight-fitting shoes. Corns are usually yellow with a clear core and may become soft, moist or red.

Hammer Toes

A toe that bends up permanently at the middle joint is called a *hammer toe*. This condition is usually caused by wearing shoes that are too tight or narrow. The tendency to develop hammer toes is inherited.

Ingrown Toenails

When the edge of a toenail grows out into the soft flesh surrounding the nail bed, there is usually inflammation, swelling, pain and a high risk of infection. *Ingrown toenails* are caused by trimming the sides of the toenail too short, wearing shoes that are too tight, or injury to the toe or toenail.

PREVENTION ✓

- Wear shoes that fit properly and have good arch support. Low-heeled shoes with a roomy toe box are best.
- If there is a high risk of trauma or injury to your toes, wear shoes with a reinforced toe box.
- Cut toenails *straight across*. Do not cut or file down on the sides.

WHAT YOU CAN DO ✓

- Relieve pressure over a painful area by wearing shoes that are roomy or open.
- Cushion the area with moleskin or pads to ease friction.
- Take aspirin or ibuprofen (Advil, Motrin) to relieve pain and inflammation. **NEVER give aspirin to children/ teenagers unless your health care provider orders it. It can cause Reye's syndrome, a rare but often fatal condition. CAUTION: Talk to your doctor or pharmacist before taking any other medications, including over-the-counter (OTC) medications, vitamins or herbal supplements.**
- For corns, soak your feet in warm water for 15 minutes, then rub the area with a pumice stone to remove thickened skin. Follow treatment by applying a moisturizing lotion. Repeat this process daily until the corn disappears.
- Remove corns, if necessary, with "corn plasters," adhesive patches containing 40 percent salicylic acid. Follow the package directions. Protect with a moleskin patch. (Both are available at drugstores.)
- For an ingrown toenail:
  - Soak your foot in warm water for 10 to 15 minutes.
  - Wedge a small piece of cotton under the corner of the nail to train it to grow outward.
  - Repeat this process daily until the nail has grown out and can be trimmed straight across.

Decision *helper*   Toe Pain
DO THESE APPLY:

- Signs of infection are present in an ingrown toenail *(redness around the area or red streaks leading away from it; swelling; warmth or tenderness; pus; fever of 101° F [38.3° C] or higher; tender or swollen lymph nodes)*   **YES** → Call Doctor Now

NO ↓

- You have a chronic illness such as diabetes or circulatory problems and a corn, wart, callus or open sore appears on your toe
- You have sudden severe pain in the big toe and no previous diagnosis of gout (see **Gout, Major Types of Arthritis,** p. 235)
- Severe pain interferes with walking or daily activities
- Your big toe begins to overlap the second toe
- Symptoms worsen or do not improve after two weeks of self-care

YES → Call Doctor

NO ↓

See **What You Can Do,** p. 274.   → Apply Self-Care

Women's Health

As a woman ages, her body undergoes a natural transformation from the childbearing years. *Menopause,* or the gradual loss of fertility, results in lower hormone levels, which in turn effect changes in body tissues and cause a decrease in bone strength. (See *Menopause,* p. 281; *Osteoporosis,* p. 238.) However, advancing age or decreased levels of hormones have little effect on sexual desire. Most older women continue to enjoy the patterns of sexual expression they had when they were younger.

Today, good preventive care such as regular breast exams and Pap smears—combined with a healthy diet and exercise—promotes well-being in women.

Breast Lumps

About half of all women develop a breast lump before they reach menopause. The vast majority of these lumps are harmless. In fact, 80 percent of all lumps that are *biopsied* (tested) are *benign* (not cancerous). But some lumps are *malignant* (cancerous). With early detection, there may be more options for treatment and a better chance to catch any cancer that may spread to other parts of the body.

Although some risk factors for breast cancer have been identified, a large percentage of women who develop the disease have no known risk factors. Having one or more of the following risk factors *does not* mean that breast cancer is inevitable:

- Being over 50 years of age
- Having a mother or sister who has had breast cancer, especially if the cancer was in both breasts or developed at an early age

- Beginning menstruation early and/or going through menopause late
- Having a first child after the age of 30, or having no children
- Having a previous diagnosis of breast cancer

NOTE YOUR SYMPTOMS ✓

A mass in the breast tissue may be hard or soft and can have a smooth or irregular contour. The size can range from microscopic to quite large. While some lumps are tender or painful, most are painless.

WHAT YOU CAN DO ✓

Screening Program

Monthly breast self-examination

By taking a few minutes to check your own breasts each month, you will become familiar with how they normally feel, enabling you to identify changes. If you still menstruate, the best time to examine yourself is two to three days after your menstrual period has ended. If you no longer menstruate, choose the same day each month to do the exam (the first day of the month, for example). Follow the six steps on page 279. Call your doctor if you discover any lumps or discharge from the nipples or if you have any concerns.

Professional breast examination

Breast exams are recommended for all women during routine checkups, beginning annually at age 40. A discussion of your breast cancer risk factors is advisable at this time.

Regular mammography

A *mammogram*—an x-ray of the breast—is generally recommended for all women beginning at age 40. Mammograms can detect lumps too small to be detected by other means.

Fibrocystic Breast Lumps

Fibrocystic breast lumps do not require treatment. Most associated pain or discomfort can be relieved by:

- Using mild analgesics such as aspirin, ibuprofen (Advil, Motrin) and acetaminophen (Tylenol). **NEVER give aspirin to children/teenagers unless your health care provider orders it. It can cause Reye's syndrome, a rare but often fatal condition. CAUTION: Talk to your doctor or pharmacist before taking any other medications, including over-the-counter (OTC) medications, vitamins or herbal supplements.**
- Wearing a larger or more supportive bra

Examining your breasts on a monthly basis is very important because the presence of cysts may make it more difficult to find a potentially dangerous lump. However, women who have benign breast lumps are not at higher risk of breast cancer.

FINAL NOTES ✓

Call your doctor as soon as possible if you think you have a breast lump or if you have unusual nipple discharge, pain or tenderness in your breast. The call could save your life.

Breast Self-Exam

Make these six steps a monthly habit:

Figure 25

In front of the mirror

1. Stand up straight with your arms at your sides; visually inspect your breasts. Check your nipples for discharge or puckering, dimpling or scaling of the skin.
2. Clasp your hands behind your head and press your hands forward. (See Figure 25.) You will feel your chest muscles tighten. Check for any change in the normal shape and contour of your breasts.
3. Press your hands firmly on your hips and lean forward. At the same time, move your shoulders and elbows forward. As in step 2, check for any change in shape or contour that seems different from the way your breasts normally look.

In the shower or bath

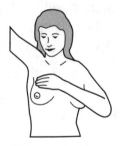

Figure 26

4. Raise one arm and with your opposite hand, press your breast firmly with your fingers flat. (See Figure 26.) Make small circles, moving from the outer edge toward the nipple each time until you have worked your way around the entire breast. Check for any unusual lump or mass, especially between the breast and underarm (including the underarm).
5. Gently squeeze the nipple. Check for a discharge. If you have a discharge at any time, call your doctor.

Lying down

6. Repeat steps 4 and 5 lying on your back. Slip a pillow or folded towel under the shoulder of your raised arm. This flattens the breast and makes examination easier.

Repeat steps 4, 5 and 6 for the other breast.

For information from the National Cancer Institute, call 1-800-4-CANCER.
Adapted from the National Institutes of Health

Pap Smear

Examination of the female reproductive organs (a *pelvic examination*) gives your doctor essential information about your gynecological health. One of the most important elements of this exam is the *Pap smear,* which tests for the presence of cancer cells in the cervix.

A *speculum,* a plastic or metal duck-billed instrument, spreads the walls of the vagina so that a scraping of the cervix and a sample of vaginal secretions can be taken.

These cells are then sent to a laboratory where a trained technician studies them under a microscope and reports the findings to your doctor. Three systems are currently used to classify Pap smears; your doctor can help you interpret your results.

Pap smears detect about 90 percent of cervical cancers, making them reliable screening procedures. Since cervical cancers are slow-growing, there is an excellent chance that regular Pap smears will detect cancer before it spreads.

Annual Pap smears are recommended for all women by most national authorities. Women over the age of 65 and women who have had hysterectomies should discuss screening recommendations with their doctors.

Menopause

Menopause, also called the "change of life," is a natural event that marks the end of a woman's menstrual cycles and her ability to bear children. It occurs for most women between the ages of 47 and 55, when production of the female hormone *estrogen* declines.

Menopause can last a few months or several years, and it is considered complete when a woman has not menstruated for a full year. Menopause eliminates the need for any form of contraception, although doctors usually recommend continuing birth control until one year after a woman's last period.

WHAT YOU CAN DO ☑

Irregular Periods

Menstrual periods usually become lighter—but can become heavier—and irregular before they stop completely. Keep a written record, including the dates of your periods, in case you need to discuss them with your doctor.

Hot Flashes

Sudden feelings of intense heat, accompanied by sweating and flushing, normally last a few minutes. They are most common at night—although they can occur any time. Hormone imbalance caused by menopause can result in insomnia and subsequent fatigue. (See *Insomnia,* p. 323.) For most women, hot flashes gradually decrease over a period of a few years and eventually disappear.

To manage symptoms of hot flashes:

- Wear loose, lightweight clothing in layers that can be easily removed.
- Drink plenty of fluids. Avoid caffeine and alcohol if they seem to bring on hot flashes.
- Exercise regularly to help stabilize your hormones and prevent insomnia.

Vaginal Dryness

Estrogen helps stimulate the production of natural lubricants in the vagina, so the loss of estrogen can result in vaginal dryness—which can make intercourse painful and lead to *vaginitis* (vaginal infection) and an increased urge to urinate (see *Vaginitis,* p. 289).

Lubricants that provide relief for many women include water-based gels (K-Y Jelly, Replens). Do not use Vaseline or other petroleum-based products. Estrogen cream, prescribed by your health care provider, may also help. Many women find that regular sexual activity decreases problems with soreness during intercourse.

Mood Swings

Hormonal and physical changes related to menopause may result in moodiness, depression, lethargy or nervousness. Try to understand that this is normal and to accept yourself—and your moods—as much as possible.

Osteoporosis

The thinning of bones (*osteoporosis*) that is caused by reduced estrogen levels results in weakened bones that are easily broken. *This silent disease usually has no symptoms and often goes undiagnosed until a bone suddenly breaks.* (See *Osteoporosis,* p. 238.)

You can take steps to prevent osteoporosis or slow its progression, however. (See *Osteoporosis, What You Can Do,* p. 239.)

Surgical Menopause

Menopause may occur early in women who have both ovaries removed for whatever reason, a procedure called *bilateral* (both sides) *oopherectomy.* This procedure may or may not accompany a *hysterectomy* (surgical removal of the uterus.) Menopausal symptoms occur suddenly due to the abrupt cessation of estrogen. Many women opt to take estrogen replacement therapy as a result. (See *HRT,* next page.)

TREATMENT OPTION ✓

Hormone Replacement Therapy (HRT)

The short-term use of hormone replacement therapy (HRT) is the mainstay for treating symptoms of menopause such as hot flashes and night sweats. (These symptoms generally last a few years and then fade away.) HRT can also help prevent vaginal and urethral thinning, and therefore reduce symptoms such as urinary urgency and incontinence. Other benefits include preventing recurrent urinary tract infections and pain with intercourse.

For some women, HRT also offers protection against *osteoporosis,* a progressive condition that weakens bones, making them fragile and prone to fracture. Alternate treatments, such as bisphosphonates, are also used to prevent and treat osteoporosis in men and women. Medications include alendronate (Fosamax) and risedronate (Actonel).

For many years, HRT was believed to prevent heart disease. Recent studies have cast doubt on its effectiveness for this purpose, however, and it is no longer recommended. Women should consult their doctors about other preventive measures for heart disease, such as lifestyle changes and cholesterol- and blood pressure-lowering drugs.

Deciding whether to use HRT is a very personal matter. It's important to weigh the benefits of HRT against your personal risks for heart attacks, stroke, blood clots, and breast cancer, which may be linked to its long-term use. Discuss the pros and cons thoroughly with your doctor and make the choice that best suits your needs and lifestyle.

See *Decision helper,* p. 284.

Decision **Menopause**
helper **DO THESE APPLY:**

- You experience even minor vaginal bleeding and:
  - You haven't menstruated in more than a year and aren't taking hormone replacement therapy
  - You are taking hormone replacement therapy and experience any unexplained vaginal bleeding
- Menopausal symptoms have become intolerable or interfere with your daily life
- You are avoiding social contacts or otherwise are unable to enjoy yourself

YES →

Call Doctor

NO

See *What You Can Do,* pp. 281 - 282.
See *Breast Lumps,* p. 276.
See *Depression,* p. 319.

Apply
Self-Care

Postmenopausal Uterine Bleeding

Postmenopausal uterine bleeding is unexpected, menstrual-like bleeding that occurs one year or more after menstruation ends. You are at increased risk of experiencing this condition if you are a woman over age 60. This is because blood vessels become more fragile as you age and the vaginal lining becomes thinner. A recent vaginal infection is also a risk factor. (See *Vaginal Discharge*, p. 288.)

Postmenopausal uterine bleeding may indicate a minor problem or a serious one, so it's important to get prompt medical diagnosis and treatment. Possible causes of the bleeding include:

- Irritation, infection or thinning of the membranes that line the *vulva* (the female external genitalia). *Atrophic vaginitis*, an inflammation of vaginal tissue due to aging of the tissue and loss of estrogen may result, causing bleeding during intercourse.
- *Hormone replacement therapy* (HRT), which stimulates the *endometrium* (uterine lining), causing sloughing away of blood and tissue similar to normal menstruation. (See *Uterine Bleeding While on HRT*, p. 286.)
- *Fibroid tumors*, uterine growths that are almost always noncancerous (see *Fibroid Tumors*, p. 286), or *polyps* (grape-shaped, usually noncancerous internal growths), or tumors of the *cervix* (the narrow outer end of the uterus).
- Cancer of the reproductive system

Diagnostic tests your doctor may recommend include blood studies, a Pap smear, *endometrial aspiration* (inserting a thin tube into the uterus and taking a sample of the uterine lining) or *dilation and curettage* (known as a D & C), which involves dilating the cervix and scraping the surface lining of the uterus.

Treatment of postmenopausal uterine bleeding may include medications or surgery, depending on the cause.

Uterine Bleeding While on HRT

With some hormone replacement therapy (HRT), it is common to have monthly periods; ask your doctor what to expect. If you are on HRT (estrogen and progestin) and have monthly cycles, you should call your doctor if:

- You are on *cyclic estrogen plus progestin therapy* and bleeding other than expected withdrawal bleeding occurs (days 10 to 15 of the month if progestin is given on days 1 to 10 of the month).
- You are on *continuous estrogen plus progestin therapy* and bleeding is heavy (heavier than a normal menstrual period), prolonged (longer than 10 days at a time), frequent (more often than monthly), or persisting longer than 10 months after the start of HRT.

If you have decided on HRT, you'll want to work closely with your doctor to find the right combination of treatment for you.

For more information on the risks and benefits of HRT, see **HRT,** p. 283.

WHAT YOU CAN DO ✓

- If you are on HRT and cycle monthly, track your monthly cycles.
- Try lubricants if you have atrophic vaginitis. (See Vaginal Dryness, p. 282.)

Fibroid Tumors

Fibroid tumors—or fibroids—consist of bundles of smooth muscle and connective tissue that develop slowly within the wall of the uterus. These growths are almost always noncancerous and can vary from the size of a pea to that of a grapefruit (the size of the entire uterine cavity).

More than 75 percent of women with fibroids experience no symptoms. When symptoms do occur, they may include:

- Heavy, prolonged or painful menstrual periods
- Frequent urination or incontinence
- Abdominal pain or pressure in the lower back
- Constipation
- Pain during sexual intercourse

Fibroids can remain unchanged for long periods and often stop growing without intervention. On the other hand, they have the potential to develop into multiple, fast-growing tumors, and—in rare cases—can be *malignant* (cancerous).

If you have symptoms of fibroids, call your doctor. Treatment can range from birth control pills (to help control vaginal bleeding) to surgery.

Decision *helper* Postmenopausal Uterine Bleeding
DO THESE APPLY:

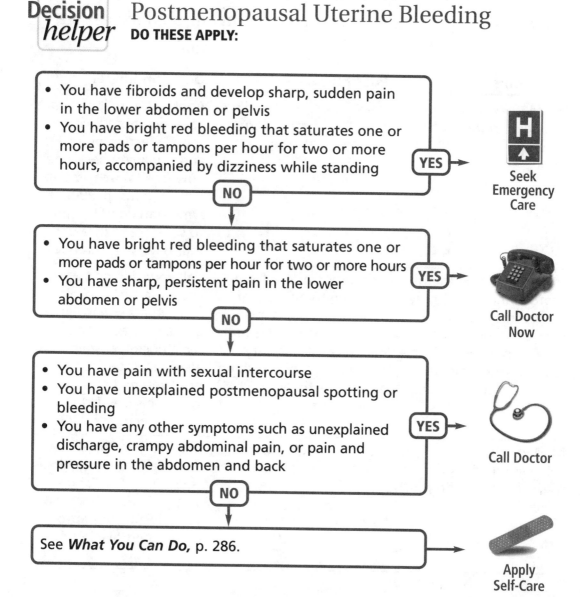

- You have fibroids and develop sharp, sudden pain in the lower abdomen or pelvis
- You have bright red bleeding that saturates one or more pads or tampons per hour for two or more hours, accompanied by dizziness while standing

YES → **H** ↑ Seek Emergency Care

NO

- You have bright red bleeding that saturates one or more pads or tampons per hour for two or more hours
- You have sharp, persistent pain in the lower abdomen or pelvis

YES → Call Doctor Now

NO

- You have pain with sexual intercourse
- You have unexplained postmenopausal spotting or bleeding
- You have any other symptoms such as unexplained discharge, crampy abdominal pain, or pain and pressure in the abdomen and back

YES → Call Doctor

NO

See *What You Can Do,* p. 286. → Apply Self-Care

Vaginal Discharge

Healthy women produce small or moderate amounts of odorless, non-irritating vaginal discharge that may increase at certain times during the menstrual cycle. Abnormal discharge is very common and has many possible causes—some that require a doctor's care.

Symptoms	Possible causes	Decision helper
White, cheesy discharge; itching; burning with urination	Yeast infection (Candida, monilia) or other forms of nonspecific vaginitis	Apply self-care if you have been diagnosed with a yeast infection before and think you have one now (see *What You Can Do, Vaginitis*, p. 290); if symptoms do not respond to self-care in three or four days, call your doctor
Frothy discharge that is profuse and white, gray-ish-green or yellowish; vaginal burning and itching; may have urinary-related symptoms (see *Urinary Tract Infections*, p. 291)	*Trichomoniasis,* a form of vaginitis and urinary tract infection, is most often sexually transmit-ted; it can also be spread via damp towels, bathing suits and—theoretically—toilet seats	Call your doctor now; if you have trichomoniasis, alert your sex partner(s) and encourage them to see a doctor; abstain from all sexual intercourse until you no longer have symptoms (see *Urinary Tract Infections*, p. 291)
Murky white, gray or yellowish discharge; distinct "fishy" odor; itching	Bacterial vaginosis or nonspecific vaginitis	May go away on its own; apply self-care for vaginitis (see *What You Can Do, Vaginitis*, p. 290); call your doctor if symptoms do not improve in three or four days

Symptoms	Possible causes	Decision helper
Vaginal discharge accompanied by severe lower abdominal pain, fever or recurrent or significant amounts of bloody discharge between periods	May indicate a serious condition	Call your doctor now (see *Sexually Transmitted Diseases*, p. 304)
Discharge in a post-menopausal woman who is not on hormone replacement therapy	May indicate other problems	Call your doctor

Vaginitis is a Common Cause

Abnormal vaginal discharge is the hallmark symptom of vaginitis, which is most often caused by yeast. Vaginitis can be the result of stress, antibiotics (which kill protective bacteria) or excessive douching. If you have diabetes, you are especially susceptible. Some forms of vaginitis can also be transmitted through sexual intercourse.

In addition to vaginal discharge, symptoms of vaginitis may include burning and itching, general pelvic discomfort, pain during intercourse, and painful or more frequent urination.

PREVENTION ✓

- Wear cotton underpants that allow for air exchange in the crotch and thighs; avoid tight-fitting pants.
- Avoid douching and the use of feminine deodorant sprays and other perfumed products.
- Wipe from front to back after using the toilet.
- If you still have a period, change tampons at least three times a day. Alternate with pads and be sure to remove the last tampon when your period is over.
- If you are prone to vaginitis, consume more acidophilus milk, buttermilk, cranberry juice and yogurt with live cultures to help the vagina maintain its natural chemical balance.

WHAT YOU CAN DO ✓

Some types of vaginitis can be treated with self-care if: 1) you have been diag-nosed with a yeast infection in the past and you suspect one now; and/or 2) you have minimal symptoms and suspect a non-specific vaginitis.

- For a suspected yeast infection, try over-the-counter (OTC) antifungal creams such as Gyne-Lotrimin or Monistat. (If you have never seen a doctor for a vaginal infection, consult one before using these products.)
- Avoid intercourse—along with douches, spermicides, tampons and contra-ceptive devices such as the sponge or diaphragm—while you have vaginitis to allow time for vaginal tissue to heal.
- Try not to scratch the area. Apply cold water compresses or ice packs to reduce inflammation and soothe irritation. For protection, place a washcloth between bare skin and ice. Warm *sitz baths* (sitting in hip-high water) may also offer you some relief.
- Call your doctor if your symptoms persist or worsen after three or four days of self-care, or if you are unsure what is causing your problem or what you should do.

FINAL NOTES ✓

In most cases, symptoms of vaginitis disappear quickly with treatment. However, vaginitis does tend to recur, and some women simply seem to be more susceptible than others. Complications can be avoided by paying attention to abnormal vaginal discharge and sensations, and getting prompt treatment.

If you experience burning and pain with urination and feel like you need to urinate more than usual, see *Urinary Tract Infections*, p. 291.

Urinary Problems

Burning or stinging pain with urination, frequent or urgent urination, or blood in the urine may all be signs of an infection in the lower urinary tract or inflammation around the urethral opening (the *urethra* is the tube that carries urine from the bladder and out of the body).

Urinary Tract Infections (UTIs)

Urinary tract infections are also known as *UTIs, cystitis* and *bladder infections.* They are most common among women, but can also affect children, infants and men. (See *UTIs, Men's Health,* p. 296.)

Symptoms may include a frequent and urgent need to urinate, pain or a burning sensation during urination, cloudy, bloody or foul-smelling urine, pain or itching in the urethra, or pressure in the lower abdomen and lower back pain.

Between 80 and 90 percent of UTIs are caused by *E. coli* bacteria, which are generally found in the digestive system. Because the female anus and urethra are very close together, bacteria can find its way from the anus into the urethra and bladder. Any irritation of the genital area (such as sexual intercourse or wearing tight pants) increases the likelihood of developing an infection.

WHAT YOU CAN DO ☑

To prevent UTIs and minimize infection once you begin to feel symptoms:
- Drink plenty of fluids (eight or more glasses of water a day), unless your fluid intake has been limited by your doctor. Cranberry juice also may be helpful.
- Avoid alcohol, coffee, tea, carbonated beverages and spicy foods.
- Wear cotton underwear, cotton-lined pantyhose and loose clothing.
- Wipe from front to back after using the toilet (to reduce the spread of bacteria from the anus to the urethra).
- Avoid sexual intercourse when symptoms are present.
- Try to urinate before and after intercourse.
- Empty your bladder frequently.

- Avoid bubble bath or bath oil, especially when symptoms are present.
- Avoid frequent douching and do not use vaginal deodorants or perfumed feminine hygiene products.
- If your doctor prescribes antibiotics, be sure to take the entire prescription as directed to help prevent a relapse or recurrence. (See *Using Medications*, p. 326.)

Urinary Incontinence

Urinary incontinence, or the inability to control bladder function, is two to five times more common in women than in men and is more prevalent with age. The condition affects about 10 to 25 percent of women under the age of 65 and about 15 to 35 percent of women over age 65. The effects of childbirth can make the uterus and pelvic floor sag, putting pressure on the bladder. In women, age-related decreases in hormone levels may also result in a thinning of the tissue lining the urethra, which can make the urethra weaken and leak urine. However, there are many preventive measures and treatments for this condition.

WHAT YOU CAN DO ☑

- If you are overweight, losing weight may help reduce pressure on your bladder. (See *Eating Right* p. 338; *Staying Active* p. 343.)
- Check with your doctor to see if your bladder has shifted. A mechanical lift (*pessary*) inserted into the vagina may help correct your bladder's position.
- Ask your doctor to check for thinning in the lining of your urethra and vagina. A topical estrogen cream or oral estrogen supplements can treat this situation. (See *HRT,* p. 283.)
- *Kegel exercises* strengthen the muscles that surround the openings of the urethra, vagina and anus. Follow these instructions:
  - While urinating, try to stop the flow of urine to identify the correct pelvic muscles.
  - Contract these muscles as if you were stopping your urine stream, but do it when you're not urinating—while sitting, standing, walking or driving.
  - Tighten your rectal muscles as if trying not to pass gas. Contract your anus, but don't move your buttocks.
  - Do these exercises every morning, afternoon and evening. Start with five repetitions and gradually work up to 20 or 30 repetitions each time. Hold each position while slowly counting to five. Try not to move your buttocks, stomach muscles or legs.

- If you take certain medications, such as diuretics, or water pills (often prescribed for heart failure and high blood pressure to increase fluid loss), ask your doctor about finding an alternative or changing the time of day you take it. They can cause *urge incontinence*, when you feel the need to urinate but can't hold back long enough.
- Check with your doctor if you experience pain, urinary frequency, or blood in the urine; you may have an infection. (See *UTIs, Women's Health,* p. 291.)

See ***Vaginal Discharge,*** p. 288; ***Men's Health,*** p. 294.

Decision *helper* Urinary Problems
DO THESE APPLY:

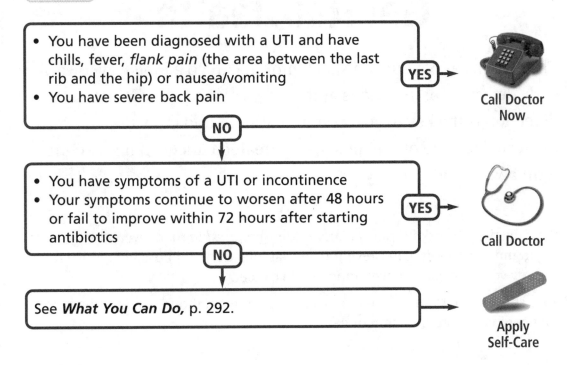

- You have been diagnosed with a UTI and have chills, fever, *flank pain* (the area between the last rib and the hip) or nausea/vomiting
- You have severe back pain

YES →

Call Doctor Now

NO

- You have symptoms of a UTI or incontinence
- Your symptoms continue to worsen after 48 hours or fail to improve within 72 hours after starting antibiotics

YES →

Call Doctor

NO

See ***What You Can Do,*** p. 292. →

Apply Self-Care

Men's Health

Although men do not experience menopause, physiological changes take place as men age that affect their health and sexuality in subtle but important ways. As the male sexual hormone, *testosterone,* begins to decline, sexual function may change. It may take more time to achieve an erection, and the penis may stay erect for a shorter period. (See *Sexual Health,* p. 303.) Illness, certain medications and too much alcohol can affect this process. The prostate tends to enlarge with age and may or may not cause any symptoms. (See *Prostate Problems,* p. 298.)

But getting regular check-ups and taking care of yourself can help prevent many age-related problems. Self-examination is equally important. Tracking your genital health takes little time and is well worth the effort.

Genital Health

Three minutes of your time each month can go a long way toward early detection of infections and cancers of the penis or testes. Early detection is the key to successful treatment and cure. (Cancer of the testicle is one of the most easily treated cancers if it is caught right away.)

Washing the penis daily, particularly under the *foreskin* that covers the tip of an uncircumcised penis, can prevent bacterial infection and possibly reduce the already very low risk of developing penile cancer.

Men should also examine their penis and testes each month for any changes that could indicate infection or cancer.

WHAT YOU CAN DO ☑️

After a warm bath or shower:

- Stand with your right leg on the side of the tub or on the toilet seat.
- Gently roll the right testicle between the thumb and fingers of both hands. Check for:
  - Hard lumps or nodules
  - An enlargement or change in the consistency of the testicle
  - A pain or dull ache in the groin or lower abdomen
- Repeat this procedure on your left side.
- Feel the *epididymis,* the spongy tube on the top and the back side of the testicle. Pain could mean an infection.
- Examine the foreskin and the head of the penis for anything unusual, including sores, warts, redness or discharge.

When to Call Your Doctor

Testicular cancer spreads quickly—within a few months—so it is important to see your doctor to rule it out as soon as possible after you find any testicular lumps or nodules.

Also discuss any enlargement of the testicle, groin pain or penile discharge with your doctor.

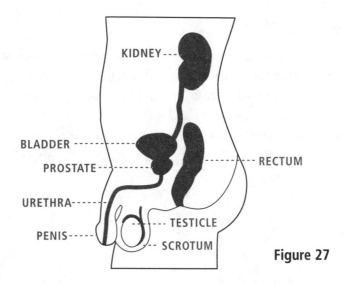

Figure 27

Urinary Problems

Problems with urination, such as dribbling, frequent or painful urination, decreased force of the urine stream, incomplete bladder emptying, or blood in the urine, can have a variety of causes from a urinary tract infection to prostate cancer.

Urinary Tract Infections (UTIs)

Urinary tract infections (also known as *UTIs, cystitis* and *bladder infections*) are most common among women (see *Women's Health, UTIs,* p. 291), but they can also affect men, children and infants. In men, most UTIs are caused by obstructions or structural problems in the urinary tract. In men over 50, the problem is often caused by an enlarged prostate gland that hinders the flow of urine out of the bladder and becomes the perfect breeding ground for bacteria.

Symptoms may include a frequent and urgent need to urinate, pain or a burning sensation during urination, cloudy or foul-smelling urine, blood in the urine, pain or itching in the *urethra* (the tube that carries urine from the bladder out through the penis), pressure in the lower abdomen, and lower back pain.

WHAT YOU CAN DO ☑

- Drink plenty of fluids to help wash bacteria away, unless your doctor has limited your fluid intake. Water is good, and fruit juices that put more acid in the urine may provide additional relief. (Cranberry juice is best.)
- Empty the bladder frequently.
- If your doctor prescribes antibiotics, be sure to take the entire prescription as directed to help prevent a relapse or recurrence. (See *Using Medications,* p. 326.)

Urinary Incontinence

Urinary incontinence (the inability to control urine) is not a normal aspect of aging, but it does affect between 5 and 10 percent of people over age 65. With the treatments available today, most can be spared the embarrassment commonly associated with this condition. Urinary incontinence is treatable in most cases and often can be completely cured. When it can't be cured, it can usually be controlled.

Types of urinary incontinence include *urge incontinence* (leaking urine as soon as you feel the urge to go to the bathroom), *stress incontinence* (leaking urine when the bladder is stressed, as when you laugh, cough or make a sudden move—usually a temporary situation for men following prostate surgery) and *overflow incontinence* (feeling like the bladder never empties completely).

Common causes of urinary incontinence include:

- Enlargement of the prostate gland (see *Prostate Problems*, p. 298)
- Damage to the urethra from prostate procedures, such as surgery or radiation treatment for cancer (see *Prostate Problems*, p. 298)
- Central nervous system disorders such as Parkinson's disease (see *Parkinson's Disease*, p. 100) or stroke (see *Stroke*, p. 93)
- Diabetes (see *Diabetes*, p. 226), urinary tract infections and certain medications

WHAT YOU CAN DO ✓

Urinary incontinence requires a visit to your doctor, who will take your medical history and possibly conduct some tests. Medications you are taking may be aggravating the condition, so talk to your doctor about that possibility.

Once a diagnosis is made, your doctor may prescribe medication to help stimulate bladder muscle contractions, or recommend surgery to tighten certain muscles or remove blockages.

In addition to a doctor's evaluation and treatment, self-care techniques may help:

- Train your bladder to urinate on a schedule. To do this, start urinating at regular times. Gradually work your way up to longer periods between urination.
- Empty your bladder as much as you can, wait a few minutes, then empty it again. This is called *double-voiding*.
- Practice *Kegel exercises* to strengthen the muscles that control urination. (See *Urinary Incontinence, Women's Health,* p. 292.)

Prostate Problems

The *prostate* (see Figure 27, p. 295), which produces some of the fluid in semen, is a donut-shaped gland that sits below the bladder and surrounds the urethra. The three most common prostate problems are prostate infection (*prostatitis*), prostate enlargement (*benign prostatic hypertrophy*) and prostate cancer.

Prostate infection

Prostate infection (*prostatitis*) is an infection of the prostate that may occur with a urinary tract infection as a result of bacteria traveling up the urethra. Prostate infection causes swelling, constriction of the urethra and urinary problems.

Symptoms include difficulty starting or stopping urination, a strong and frequent urge to urinate while passing only small amounts of urine, pain or discomfort in the area behind the *scrotum* (the "sac" of skin that encloses the testes), low-back or abdominal pain, and pain and burning during urination or ejaculation. Fever and chills, a general ill feeling, and blood in the urine or pus-filled discharge are also possible.

The prostate can also become inflamed without bacterial infection, causing chronic pelvic pain syndrome. Symptoms are similar to bacterial prostatitis; the cause is unknown.

WHAT YOU CAN DO ☑

A prostate infection requires a doctor's diagnosis and antibiotics, although self-care may be helpful as well. Chronic pelvic pain syndrome may respond to self-care alone.

- Drink lots of fluids—both water and fruit juices.
- Avoid alcohol, caffeine, carbonated beverages and spicy foods.
- Ejaculate three or four times a week.
- Try warm baths or over-the-counter (OTC) pain relievers such as aspirin, acetaminophen (Tylenol) or ibuprofen (Advil, Motrin) to soothe the pain. **NEVER give aspirin to children/teenagers unless your health care provider**

orders it. It can cause Reye's syndrome, a rare but often fatal condition. CAUTION: Talk to your doctor or pharmacist before taking any other medications, including over-the-counter (OTC) medications, vitamins or herbal supplements.

- Practice stress-management techniques if you experience anxiety or stress with prostate symptoms. (See *Stress*, p. 313.)

Prostate enlargement

Prostate enlargement (*benign prostatic hypertrophy or BPH*) is a noncancerous increase in the size of the prostate gland that appears to be part of the normal aging process; four out of five men between 50 and 60 years of age have this condition. It is not usually a serious problem, but it can become severe enough to compress the urethra and hinder the flow of urine as you urinate.

The hallmark symptom of BPH is *nocturia,* which is the need to get up at night to urinate. Other common symptoms include difficulty starting, stopping or maintaining the flow of urine; a decrease in the force or volume of urine flow; or increased frequency of urination. Symptoms that develop as a result of the condition include increased fatigue (due to difficulty getting back to sleep at night because of nocturia) and mild dehydration (if fluid intake is decreased to avoid having to get up at night).

WHAT YOU CAN DO ✓

- Avoid the use of caffeine, *diuretics* (medications known as water pills that increase fluid loss), alcohol and any over-the-counter (OTC) medications that have warnings related to causing urine retention, such as decongestants.
- Take plenty of time to urinate. Sit on the toilet instead of standing.
- Do not limit your fluid intake unless your doctor puts you on a fluid restricted diet. Try to drink two quarts of water and other fluids throughout the day to help prevent urinary tract infections.
- Don't drink fluids after the evening meal. Empty your bladder before bedtime.
- If you have nocturia, leave a night light on and make sure the path to the bathroom is clear to decrease the risk of falls. You might prefer to keep a urinal at the bedside to avoid getting up at all—especially if you tend to feel dizzy or lightheaded when you first get out of bed.

Prostate cancer

Prostate cancer grows slowly in many cases, remaining within the prostate and causing no health problems. In other cases, however, it spreads aggressively and can become life-threatening. (Prostate cancer is the second leading cause of cancer death in men in the United States.)

Symptoms include decreased strength of the urine stream, difficulty getting urine started or completely stopped, frequent and painful urination, hip or lower-back pain, and blood or pus in the urine.

WHAT YOU CAN DO ✓

While prostate surgery is successful in many cases for localized prostate cancer, it can also result in impotence and urinary incontinence. As a result, men who are diagnosed with the disease may face a difficult dilemma: whether to undergo treatment and take the risk of side effects, or opt for "watchful waiting" and risk the possibility that the cancer will spread.

Watching and waiting—a process in which your doctor closely monitors your condition without treating it—may be appropriate in some situations (for example, if your tumor is small and appears to be growing slowly).

If you and your doctor decide to watch and wait, you'll want to discuss how often you need to go in for checkups. Over time, if your doctor notices a steady increase in your prostate-specific antigen (PSA) level (a sign that the cancer could be spreading), it may be time to discuss a different treatment path.

Important questions to ask your doctor:

- What are my treatment options?
- What are the risks, benefits and possible side effects of each option?
- How will treatment affect my sex life?
- Will the treatment be painful, and if so, how will you treat the pain?
- Will I need to change my normal activities? If so, how and for how long?
- How often will I need to have checkups?

If there is pain associated with urination or ejaculation and an unusual discharge from the penis, see *Sexually Transmitted Diseases,* p. 304. If the question concerns painful or swollen testes or the penis, see p. 302.

If you've seen the doctor but still experience urinary leakage on occasion, try keeping a urine receptacle close by or using incontinence pads to absorb urine, protect clothing and prevent odor. Comfortable, inconspicuous and disposable pads are readily available at grocery stores or drugstores.

Decision *helper* Urinary Problems
DO THESE APPLY:

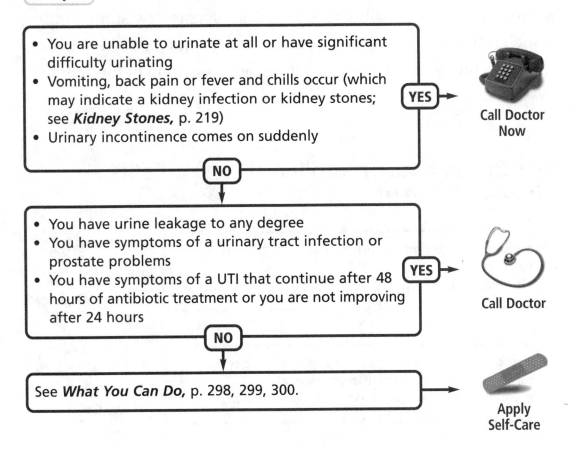

- You are unable to urinate at all or have significant difficulty urinating
- Vomiting, back pain or fever and chills occur (which may indicate a kidney infection or kidney stones; see *Kidney Stones,* p. 219)
- Urinary incontinence comes on suddenly

YES → Call Doctor Now

NO ↓

- You have urine leakage to any degree
- You have symptoms of a urinary tract infection or prostate problems
- You have symptoms of a UTI that continue after 48 hours of antibiotic treatment or you are not improving after 24 hours

YES → Call Doctor

NO ↓

See *What You Can Do,* p. 298, 299, 300.

Apply Self-Care

Painful or Swollen Testes or Penis

Pain, lumps, swelling or changes of any kind in the testes or penis—even if they do not cause pain—may be signs of a problem that needs prompt attention. Possible causes include *torsion* (twisting) of the testicle; internal damage to the testicle due to injury; infection of the lymph glands; a recent case of mumps; accumulation of fluid; or a cyst or tumor.

Decision *helper*   Painful or Swollen Testes or Penis
DO THESE APPLY:

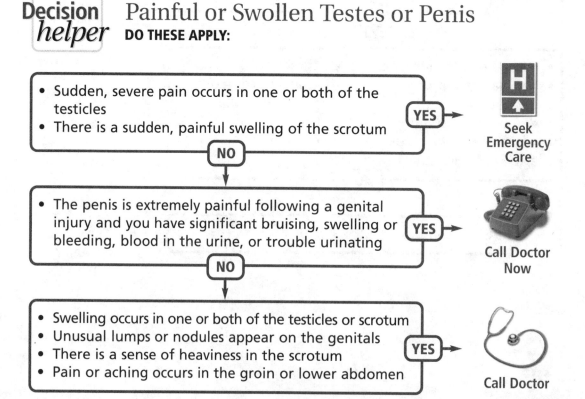

- Sudden, severe pain occurs in one or both of the testicles
- There is a sudden, painful swelling of the scrotum

YES → Seek Emergency Care

NO

- The penis is extremely painful following a genital injury and you have significant bruising, swelling or bleeding, blood in the urine, or trouble urinating

YES → Call Doctor Now

NO

- Swelling occurs in one or both of the testicles or scrotum
- Unusual lumps or nodules appear on the genitals
- There is a sense of heaviness in the scrotum
- Pain or aching occurs in the groin or lower abdomen

YES → Call Doctor

Sexual Health

Just as diet and exercise are important for a healthy heart, maintaining sexual health is important for overall well-being. Sexuality is an important part of life. While many physiological changes may occur with aging, the desire for sexual intimacy (*libido*) does not diminish. Research shows that most men and women remain as sexually active in their later years as they were as young adults.

Many postmenopausal women fear that they will no longer have the desire for sex. Yet many report a renewed interest—partly attributed to the freedom from becoming pregnant and from parenting kids that are now grown and out of the home. Lubricants or hormone replacement therapy (HRT) can help eliminate discomfort caused by menopausal symptoms. (See *HRT*, p. 283.)

Men often worry that they will no longer be able to achieve and maintain an erection. While it is true that the process may take a little longer, this is not a sign of erectile dysfunction (*impotence*). Although the fear of having a heart attack from sex shouldn't be discounted, studies show that the risk is no greater than that caused by getting out of bed in the morning. However, anxiety about sex can lead to lower performance and decreased enjoyment.

The key for a satisfactory sex life at any age is communication. Taking time to enjoy each other allows a woman's natural lubrication process to work and assists a man in achieving and sustaining an erection. It also creates a greater sense of intimacy.

Older adults who understand the physiological and emotional changes of aging and who give their sexuality the same care and attention they do any other aspect of their health are likely to have the most satisfying sex lives. While sperm counts generally decline in older men, the ability to father a child continues. Birth control practices may still be necessary if the female partner is of child-bearing age. Likewise, age does not protect against sexually transmitted diseases (STDs). Older adults having sexual relations outside of a long-term relationship should take the same precautions as younger adults. (See *Safe Sex*, p. 311; *Prevention, HIV*, p. 307.)

Illness and certain medications can diminish libido and cause erectile dysfunction and other problems; discuss these issues with your doctor.

Sexually Transmitted Diseases (STDs)

Most sexually transmitted diseases (STDs) can be prevented by following basic safe sex measures. AIDS poses special risks, including transmission by needles. Although genital herpes is an incurable STD, it can be managed with self-care and medical treatment. Always consult your doctor for diagnosis and treatment.

Signs	Diagnosis	Final Notes
Chlamydia: Caused by bacteria		
General pelvic pain; vaginal discharge, discomfort during sexual intercourse, and/or burning urination (which can occur in both men and women); scrotal swelling or pain in men	Pelvic exam and/or test or culture from the cervix or penis	Treated with antibiotics; if untreated, Chlamydia can cause pelvic inflammatory disease (PID), infertility and complications in pregnancy; and prostatitis, epididymitis or urethritis in men
Genital Herpes: Caused by a virus		
Clusters of blisters in genital, anal or mouth areas; turn into ulcers or sores and heal in one to three weeks; accompanied by mild flu-like symptoms (see *Genital Herpes*, p. 308)	Physical exam; viral culture	Treated with antiviral acyclovir; self-care includes warm sitz baths, cool compresses soaked in aluminum acetate solution (Domeboro, Bluboro, Burow's), witch hazel compresses, a hair dryer set on low to dry blisters, non-prescription pain relievers

Sexually Transmitted Diseases

Signs	Diagnosis	Final Notes
Genital Warts (HPV): Caused by a virus		
Small, fleshy growths in genital, anal or mouth areas; singular or in clusters	Physical exam; can be confirmed by biopsy	Cryotherapy, topical medications, surgical removal; genital warts often reappear after treatment
Gonorrhea: Caused by bacteria		
Men: mucous discharge from penis; slow, painful or difficult urination; **Women**: mucous vaginal discharge; vaginal itching; painful or burning urination	Physical exam and culture of discharge	Untreated gonorrhea can lead to pelvic inflammatory disease (PID) or cause arthritis, infertility and other serious problems; treated with antibiotics
Human Immunodeficiency Virus (HIV): Caused by a virus		
See *HIV*, p. 307	Physical exam and lab tests	Drug treatments for HIV and AIDS are aimed at prolonging life and preventing replication of the virus
Syphilis: Caused by bacteria		
Painless sore on genitals, anus or in mouth two to four weeks after infection, hardening into a painless ulcer then disappearing; swollen lymph nodes, fever, and/or rashes four to six weeks after infection	Blood test, examination of fluid from a sore	Untreated syphilis can lead to blindness, brain damage and heart disease; treated with antibiotics

chart continues next page

Sexually Transmitted Diseases *continued from previous page*

Signs	Diagnosis	Final Notes
Trichomoniasis: Caused by protozoa		
Women: may have no symptoms or: painful or more-frequent-than-usual urination; large amount of white, grayish-green or yellowish vaginal discharge that is offensive in odor; possible burning sensation in vagina with spotting of blood; uncomfortable or swollen pelvic area; painful sexual intercourse; and itchy vulva **Men:** Generally no symptoms: possible frothy discharge from the penis and urinary symptoms	Microscopic examination or culture of discharge	May cause complications such as infections of the urethra or bladder; complications of pregnancy for women; prostate infection for men; treated with a special type of antibiotic

You can greatly reduce the likelihood of contracting STDs by practicing safe sex:

- Always use a latex condom—if you're having sex outside of a long-term relationship.
- Practice monogamy (sex with one person).
- Ask your partner to be tested for STDs.
- Avoid sex with infected individuals.

See *Safe Sex,* p. 311.

Human Immunodeficiency Virus (HIV)

The human immunodeficiency virus (HIV) causes acquired immunodeficiency syndrome (AIDS). If you test positive for HIV, you carry the virus and can infect others but may not have symptoms of the illness for some time. For adults, the average period from infection with the virus to development of AIDS is six to 10 years. After AIDS develops, death usually occurs within two or three years.

HIV is spread by unprotected sexual intercourse; sharing needles or syringes with someone who has HIV; receiving contaminated blood, blood products, organs for transplantation or semen for artificial insemination. It can also spread from mother to fetus during pregnancy or delivery or from mother to infant through breast-feeding.

An estimated 36 million people have HIV/AIDS worldwide and the number is growing.

NOTE YOUR SYMPTOMS ✓

Some people experience symptoms of an acute viral infection within a few months after exposure. The symptoms typically last one to two weeks and resemble infectious mononucleosis: swollen glands, sore throat, fever, *malaise* (feeling lousy) and skin rash. (See *Swollen Glands*, p. 152.) Years may pass before illnesses associated with AIDS appear, including:

- Infections of the lungs, brain, intestines, skin, etc.
- Cancers
- Excessive weight loss (*wasting*)
- Lung diseases such as tuberculosis and recurrent pneumonia
- HIV dementia

PREVENTION ✓

Practice safe sex, which can help prevent HIV and other STDs. Don't use intravenous (IV) drugs, or share needles or syringes.

See *Safe Sex,* p. 311.

NOTE: HIV is not transmitted through saliva, tears, sweat or feces, nor can it be transmitted through mosquito bites, donating blood or contact with inanimate objects such as toilet seats. An infected person who is coughing, talking or eating poses no risk of spreading HIV to others.

Testing for HIV

- Do you suspect you have been exposed to HIV? If so, get tested immediately and repeat the test in six months. Continue testing every three to six months for as long as your high-risk behavior continues.
- Have you had a positive HIV test, but no symptoms of AIDS? Schedule follow-up visits and tests with your doctor.
- Cooperate with your doctor and public health officials in identifying your sex partner(s) so they may be alerted to the possibility of exposure to HIV.

WHAT YOU CAN DO ☑

There is no vaccine for HIV infection and no drug that can cure HIV. Your best strategy for dealing with it is prevention; practice safe sex or abstain from it.

Drug treatments for HIV and AIDS are aimed at prolonging life by preventing replication of the virus. In general, combinations of drugs appear to be most effective. People who test positive for HIV often experience depression and job-security issues, as well as major social and financial challenges. For more information on counseling resources, contact the Centers for Disease Control and Prevention National STD and AIDS hotline, 1-800-342-2437. **Always consult your doctor for diagnosis and treatment.**

Genital Herpes

Herpes simplex virus type 2 causes genital herpes, which infects the genital and *anorectal* (anus and/or rectum) areas. Herpes simplex virus type 1 typically causes fever blisters/cold sores on the lips and mouth. *Herpes* viruses can cause conditions such as chickenpox and mononucleosis.

However, herpes simplex virus type 1 *can* infect the genital area, usually through oral sex, and herpes simplex type 2 can infect the lips or mouth. Once either virus enters the body, you can never be completely free of it. (To avoid genital herpes, always practice safe sex; see *Safe Sex*, p. 311.) However, you can help limit the spread of infection and reduce the discomfort of an outbreak.

During the first outbreak of genital herpes, blisters turn into well-defined ulcers or sores and form crusts that heal within one to three weeks. After the first outbreak, many people experience periodic but milder attacks as smaller clusters of blisters appear; these can last up to 10 days.

WHAT YOU CAN DO ☑

Although there is no cure for genital herpes, these measures can help relieve your discomfort:

- Take five- to 10-minute *sitz baths* (soaking in hip-high, warm water), which can soothe and help promote healing.
- Apply cool compresses soaked in aluminum acetate solution (Domeboro, Bluboro, Burow's) or gently dab herpes sores in the genital or rectal area with pads soaked in witch hazel.
- Use a hair dryer set on low to help dry up blisters.
- Take steps to reduce stress and anxiety to help prevent outbreaks. (See *Stress*, p. 313.)
- Try nonprescription pain relievers (aspirin, acetaminophen or ibuprofen). **NEVER give aspirin to children/teenagers unless your health care provider orders it. It can cause Reye's syndrome, a rare but often fatal condition. CAUTION: Talk to your doctor or pharmacist before taking any other medications, including over-the-counter (OTC) medications, vitamins or herbal supplements.**
- Wash your hands frequently to prevent spreading the disease.

Alerting your sex partner(s)

You will have to tell your sex partner(s) that they have been exposed to the virus so they can be evaluated by a doctor, treated if necessary, and advised to continue checking themselves for herpes outbreaks. If you are hesitant to talk to your sex partner(s), ask your doctor for advice.

Living with herpes

Most people with genital herpes experience itching, tingling or burning in the affected area a day or two before blisters appear. Acyclovir (Zovirax) is the drug most often prescribed for outbreaks. Daily treatment does not eliminate the risk of transmitting the virus, however. Until all sores have healed, the herpes virus is highly contagious.

Avoid sex until all the sores have healed. Because the virus can be spread even when there are no apparent sores, always use a latex condom for your partner's safety. Even though infection can still occur if condoms are used, some protection is better than none. Genital sores from any cause increase the risk of HIV or AIDS. Always practice safe sex.

See *Safe Sex*, p. 311.

FINAL NOTES ☑

The Centers for Disease Control and Prevention (CDC) can provide you with more information about STDs. Call the CDC National STD and AIDS Hotline at 1-800-342-2437.

Decision *helper* Sexually Transmitted Diseases (STDs)
DO THESE APPLY:

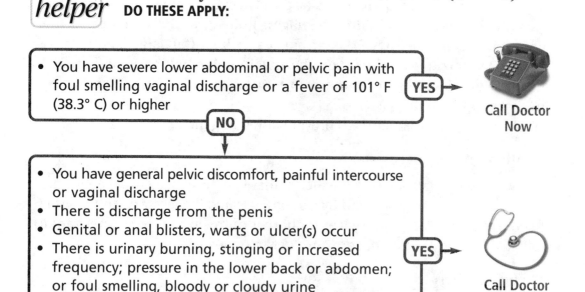

* You have severe lower abdominal or pelvic pain with foul smelling vaginal discharge or a fever of 101° F (38.3° C) or higher   **YES** →

NO

Call Doctor Now

* You have general pelvic discomfort, painful intercourse or vaginal discharge
* There is discharge from the penis
* Genital or anal blisters, warts or ulcer(s) occur
* There is urinary burning, stinging or increased frequency; pressure in the lower back or abdomen; or foul smelling, bloody or cloudy urine   **YES** →
* You may have been exposed to an STD or are currently infected

Call Doctor

Safe Sex

Prevention is the *only* defense against AIDS and the best defense against other sexually transmitted diseases (STDs). Anyone can get AIDS. There is no vaccine to prevent HIV (the virus that causes AIDS) and no cure for AIDS once you have it. It's what you do—not who you are—that puts you at risk.

WHAT YOU CAN DO ☑

Prevention

- Eliminate your risk entirely through *abstinence* (not having sex with anyone) or through *mutual monogamy* (having sex only with a non-infected partner who has sex only with you).
- Unless you are in a monogamous relationship and you and your partner have tested negative for HIV for six months or longer (or you have been in a mutually monogomous relationship since the late 70s):
  - Use a latex condom each time you have sex.
  - Avoid unprotected vaginal, oral and anal sex.
- Don't use "natural" skin condoms. Only latex condoms protect against HIV/STDs. In addition:
  - Always check the condom for tears.
  - Cover the erect penis with the condom before any sexual contact.
  - Keep the condom snugly in place until sexual contact is over.
- If needed, use a water-based lubricant, such as K-Y Jelly, during intercourse. Avoid petroleum-based products, which can weaken the latex barrier.
- Get to know your sexual partner(s) before you have sexual relations, and limit the number of partners you have.

Heterosexual and homosexual behaviors that put you at high risk for contracting
HIV and other STDs include having sex with:
- Intravenous (IV) drug users, or anyone who has had sex with an IV drug user
- Someone who has or has had numerous sexual partners
- Someone who has or has had an STD such as genital herpes, syphilis,
  gonorrhea or any open genital or oral sore
- Someone who received a blood transfusion or blood products between
  1978 and 1985 and has not been tested for HIV
- Male or female prostitutes
- Individuals with questionable HIV status

Mental Health

Aging has its rewards—time to travel, pursue hobbies and enjoy friends and family. But the challenges of growing older—retirement, possible physical problems, the use of certain medications and the loss of friends and loved ones—can contribute to stress, anxiety, depression and grief.

By staying physically and mentally fit through exercise, a nutritious diet, work or other intellectually stimulating activities, you will be better prepared for what could be some of the best years of your life.

Stress

Anyone who has been late for an important appointment or struggled with the family finances knows that stress is a normal and even useful occurrence. Stress in itself is neither good nor bad, but how a person reacts to stress can have a huge impact on his or her well-being.

In stressful situations or emergencies, our bodies automatically increase production of certain hormones. This results in a rise in heart rate and blood pressure, a tensing of muscles to prepare the body for action, an increase in perspiration to cool the body, faster respiration to raise the oxygen supply, and dilation of the pupils to improve vision. These responses, known as the "fight or flight" response, were once vital to the survival of the human race.

Today, we're rarely in life-or-death situations, but our bodies still react to stress in the same old ways. This is particularly clear during times of major life changes such as divorce, illness, loss, unanticipated change or retirement.

Studies show that some older adults tend not to have a "fight or flight" reaction, but rather a passive "freeze" reaction to stress. Inactivity, acceptance, contemplation, apathy and neutrality are quiet responses to common crises, such as illness, loss or unanticipated change. Anxiety, fear or dread without obvious cause or threat, is one way to react to stress. (See *Anxiety,* p. 316.) Grief over the loss of a loved one or something dear to us is another example. (See *Grief,* p. 321.) Stress also can cause depression that might show itself as reclusiveness, irritability or pessimism.

In extreme cases of stress, such as war or natural disaster, post-traumatic stress disorder (PTSD) can develop. It's characterized by the persistent "re-experiencing" of the stressful event with flashbacks and sometimes hallucinations. Other symptoms include avoiding thoughts and feelings about the event, emotional withdrawal, insomnia, irritability, and an exaggerated startle response.

WHAT YOU CAN DO ✓

The physical symptoms of stress can be alleviated if you recognize the sources of stress. For example, if isolation and inactivity are contributing to persistent joint tension or pain, you cannot solve the problem by simply treating the pain. The key is to find ways to minimize or manage the causes of stress.

Look for Creative Solutions

- Would joining a group that engages in some physical activity reduce the stress of isolation and inactivity?
- Are there other people in your neighborhood you could walk with?
- Can home chores be rearranged or taken over by others?

Consider Other Stress Management Tools

- Exercise regularly.
- Pursue hobbies.
- Talk things over with a friend.
- Cry, if that helps you feel better.
- Try stretching, meditation or other muscle-relaxation techniques. The following may be helpful:

Deep breathing: While sitting or lying down, close your eyes and tilt your head forward. Inhale and exhale naturally through your nose. As you exhale, without holding your breath, pause and count "one thousand one, one thousand two." Exhale completely. Repeat for several minutes.

Clearing the mind: Give yourself a mental break by focusing your thoughts on a single, peaceful word, thought or image for five to 10 minutes a day. Reduce distractions as much as possible, sit comfortably and begin deep breathing, as described above. Concentrate on your single thought. Stretch and exhale as you complete the exercise.

Tensing and relaxing: Stretch out comfortably on a carpeted or padded floor. Starting with your toes, tense each group of muscles for five to 10 seconds, then release the tension and relax for 10 to 20 seconds. Continue alternating the tensing and relaxing of your muscles, moving up and down your legs; through your back, neck and shoulders and down your arms. Repeat the process in areas that seem particularly tense.

Stretching: Muscle tension is a physical response to stress, inactivity and (sometimes) overuse. To loosen tight muscles, take a break and try some of these stretches. Remember, it's always a good idea to check with your doctor before starting any new exercises. **If any of the following exercises cause pain, stop them immediately and consult your doctor.**

Back stretch: While sitting on a firm chair, reach out with your hands and bend forward so your upper body rests on your lap. Stretch your arms toward the floor and relax your head and neck. Hold the stretch for a minute, then place your hands on your thighs and press yourself back up to a seated position.

Neck stretch: While looking straight ahead, slowly tilt your head toward one shoulder, then the other. (Do not lift your shoulders or move your head in jerking motions.) Repeat this movement five times.

Shoulder and arm stretch: Lock your hands together by intertwining your fingers; then stretch your arms over your head, with your palms facing up. Hold this stretch for about 30 seconds and repeat it five times with a rest between stretches.

Passive back stretch: Lie with your back on the floor, and rest your knees and lower legs above you on a chair so that your legs are bent at a right angle. As you relax in this position, gently press your lower back against the floor for several minutes. When finished, bring your knees down to the floor to the left or right, and roll over on your side before getting up.

Leg stretch: While standing, place the back of one heel on a low stool or footrest while keeping both legs relatively straight. Slowly lean forward by bending at your hips, reaching for the elevated foot, and keeping your lower back straight. Hold the stretch about 30 seconds and repeat it several times. Stretch the alternate leg in the same manner. (Do not attempt this stretch if you have balance difficulties.)

Upper body stretch: Stand with your legs shoulder-width apart. Reach over your head with your right arm and bend to the left at your waist. Hold the stretch for 30 seconds, being careful not to twist your right hip forward. Switch sides and bend in the opposite direction.

Try to Keep Things in Perspective

- Let go of things that are beyond your control.
- Imagine the worst that could happen in any given situation, the likelihood that it will occur and how you will handle it if it does.
- Consider whether you will even remember this event in a few months or years.

During extremely stressful situations, such as the death of a spouse, close friend or pet, acknowledging your feelings of sadness and loss is an important step toward emotional healing. (See *Grief,* p. 321.)

Anxiety

For older adults, anxiety can be a response to helplessness, isolation and insecurity. Some anxiety is normal; it becomes a disorder when physical and emotional symptoms become overwhelming and interfere with daily life.

Some of the physical symptoms of anxiety include trembling, muscle tension, restlessness, fatigue, breathlessness, a pounding heart, sweating, cold and clammy hands, dry mouth, dizziness, chills or hot flashes, frequent urination or diarrhea, and nausea.

Emotional symptoms are apprehension, excessive worrying, a feeling that something bad is going to happen, poor concentration, excessive startle response, insomnia, irritability or agitation, and depression.

Post-traumatic stress disorder (p. 314) is another example of an anxiety disorder.

WHAT YOU CAN DO ☑

Recognizing and accepting anxiety about certain fears and situations is the first step in reducing symptoms. For example, if you are alone for the first time in your life, it's only natural to feel anxious. Seek out friends, family or a support group and talk about your concerns. Find ways you can either accept or change your situation. Consider whether too much caffeine or medications might be making you anxious. One of the best things you can do is to develop positive expectations for the future. As with any stress-related medical concern, finding the cause of the anxiety is important in eliminating the symptoms.

Hyperventilation Syndrome

Hyperventilation occurs when you breathe too fast. The result is that too much oxygen is taken into your system and the carbon dioxide level in your blood is lowered.

Hyperventilation makes you feel out of breath and can bring on dizziness or numbness and tingling of the hands, feet and mouth. In severe cases, there can be chest pain, spasms of the heart muscles or even unconsciousness.

Hyperventilation syndrome occurs if this happens repeatedly due to anxiety. It usually occurs in anxious or nervous people who develop concerns about their ability to breathe. Hyperventilation syndrome can also be a reaction to severe pain or panic attacks. The cause needs to be determined to eliminate the symptoms.

WHAT YOU CAN DO ☑

If you know someone who has a history of hyperventilating, let him or her know if you notice this tendency. Sometimes people are unaware they are doing it. The goal is to get the person to breathe slower—about one breath every five seconds.

When a person is hyperventilating, he or she should try breathing into a paper bag for five to 15 minutes so that carbon dioxide is taken back into the lungs. The bag should be held loosely over the nose and mouth.

Lump in the Throat

The feeling of a lump in the throat is a common symptom of anxiety. The lump makes it difficult to swallow and usually comes and goes, heightened by anxiety and tension. The symptoms seem worse when you concentrate on swallowing.

Several serious diseases can cause swallowing difficulties. In these cases, the symptoms usually develop slowly, begin while the individual tries to eat solid foods, and progressively gets worse. This condition—more commonly seen in people over 40—can result in weight loss. Call your doctor if you develop these symptoms.

FINAL NOTES ✓

If you feel you can't cope with a problem, talk to a health care professional, counselor, psychiatrist or a member of the clergy. These steps might be particularly helpful if you can't identify the cause of stress but are having troublesome symptoms.

Seek immediate emergency care if you are thinking about suicide or doing physical harm to yourself or others. Call your doctor if you use alcohol or drugs to relieve stress.

Depression

Major depression is a potentially life-threatening physical and mental illness. The classic symptoms are hopelessness and a loss of pleasure in activities that used to be enjoyable. Major depression can be triggered by severe life stresses including the death of a loved one, divorce, serious financial difficulty, chronic illness and chemical dependency—particularly on alcohol.

Older adults are often faced with the additional strain of giving up a former residence, moving to a retirement or nursing home, being alone, fighting illness, experiencing chronic pain, losing a meaningful occupation, or having the nagging feeling that they simply aren't useful anymore.

While chronic illness of any sort can cause depression, some illnesses, such as lupus and Parkinson's disease, seem to include depression as one of their symptoms. Certain medications, including some used to treat high blood pressure and Parkinson's disease, also can cause depression.

Depression can come and go in waves, but the inability to recover from these episodes signals the likelihood of a potential problem requiring some level of professional care.

Unfortunately, despite gains in the past few years, a stigma is still attached to undergoing or seeking treatment for mental illness. Some people may avoid acknowledging their depression to avoid this stigma.

NOTE YOUR SYMPTOMS ✓

Common signs of depression include:

- Unintentional weight loss or gain
- Abnormal sleeping patterns
- Fatigue
- Feelings of worthlessness
- Excessive or inappropriate feelings of guilt

- A decreased ability to concentrate
- Recurrent thoughts of death or suicide
- A suicide attempt
- Withdrawal
- Irritability, anxiety, sadness

People with major mood swings—from depression to elation—may be suffering from a different condition known as *bipolar affective disorder,* previously called manic-depressive illness.

Another form of depression is *seasonal affective disorder,* or SAD. SAD is caused by a lack of exposure to sunlight and often occurs during the winter months, especially among people who live in northern regions.

Symptoms can include lethargy, irritability, chronic headaches, increased appetite, weight gain and the need for more sleep. Episodes may last for several weeks or months.

Many SAD sufferers benefit from *phototherapy,* a medically supervised therapy that consists of daily exposure to intense full-spectrum lights (the ultraviolet wavelengths are filtered out to protect the skin). Relief usually begins in about a week. A vacation to sunnier climates, like Hawaii or the Caribbean, is a much more pleasant, but short-term, solution.

WHAT YOU CAN DO ✓

Some activities that are helpful in cases of mild depression include:

- Getting regular exercise
- Joining a support group or getting involved in group activities
- Talking to someone about your problems
- Decreasing the use of alcohol or other drugs

Major depression is a chronic, debilitating illness that can last from weeks to years. A vast majority of people who suffer from depression would benefit from some form of intervention, in the form of medication, *psychotherapy* (counseling) or both.

Seek emergency care if you have serious thoughts of suicide, with or without a specific plan, or if you have made a suicide attempt. If someone you know has threatened suicide, take those threats seriously. Call a crisis hotline or encourage the person to seek help.

Grief

Grief is a normal response to extreme loss and plays an important role in accepting the transitions of life. Unresolved grief, however, can lead to chronic depression. No one can tell another person how to grieve, but there are generally recognized stages of grief that many people go through. Knowing these may help you deal with some of your own emotions or offer support to another who is grieving.

Stages of grief

Shock and denial: Being unable to believe that the loss has occurred. After a death, the griever may behave as if the dead person is still alive and may "see" or "hear" the person.

Anger: The need to point blame for the loss. Mourners may be angry at a boss for the loss of a job, or at friends, themselves or the deceased after a death.

Depression: Being overwhelmed by the loss and experiencing some or all of the symptoms listed on pages 319 - 320.

It's important to know that grief is an individual process and that a significant loss causes a wide range of feelings. The grief process can be lengthy or short, and the only measure of "successful" grieving is the griever's eventual acceptance of or ability to cope with the loss. There is no "right" order in which to experience the phases of grief. In fact, some of the stages may not be experienced at all.

See *Decision helper,* p. 322.

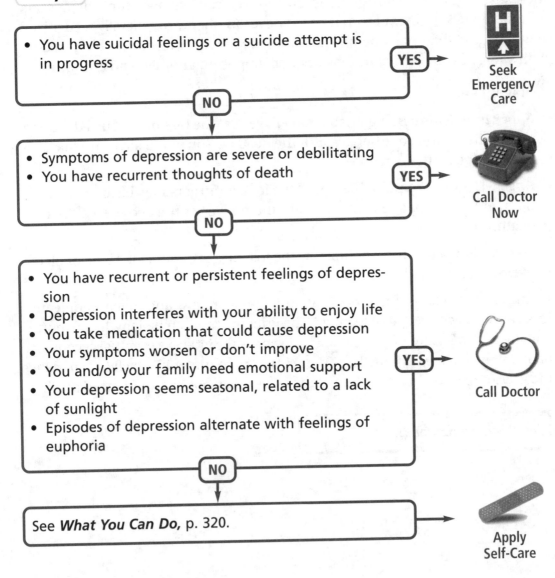

Decision **helper** Depression

DO THESE APPLY:

- You have suicidal feelings or a suicide attempt is in progress   **YES** →

H ↑
Seek Emergency Care

NO ↓

- Symptoms of depression are severe or debilitating
- You have recurrent thoughts of death   **YES** →

Call Doctor Now

NO ↓

- You have recurrent or persistent feelings of depression
- Depression interferes with your ability to enjoy life
- You take medication that could cause depression
- Your symptoms worsen or don't improve
- You and/or your family need emotional support
- Your depression seems seasonal, related to a lack of sunlight
- Episodes of depression alternate with feelings of euphoria   **YES** →

Call Doctor

NO ↓

See *What You Can Do,* p. 320.   →

Apply Self-Care

Insomnia

Insomnia is the inability to enjoy adequate or restful sleep. It can be defined as difficulty falling asleep, frequent awakenings during the night, or waking up too early in the morning.

Acute, *transient* insomnia lasts for less than four weeks and may be due to stress, acute illness or injury, or changes in the sleeping environment.

Chronic insomnia (lasting more than a month) may be caused by depression, anxiety disorders, manic disorders, chronic pain syndromes, heart and circulation disorders, kidney disease, menopause, or *sleep apnea,* in which breathing is temporarily interrupted by airway obstruction. More than 300 over-the-counter (OTC) and prescription drugs also can contribute to acute and chronic insomnia, including alcohol, caffeine, cardiac medications, nicotine, amphetamines and decongestants.

Behaviors that can cause or aggravate insomnia include vigorous exercise or mental exertion before bedtime, chronic use of sleeping pills, staying in bed too long in the morning or napping too much during the day.

WHAT YOU CAN DO ✓

Practice any of the following to promote restful sleep:

- Exercise on a regular basis (but avoid exercising within two hours of bedtime).
- Take a warm bath or drink warm milk before bed.
- Establish a regular bedtime routine that includes relaxing activities such as reading for pleasure.
- Reserve the bedroom for sleep and sex.
- Avoid drinking alcohol and smoking before bedtime.
- Drink caffeine in moderation, before noon only.
- Do not nap.

You can gain insights into improving your sleep by keeping a diary of your sleep patterns and behaviors.

Decision *helper*   Insomnia   **DO THESE APPLY:**

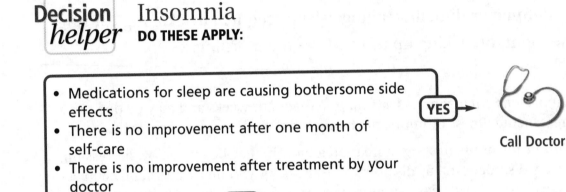

- Medications for sleep are causing bothersome side effects
- There is no improvement after one month of self-care
- There is no improvement after treatment by your doctor

YES → Call Doctor

NO

See *What You Can Do,* p. 323.

→ Apply Self-Care

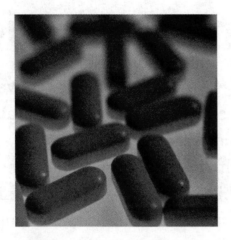

SECTION 4
Medications

Using Medications

The body's response to medications changes over the years. In later life, the body becomes more sensitive to chemicals and drugs. A dose of medicine that is correct and safe for a young adult often needs to be in a different form or amount for a child or an older adult. Age affects the body's ability to absorb, use and eliminate medications. This may cause the medicine's effects to last longer and the level of medication in the bloodstream to be higher than desired. A 65-year-old is twice as likely to have unwanted side effects from medicines as a 35-year-old, and an 80-year-old is four times more likely to experience side effects.

Modern medicines can help keep our lives more active and comfortable. Unfortunately, medications are often overused in the older population. If you are over the age of 65, you are likely to be taking at least four medications. All medicines (prescription and nonprescription) have the risk of interacting and producing undesired results. Nearly one in seven hospitalizations of older adults is due to problems with medications.

OTC and Prescribed Drugs

All medications must be cautiously and wisely used. *Over-the-counter* (OTC) drugs—those that do not require a prescription—can have as many side effects as prescription drugs. In fact, many of today's OTC drugs are medications that were once available only by prescription. One of the most common OTC drugs, aspirin, is a very effective and useful medicine that can affect the body's temperature system; relieve pain; decrease inflammation; alter blood clotting; and help decrease the risk of heart attack, stroke and cancers in the digestive system; but it can also irritate the stomach lining and affect kidney function. Because of its widespread use, aspirin is often mistakenly thought to be harmless.

Some of today's medicines are based on historical herbal and natural preparations that can affect the body. **All medications, both OTC and prescribed, as well as herbal or "home remedies" and high doses of vitamins and health tonics can affect the body's response and alter the action of other drugs you take.**

Follow Directions

- **Ask your doctor or pharmacist about how to take your medicines.** Find out how much, how often and when. It is important to know which can be taken together and which should be taken with food.
- **Ask your doctor how long you may need to take a particular drug.** If more is needed, have your prescription refilled before running out of the medication. It is important not to miss doses.
- **Ask your doctor or pharmacist about the medicine.** Know why you are taking it, what you can expect from it and how soon, what side effects you should report, what you should do if you miss a dose, and when you need to check back.
- **Establish a routine and particular location for your medications.** Unless young children are around, set out all of your medicines for the week using a special medication holder, egg carton or cupcake pan, especially if you have trouble remembering whether you've taken your daily doses. Or, use a calendar and mark off when you have taken your medicines. Take your medicines at a time of day that is easy to remember, like mealtimes or bedtime, or set a timer to remind you. If you still have trouble remembering, a family member, friend or visiting nurse can assist you in setting up a system and give you a reminder call.
- **If you have difficulty with your medication schedule, talk to your doctor.** There may be a way to simplify the schedule or find alternative medicines.
- **Never abruptly stop a prescribed medication without first consulting your doctor.** Some medicines must be tapered off slowly to be safe; some of your other medicines may need to be adjusted when one is stopped.

WHAT YOU CAN DO ✓

- Tell all of your doctors and pharmacists about all of the medicines you are taking (OTC and prescription) to prevent a reaction between drugs. Having all of your prescriptions filled at the same pharmacy is a good idea.
- Bring a written list of all of your medicines or all medicine bottles to your medical appointments.

- Read labels of all medicines carefully for correct usage and potential side effects.
- Take the correct dosage as prescribed—no more and no less.
- Consult your doctor and pharmacist before taking *any* OTC drug, particularly if you are taking an *MAO* (monoamine oxidase) inhibitor or if you have a serious chronic condition such as asthma, diabetes, epilepsy, glaucoma, enlarged prostate, dementia, high blood pressure or heart disease.
- Never share or trade prescription drugs with anyone. The interaction of medications you take needs to be considered by your doctor for safety, and some drugs may have adverse side effects because of a condition you may have. (See *Medications That Can Cause Problems,* this page.)
- Store all medications out of the reach of children.
- Throw out medications when they reach their expiration date.
- Ask your doctor if there are other treatment options that may not include drugs, or if a less expensive but equally effective generic form of the drug is available.
- When starting a new medicine, ask your doctor if there are sample packages. If a sample is available, try the new medicine for a few days to see if you have any intolerable side effects before having the prescription filled. Once a prescription has been filled the medication cannot be returned.

A properly stocked home medicine cabinet can help you be prepared for common illnesses and minor emergencies and help you avoid unnecessary trips to the doctor and pharmacy. (See *First-Aid Supplies,* p. 336.)

Medications That Can Cause Problems with Certain Health Concerns

In addition to notifying your doctors and pharmacists about all the medications you take—to guard against any possible drug interactions—it's important to tell them about other medical conditions you have, even if these conditions seem unrelated to your current concern. Some prescription or OTC medications commonly taken for one condition can have adverse effects on your health. The chart on the following pages lists some common health concerns and some of the medications that should be discussed with your doctor; they are not the only ones.

Disease/Drug Interactions

If this health concern applies to you:	These medications should be discussed with your doctor:
Heart Failure	Some eye drops used to treat glaucoma (such as timolol, Betagan C); calcium channel blockers (such as verapamil, nifedipine, diltiazem); and some antacids containing calcium, aluminum or sodium (such as Rolaids, Tums, Mylanta or Bromo-Seltzer)
Dementia	Most antihistamines (contained in many cold, allergy and sleeping pills); antidepressants or antipsychotics (such as Elavil or Stelazine); gastrointestinal antispasmodics (such as dicyclomine, Bentyl, Pro-Banthine); and *opioid* (narcotic) pain killers (such as Demerol, codeine) or any medications that impair memory or judgment
Depression	Beta blockers (such as Inderal, Tenormin, Corgard, Lopressor); and indomethacin, a nonsteroidal anti-inflammatory and *analgesic* (pain killer)
Diabetes	Beta blockers (such as Inderal, Tenormin, Corgard, Lopressor); corticosteroids (such as prednisone, betamethasone); laxatives that contain large amounts of *dextrose* (sugar); most antihistamines and decongestants; and Vasodilan, a medication commonly given for senility
Enlarged Prostate	Some eye drops used to treat glaucoma (such as timolol, Betagan C); beta blockers (such as Inderal, Tenormin, Corgard, Lopressor); calcium channel blockers (such as verapamil, nifedipine, diltiazem); gastrointestinal antispasmodics (such as dicyclomine, Bentyl, Pro-Banthine); certain antidepressants (such as Elavil, doxepin, imipramine); and any drugs containing atropine (an ingredient in many cold pills)

chart continues next page

Disease/Drug Interactions *continued from previous page*

If this health concern applies to you:	These medications should be discussed with your doctor:
Gastric Ulcers	Aspirin or ibuprofen (sometimes used in cold and allergy medications); niacin supplements (for treating high cholesterol and vitamin B₃ deficiency); and corticosteroids (such as prednisone, betamethasone)
Glaucoma	Most antihistamines (contained in many cold, allergy and sleeping pills); antidepressants or antipsychotics (such as Elavil or Stelazine); gastrointestinal antispasmodics (such as dicyclomine, Bentyl, Pro-Banthine); and many antidyskinetics that are used to treat Parkinson's disease (such as Cogentin, procyclidine)
Erectile Dysfunction (impotence)	Many drugs used to treat high blood pressure: beta blockers (such as Inderal, Tenormin, Corgard, Lopressor), Aldomet and Catapres; *opioids* (narcotics), such as codeine, Darvon, Percocet; barbiturates (such as phenobarbital); and medications used to treat ulcers (such as Tagamet)
Incontinence	Diuretics (such as Lasix, hydrochlorothiazide); antihistamines (contained in many cold, allergy and sleeping pills); sleeping pills and tranquilizers (such as benzodiazepines, Valium); *opioids* (narcotics), such as Darvon, Percocet; and gastrointestinal antispasmodics (such as dicyclomine, Bentyl, Pro-Banthine)
Kidney Failure	Certain medications that are excreted primarily by the kidneys (such as aspirin, ibuprofen); medications used to treat heart failure, high blood pressure or scleroderma (such as captopril, Vasotec); and potassium and vitamin A supplements

Home Pharmacy

A properly stocked home medicine cabinet can help you prepare for common complaints and emergencies and help you avoid unnecessary trips to the doctor and pharmacy. The following are some suggested items for your "home pharmacy" and first-aid kit. **But remember to talk to your doctor or pharmacist before taking any other medications, including over-the-counter (OTC) medications, vitamins or herbal supplements.**

Nonprescription Drugs

How it works	Risks	Comments
Acid Reducers		
Decrease gastric acid production	Interact with some medicines and foods and should not be used in the presence of some diseases; read directions carefully	Don't use longer than two weeks without seeing your doctor
Antacids		
Relieve heartburn or stomach upset by neutralizing acid	Some can cause constipation, others loosen stools; some brands are high in sodium and should be avoided by those on low-salt diets	Avoid long-term use

chart continues next page

Nonprescription Drugs *continued from previous page*

How it works	Risks	Comments
Antidiarrheals		
Relieve diarrhea by thickening stools and/or slowing intestinal spasms	Do not use if you have a fever; prolonged use can lead to constipation or absorb bacteria that aid digestion. **Do not give Pepto-Bismol to children/ teenagers, it can cause Reye's syndrome (due to an aspirin-like ingredient), a rare but often fatal condition.**	Diarrhea is the body's way of flushing out infection, so use antidiarrheals only when necessary; replace body fluids depleted by diarrhea; drugs with bismuth may darken the tongue or stools; consult doctor before using attapulgite (Kaopectate) or loperamide (Imodium) for children under 3 years of age
Antifungal Preparations		
Clear up skin fungal infections, such as athlete's foot and jock itch	Few risks; preparations with selenium sulfide can burn skin if used excessively	
Antihistamines/Decongestants		
Antihistamines dry mucous membranes to relieve runny nose, watery eyes and itching; *decongestants* shrink swollen membranes; buy one or the other, rather than a combined medication, to treat specific symptoms	Some antihistamines can cause drowsiness; decongestants can cause agitation or insomnia; both can cause problems for people with certain medical conditions	Consult doctor before giving either antihistamines or decongestants to children under 12 months of age

Nonprescription Drugs

How it works	Risks	Comments
Antiseptics		
Clean wounds and prevent infection	**Do not use.** Harsh antiseptics like iodine, mercurochrome, Merthiolate and full-strength hydrogen peroxide can harm delicate tissues and inhibit healing; plain soap and water is all that is needed to cleanse wounds	Wash wounds thoroughly with plenty of soap and running water
Cough Suppressants/Expectorants		
Suppressants control the coughing reflex to reduce dry, hacking coughs; *expectorants* thin mucus to make it easier to expel phlegm	Some should not be taken by people with certain health conditions; can interact with sedatives and some antidepressants; can contain alcohol; read directions carefully	Coughs help remove phlegm to clear respiratory tract, so suppressing them may be counter-productive; products with guaifenesin help you cough up phlegm; those with dextromethorphan suppress coughs
Laxatives		
Stimulate intestines to prompt bowel movement during constipation; bulking agents soften stool	Few side effects if taken as directed; regular use can decrease muscle tone in the intestines and cause reliance on laxatives	Take laxatives with plenty of water; regular use can interfere with the body's absorption of vitamin D and calcium

chart continues next page

Nonprescription Drugs *continued from previous page*

How it works	Risks	Comments
Nasal Sprays/Nose Drops		
Shrink swollen mucous membranes to encourage free breathing; relieve runny nose and post-nasal drip	Should not be used for more than three days in a row; prolonged use can cause more swelling than before using the spray or drops	Less likely than oral decongestants to interact with other drugs; provide temporary relief
Nonsteroidal Anti-inflammatories (NSAIDs) (aspirin, ibubrofen, naprosyn)		
Help relieve swelling and pain in muscles and joints, as well as fever	NSAIDs can pose danger to those on blood thinners; do not exceed dosage limits; aspirin can irritate the stomach, cause bleeding or ulcers, and is the most common cause of child poisonings; aspirin and ibuprofen should be taken with food to avoid stomach irritation. **NEVER give aspirin to children/ teenagers unless your health care provider orders it. It can cause Reye's syndrome, a rare but often fatal condition.**	Daily, low doses of aspirin may help prevent heart attack, stroke and the risk of cancers in the digestive system; naprosyn is similar to ibuprofen in its uses and risks
Pain/Fever Medication (acetaminophen) — also see Nonsteroidal Anti-inflammatories (NSAIDs) above		
Reduces fever and pain	Excessive use of acetaminophen can contribute to liver damage, especially in heavy drinkers	Acetaminophen is ineffective against inflammation; available in liquid form; milder to stomach than NSAIDs; do not exceed dosage limits

Nonprescription Drugs

How it works	Risks	Comments
Skin Irritation Medication (hydrocortisone)		
Acts as an anti-inflammatory to temporarily relieve itching from rashes, insect bites, hives and poison ivy	Excessive use can damage the skin; generally safe if used for two weeks or less; should not be used on infected skin or near eyes	Suppresses the itch reflex, but does not cure the rash; use only as much as rubs easily into the skin
Other Topical Anti-itch Medications (calamine, pramoxine, aloe vera)		
Relieve itching in a variety of ways—cooling, mild anesthetic, soothing	Topical anti-itch medications containing antihistamines may be skin-sensitizing	Avoid use on open sores or wounds

First-Aid Supplies

In addition to over-the-counter (OTC)/nonprescription drugs, a well-stocked home medicine cabinet should include some first-aid supplies and a first-aid manual. You can put together the elements of a first-aid kit by gathering the items listed here, or you can purchase first-aid kits for your home, car, boat or other use at drugstores or through organizations such as the American Red Cross. First-aid manuals are also available at these locations.

First-Aid Items/Uses

Assorted Band-Aids/Butterfly Bandages: Cover and protect small scrapes and cuts from dirt and moisture; butterfly bandages can bring the edges of a cut together

Tweezers: Help remove large dirt particles from wounds and dislodge splinters

Ice Bag: Reduces swelling from injuries; can provide relief from headaches

Cotton/Cotton-tipped Swabs: Useful in cleaning wounds and lifting foreign matter from eyes; do not use inside the ear

Thermometer: Helps detect fever; electronic thermometers are preferred

Gauze Pads/Adhesive Tape: Large bandages for wounds or scrapes that can't be covered with adhesive bandages

Sharp Scissors: For cutting gauze rolls and removing jagged edges from scraped or torn skin

Heating Pad: Speeds the healing process after swelling subsides; may relieve headaches; always set on low

Anaphylactic Kit (for people with previous severe allergic reaction)**:** To treat life-threatening allergic reactions; available by prescription

SECTION 5
Prevention

Getting and Staying Healthy

There are many steps you can take to slow the effects of aging and maintain your good health. Excellent places to start include eating a healthy diet; controlling your weight; staying active; avoiding alcohol and tobacco; getting necessary checkups, screenings and immunizations; and preventing accidents and injuries.

Most of these healthy behaviors—especially avoiding alcohol and smoking, eating a low-fat diet and exercising—may also decrease your risk of cancer, heart disease and diabetes. (See index for specific topics.)

The good news is that it's never too late! By adopting a positive attitude and making healthy lifestyle choices, you can dramatically enhance the quality of your life.

Eating Right

Making wise food choices is an important element in a healthy lifestyle for people of all ages, and it is even more important as you get older.

Malnutrition (not consuming enough foods containing proper nutrients) is a common problem among older adults. One reason is that the body's ability to absorb nutrients declines with age. Taking multiple drugs—as many older adults do—can hamper the body's ability to absorb nutrients and also diminish your appetite. (See *Using Medications,* p. 326.) What's more, the tongue loses some of its taste buds as you age, so foods that were once flavorful may taste bland and unappealing. Dental problems may also make it more difficult to eat. (See *Mouth Concerns,* p. 161.) Other factors that may contribute to malnutrition include the expense of buying food or meals, the isolation of eating alone and the effort of fixing meals.

Just as detrimental as not eating *enough* of the right foods is eating *too much.* Excessive body weight stresses the heart, muscles and bones. It increases the likelihood of heart disease, diabetes, as well as hernias, hemorrhoids, gallbladder disease and varicose veins. It can also aggravate arthritis and other chronic conditions.

A healthy diet—low-fat, low-calorie, high-fiber—combined with regular exercise (see *Staying Active,* p. 343) reduces these risks by controlling blood sugar levels, lowering blood pressure and cholesterol levels and helping you stay strong and healthy.

Diet and Nutrition

The goal of a healthy diet is to eat a wide range of foods every day from each of the major food groups: the bread, cereal, rice and pasta group; the vegetable group; the fruit group; the milk, yogurt and cheese group; and the meat, poultry, fish, dry beans, eggs and nuts group. Stay away from foods that are high in fat and sugar. They provide calories, but not the nutrients you need.

The Food Guide Pyramid (see Figure 28) illustrates the six basic food groups and the daily amounts of various foods you should eat to get all the needed nutrients. Select the bulk of your food from the lower levels of the pyramid, with emphasis on fruits, vegetables and whole grains (whole-grain, rather than refined rice, pasta and bread).

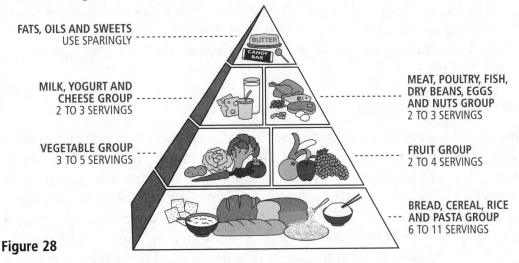

FATS, OILS AND SWEETS
USE SPARINGLY

BUTTER
CANDY BAR

MILK, YOGURT AND
CHEESE GROUP
2 TO 3 SERVINGS

MEAT, POULTRY, FISH,
DRY BEANS, EGGS
AND NUTS GROUP
2 TO 3 SERVINGS

VEGETABLE GROUP
3 TO 5 SERVINGS

FRUIT GROUP
2 TO 4 SERVINGS

BREAD, CEREAL, RICE
AND PASTA GROUP
6 TO 11 SERVINGS

Figure 28

U.S. Department of Agriculture/U.S. Department of Health and Human Services

Cutting Back on Fat

While some dietary fat is essential for good health, most people consume too much of it. Excessive dietary fat contributes to aging and certain diseases such as atherosclerosis (see *CAD*, p. 181) and cancer. Evidence is especially strong for the connection between dietary fat and colon cancer. (See *Colon Cancer*, p. 224.) Foods most strongly associated with an increased risk of colon cancer are beef, pork and lamb. Other especially high-fat foods include whole milk, butter, eggs and other animal fats.

To limit your fat intake:

- Eat grains and beans or legumes—instead of animal protein—whenever possible. Fish and skinless poultry (such as turkey or chicken) are animal proteins that are lower in fat. When you eat red meat, use leaner cuts.
- Try nonfat or low-fat milk, yogurt and cheese.
- Substitute fresh vegetables, graham crackers or low-fat yogurt for fat-laden snacks such as potato chips or cookies.
- Use oils sparingly and choose those lowest in saturated fat and cholesterol: canola, corn, olive, sesame, soybean and sunflower.
- Try steaming, boiling, baking, grilling or braising. Sauté foods in broth, water or wine instead of oil.
- Because food-package claims can be misleading, read their labels carefully for information related to fat. (Every U.S. food product label now displays a "Nutrition Facts" section.) Avoid buying foods with more than three grams of fat per 100 calories. Look for "fat-free" (less than 0.5 gram of fat per serving) and low-fat (three grams of fat or less per serving) products, and lean or extra lean meats.

Good Cholesterol/Bad Cholesterol

Watch your cholesterol. Cholesterol has two components: low-density lipoprotein (LDL) and high-density lipoprotein (HDL). LDL is called the "bad" cholesterol because it can make cholesterol gather on the walls of your arteries, contributing to coronary artery disease. HDL, the "good" cholesterol, prevents blockage of the arteries by carrying cholesterol away from coronary artery walls. In general, your LDL should be below 130 mg/dL (milligrams per deciliter) and your HDL should be above 40 mg/dL. Your total cholesterol should be below 200 mg/dL.

To lower your LDL and raise your HDL, exercise regularly and, if you smoke, start taking steps to kick the habit. Also, eat foods with reduced cholesterol or less than one gram of saturated fat per 100 calories. Use fats and oils sparingly and choose those lowest in saturated fat and cholesterol: canola, corn, olive, safflower, sesame, soybean and sunflower. Avoid "trans-fatty acids," which are listed as "hydrogenated" or "partially hydrogenated" fat in the ingredients of many packaged and fast foods and margarines.

Fiber and Salt

Eat more fiber. The fiber in fruits, vegetables, beans and peas helps lower cholesterol and reduce your risk of heart disease. Fiber in whole-grain products provides bulk to give you a "full" feeling, and both types help prevent constipation.

Go easy with the salt shaker. Excess salt can raise your blood pressure and increase your risk of stroke, heart attack or kidney failure. Season foods with spices and herbs instead and watch out for high levels of salt in canned and packaged foods.

Sugar and Starch

Your ability to digest large amounts of sugar and refined grains, which are broken down into glucose in the body, rapidly decreases as you get older. This means your *glucose* (blood sugar) climbs higher after eating sugar than it did when you were younger. While it's not necessary to avoid these foods completely, it's wise to eat them in moderation.

It is not uncommon for older adults to develop *diabetes* (an elevation of glucose caused by inadequate amounts of insulin in the body), so alert your doctor if you notice any of the symptoms. (See *Diabetes*, p. 226.)

Vitamins and Herbal Supplements

If you're eating a well-balanced diet that includes fresh fruits and vegetables, meat and dairy products, taking vitamin and mineral supplements is usually not necessary. If you have trouble eating a well-balanced diet, however, taking multivitamins may be helpful. Your doctor can advise you on appropriate and safe dosages. Also, if you have *osteoporosis* (loss of bone mass) or are at high risk for the disease, ask your doctor about calcium and vitamin D supplements. (See *Osteoporosis*, p. 238).

Herbal supplements sold in health food stores are very popular these days for everything from treating the flu to helping you lose weight. Unfortunately, there is limited scientific proof that herbal supplements can actually help you. What's more, most are not currently evaluated for safety and effectiveness, so taking them may be risky. At the very minimum, don't take them for serious diseases such as cancer, heart disease and arthritis. Also, keep your doctor informed about any supplements you're taking to avoid interactions with other medications. (See *Using Medications*, p. 326.)

* **CAUTION: Talk to your doctor or pharmacist before taking any other medications, including over-the-counter (OTC) medications, vitamins or herbal supplements.**

Maintaining a Healthy Weight

If weight loss is a goal for you, avoid the impulse to slim down rapidly. As appealing as this may seem, it frequently leads to a frustrating and unhealthy "yo-yo" cycle of quick weight loss followed soon afterward by weight gain.

By concentrating instead on long-term, sensible dietary changes and regular exercise, your weight should gradually normalize and your health should improve. Talk to your doctor about establishing reasonable weight loss goals.

Staying Active

Many people become less physically active as they age—so it becomes more and more important to get enough exercise. Older adults benefit from regular exercise as much as younger people. Age doesn't have to be an automatic limitation and it's never too late to begin. In fact, most people find that—as they exercise and become more physically fit—they feel better and have more energy.

Regular exercise can lower your blood pressure, prevent constipation and improve sleep. It also reduces your risk of serious illnesses (and their complications) such as diabetes (see *Diabetes*, p. 226), coronary artery disease (see *Heart Disease*, p. 181) and cancer. Exercise also improves strength and stamina; controls weight; reduces stress levels; improves your ability to cut down or stop smoking (see *Smoking Cessation*, p. 346); makes you less likely to experience shortness of breath or fatigue; and improves your overall quality of life. Exercise is a vital component of good health—whatever your age.

Choosing an Exercise Program

You don't have to be an athlete to benefit from exercise, and it doesn't have to take a lot of time. Many extremely beneficial forms of exercise don't require any special athletic abilities, in fact.

The Surgeon General advises adults to exercise at least 30 minutes on most, if not all, days of the week. You can split these into several 10 or 15-minute sessions. Regular and brisk exercises such as walking, jogging, cycling and swimming are excellent ways to improve the efficiency of your heart and lungs and burn a significant amount of calories. Informal exercise—such as using the stairs instead of the elevator, playing golf, bowling, strolling with friends, doing housework or gardening—offer health benefits to a lesser but still important degree, including increasing your flexibility and muscle strength. In addition, light exercise can be fun and pleasurable, and it can provide opportunities for socializing.

The key to a successful exercise program is choosing an activity—or activities—that you will enjoy on a regular basis for months and years to come. It's also important to consider your physical capabilities. If you have heart or lung problems, start with slow walking or stretching in place. If you suffer from arthritis, you'll want to choose an activity that doesn't cause further pain (swimming is an excellent choice). If you have problems with your balance, exercise while seated.

Consult your doctor before starting any exercise program. If you've had a heart attack, surgery, joint problems or other chronic or acute illnesses, your doctor can help you choose a program that is safe, effective and right for you. If you have temporary or permanent physical limitations, a physical therapist can recommend modified exercises that suit your situation.

Before getting started, also make sure you have athletic shoes that provide cushioning, heel and ankle support and stability. Some athletic shoes are designed for specific activities such as running, aerobics and walking. Cross-training shoes combine characteristics of many types of athletic shoes and can be used for multiple activities.

Well-rounded exercise

A well-rounded exercise program includes:

- **A warm-up period and stretching exercises.** Cold muscles injure easily, so it's essential to warm up before stretching. Just do your regular exercise activity at an easy pace for five to 10 minutes. Next, begin slowly stretching specific muscle groups—shoulders, back, hips, thighs, calves and ankles—to help your muscles limber up and prevent stiffness. Stretch slowly and avoid bouncing and jerking movements.
- *Aerobic* **(endurance) exercises** (brisk walking, jogging, cycling, swimming, dancing, cross-country skiing or jumping rope). Aerobic exercises raise and sustain your heart rate for a period of time, burn calories and strengthen your heart and lungs. Whichever exercises you choose, they should be sustained for at least 12 to 15 minutes for you to achieve cardiovascular benefits. You should be able to talk or laugh without difficulty while you exercise—even during the most strenuous parts. If you can't, slow down.

- **Strengthening exercises** (push-ups, sit-ups, pull-ups or working with barbells, elastic bands or weight machines). These exercises strengthen your abdominal and back muscles (decreasing the risk of back injury) and the muscles around knee joints (protecting the knees from injuries).
- **A cool-down (recovery) period.** Slow down gradually, then exercise at a relaxed pace for at least five minutes. Never stand still after vigorous exercise. In cold weather, warm up and cool down indoors.

Starting slowly and overcoming setbacks

The most common cause of injury is exercising too aggressively, too soon. Instead, start gradually and slowly increase the time and intensity of your exercise program. This will give your muscles and joints time to adjust to exercising. Also, a gradual start will increase the likelihood that you will stick with your program until it becomes routine.

If you skip exercising for a day or two, don't get discouraged. Just get back into your routine as soon as you can. If the exercise you've chosen is too strenuous or causes injuries, slow down or switch to something else. If you can keep up your exercise program for the first month, it will most likely become a regular habit you look forward to and enjoy.

Smoking Cessation

Each year, approximately 430,000 Americans die as a result of using tobacco, and many of them are older adults.

Cigarettes, pipe tobacco, cigars, snuff and chewing tobacco all contain *nicotine,* a highly addictive and unhealthy substance. Using tobacco increases your risk of developing numerous illnesses such as coronary artery disease (CAD), strokes, emphysema, chronic bronchitis, pneumonia, atherosclerosis, lung cancer and a variety of other cancers. (Although chewing tobacco may not threaten the respiratory system, it can still cause a number of health problems, including cancer of the mouth.)

Smoking tobacco can worsen symptoms of asthma and allergies and, even if you don't smoke, evidence shows that inhaling *secondhand smoke* (smoke from others who are smoking) can still make you ill. In addition, smoking is one of the leading causes of accidental death due to fires among older adults. (See *Fires,* p. 357.)

It's Never Too Late

The more you have smoked over your lifetime, the more likely you are to develop smoking-related illnesses. However, it's *never* too late to stop smoking and enjoy positive health benefits. Within 12 hours of your last cigarette, your body begins to repair the damage to your heart and lungs. Your risk of lung cancer starts to decline about one year after you kick the habit, and by the time you've been a nonsmoker for 10 or 15 years, your risk of cancer is about the same as that of people who have never smoked. Kicking the habit may not be easy— but it's definitely worth the effort.

Kicking the Habit—Forever

The first step in giving up tobacco products is to resolve to become—and remain—a non-user. The next step is to find ways to replace the mental and physical pleasures of nicotine with other less harmful substitutes—a process that takes planning, preparation, perseverance and moral support.

Preparing to quit smoking

- Begin "getting in shape" for quitting by incorporating regular physical activity into your lifestyle (see *Staying Active*, p. 343), adopting a healthy diet (see *Eating Right*, p. 338), and practicing relaxation skills (see *Stress*, p. 313). These lifestyle improvements can provide pleasurable sensations similar to the ones you're getting from nicotine.
- Choose a partner who's readily available to give support and encouragement. (It's most effective if this person does not use tobacco.) Tell other friends and family members you are quitting and ask for their support.
- Consider quitting with someone else. You can offer each other support and help each other through difficult times.
- Start cutting back on tobacco gradually and set a date for quitting completely (within a month or six weeks, for example).

Once you quit smoking

- Have your car, carpets and upholstery cleaned as soon as you quit smoking; then make your car and home nonsmoking environments for any friends or family members who still use tobacco.
- Brush your teeth as soon as you wake up in the morning and right after meals so you have a fresh taste in your mouth.
- If you associate coffee with smoking, drink tea or another beverage instead. Or have coffee while doing an activity that keeps your hands busy, so you can minimize the urge to reach for a "smoke."
- Keep low-calorie snacks, sugarless gum or toothpicks on hand.
- Sit in nonsmoking sections of restaurants. Plan other activities in nonsmoking environments such as shopping centers and movie theaters.
- Congratulate and reward yourself frequently for quitting.

Handling setbacks

If you backslide on occasion (by having a cigarette or two), recognize the lapse as a small setback. Just get rid of any tobacco you may have bought, figure out the reason for the lapse, and make plans for how you're going to better handle the situation next time. That might involve getting out of the house for a walk, taking a shower or calling your partner or another supportive friend.

Getting help

While some people are able to quit using tobacco without any formal help, others need assistance—and it's readily available. For example, nicotine replacement products like patches and gum help many people minimize withdrawal symptoms after they've stopped smoking. Talk to your doctor if you're interested in one of these approaches. Smoking cessation workshops and support groups are also helpful.

For information about programs in your area, contact your local chapter of the American Cancer Society or the American Lung Association.

Alcohol Use

Drinking alcohol in moderation—a glass of wine or a beer with dinner, for example—is usually nothing to be concerned about. However, remember that your body may react differently to alcohol than it did when you were younger and your tolerance for alcohol may be reduced.

Alcohol abuse is a serious problem that needs prompt attention. Until recently, older problem drinkers tended to be overlooked by both health professionals and the general public due to perceived low numbers. This is because chronic problem drinkers—who abuse alcohol off and on for most of their lives—often die before becoming older adults. Also, older adults—who may be retired or have fewer social contacts—often hide their drinking problems, and family members, friends and medical professionals may not see the signals. Alcohol abuse can occur at any age, even if the problem doesn't materialize until late in life.

Heavy drinkers experience an increase in health risks, including *cirrhosis* (a severe, chronic disease of the liver); obesity; high blood pressure; cancer of the esophagus, throat and mouth, as well as breast cancer in women; and traffic accidents or accidents at home.

Some alcoholics develop a form of *dementia* (memory problems) or *asterixes* (tremor or jerky movements), and alcoholism may cause or accelerate *osteoporosis* (progressive loss of bone mass). (See *Osteoporosis*, p. 238.) Among older adults, one of the most frequent problems brought on by excessive use of alcohol is depression, which can have a negative impact on all areas of a person's life. (See *Depression*, p. 319.)

Overcoming Alcoholism

The good news is that many people successfully overcome alcoholism. The first essential step is to acknowledge that you—or your spouse, child, coworker or friend—have a problem with alcohol and that continuing to drink can cause serious, if not deadly, consequences. (One of the heartbreaking symptoms of the disease is that the alcoholic often doesn't realize—or denies—there is a problem.)

The next step is to get help. (Individuals with a dependency or addiction to alcohol are rarely able to stop drinking permanently on their own.) A few of the most successful and well-known resources that are available in most communities include:

- Alcoholics Anonymous (AA), which uses a self-help group approach to help the alcoholic fully understand the seriousness of the problem, and begin—and stick with—a recovery program.
- Al-Anon, a program for family and friends of alcoholics.
- Alateen, a program similar to Al-Anon but specifically for teens and children in families where a drinking problem exists.

Other resources include alcohol treatment programs, your health care professional, public health departments, mental health agencies or—if one is available to you—an employee assistance program.

Catching Problems Early

Some medical tests are unnecessary, costly and overprescribed. Others, however, play an important role in increasing your longevity and quality of life, while saving thousands—or even hundreds of thousands—of dollars in the long run by catching potentially serious problems early.

Here are a few of the preventive tests that are recommended for **healthy adults over 50.** If you have a serious medical condition or other high-risk factors, your doctor may recommend more frequent testing or additional tests or procedures.

Preventive Exams/Tests

Who Needs It	How Often
Complete Physical	
All adults	Every one to three years until age 75, then yearly
Sigmoidoscopy, Colonoscopy or Barium Enema (to detect colon/rectal cancer)	
Adults 50 years and over	Every five to 10 years, depending on test
Fecal Occult Blood Testing (stool test for early detection of colon/rectal cancer)	
Adults 50 years and over	Every year
Digital Rectal Exam (to detect prostate cancer)	
Men 50 years and over	Every year
Glaucoma Screening	
Everyone over age 40	Every two years or on your doctor's advice or every year if there is a family history

chart continues next page

Preventive Exams/Tests *continued from previous page*

Who Needs It	How Often
Pap Smear (to detect cervical cancer)	
All women	Annually. If you've had a hysterectomy or are over the age of 65, check with your doctor for frequency recommendations.
Professional Breast Exam	
All women during routine checkups	Every year. (A monthly self-exam is also recommended; see *Breast Self-Exam,* p. 279.) Discuss risk factors at your professional breast exam appointment.
Mammogram	
All women age 40 and over	Every year
Blood Pressure Measurement	
All adults	Every two years
Cholesterol Screening (to detect high blood cholesterol levels, which may lead to atherosclerosis)	
All adults; adults over 75, check with your physician	Every five years
Glucose	
All adults age 45 and older	If tested normal once, repeated at three-year intervals or on your doctor's advice
Electrocardiogram or EKG (to detect coronary artery disease)	
Not recommended for routine screening of people without symptoms	Selectively on your doctor's advice

Preventive Exams/Tests

Who Needs It	How Often
Exercise Stress Test (to screen for coronary artery disease)	
Men over 40 or women over 50 who have two or more major risk factors for heart disease (high cholesterol, high blood pressure, smoking, diabetes, family history of early onset of heart disease). Not recommended as routine for people without symptoms	Selectively on your doctor's advice
Chest X-ray	
Not recommended as routine for people without symptoms	Selectively on your doctor's advice
Common Lab Tests (CBC, urinalysis, thyroid, liver, kidney, syphilis, tuberculin)	
Not recommended as routine for people without symptoms or a significant history of exposure	Selectively on your doctor's advice
Osteoporosis Screening	
Baseline test recommended for women at high risk and every two years if no new risk factors exist	Selectively on your doctor's advice

Immunization Schedule

A thorough immunization plan is an important lifetime health investment that protects you against a host of life-threatening diseases such as influenza and tetanus—and it continues to be a very important part of life as you get older.

Key immunizations you need follow. Ask your doctor if you need others as well:

- A *pneumococcal vaccine* to decrease the likelihood of getting pneumonia and reduce the severity of the disease if you do get it. The current recommendation is one dose for people over age 65 who have never been vaccinated for pneumonia. Anyone with a disease that affects their immunity needs a pneumonia shot, too.
- An *influenza vaccination* (given annually) to protect you against the flu—an illness that can be very serious and even life-threatening among older adults.
- A *tetanus diphtheria (Td) booster* every 10 years for adults (everyone needs to have completed a primary series of three shots), or every five years if you get a dirty wound, to fend off tetanus (also known as "lockjaw").

Develop a schedule with your doctor to make sure you stay current on your immunizations, and keep your own record of vaccines at home.

Safety

Injuries due to falls and fires are among the leading causes of accidental death for older adults. While the frequency of accidents doesn't necessarily increase with age, the serious injuries that can result do. This is because your body becomes less able to withstand injury as you grow older. By planning ahead, you can considerably reduce your risk of most accidents.

Falls

Each year, about one-third of adults over age 65 suffer falls, and 10 to 15 percent of them are significantly injured. A serious fall can limit your level of activity—due to injuries and the fear of falling again—so it pays to take extreme care to avoid falling in the first place.

Falls among older adults frequently result from slowed reaction time, lack of conditioning, poor vision or hearing, diseases such as osteoporosis that weaken the bones (see *Osteoporosis*, p. 238), or dizziness that can result from several factors, including medication. (See *Dizziness and Vertigo*, p. 85; *Using Medications*, p. 326; *Home Pharmacy*, p. 331.)

PREVENTION ☑

- **Keep your body as strong as possible** by eating right (see *Eating Right*, p. 338), exercising regularly (see *Staying Active*, p. 343) and taking steps to avoid or reduce the progression of osteoporosis. Your eyes and ears contribute to balance, so have them checked regularly. (See index for specific topics.)
- **Carefully inspect your home**, asking yourself: "Where are the places I'm likely to fall, and what can I do to reduce my risks?" and "What is my physical condition, and what are the compensations I can make?" Your list might include putting non-skid tape in the bathtub, adding handrails along staircases, getting rid of throw rugs that may slide under you, padding sharp corners or improving lighting.

- **Avoid excessive alcohol consumption.** As you grow older, you become more sensitive to alcohol and other drugs so your reflexes may be impaired by much less alcohol than they did when you were younger. (See *Alcohol Use*, p. 349.)
- **Make a habit of getting up slowly.** A normal drop in your blood pressure when you stand up—caused by your heart's inability to speed up as quickly as it used to—can result in dizziness that contributes to falls. (See *Heart Disease*, p. 181.)
- **Don't stand on a stool or chair** to reach items stored up high. Have someone help you get them down—then move them to a spot within easy reach.
- **Use a cane or walker** if you have problems with balance.

> For information about other precautions—such as getting a personal response system for your home or wearing a medical-alert bracelet—see *Be Prepared*, p. 18.

Traffic Safety

Automobile accidents cause a significant number of deaths among older adults and are frequently the result of slowed reaction time and impaired vision or hearing. However, practicing a few precautions can help you maximize your safety.

PREVENTION ✓

Driving an automobile

- Enroll in a safe-driver training course to refresh your driving skills.
- Schedule yearly eye examinations. Ask your ophthalmologist whether you have experienced any vision changes that may impact your driving abilities.
- If you wear glasses or a hearing aid, use them when you drive, if appropriate.
- If you don't have to be on the road during rush hour, don't. If you know your vision is worse after dark, avoid driving at night.
- Keep a car window open a bit so you can hear sirens and other warning signals more easily. When using your car radio, keep the volume down.
- Don't drive if any of your medications impair your driving ability.
- Take frequent breaks on long drives to rest your eyes and stretch your muscles.
- Wear your seatbelt while in all motor vehicles and place children in proper car seats.

As a pedestrian

- Wear light-colored and/or reflective clothing when walking after sundown.
- When looking to the left and right before entering an intersection, use extra caution if your vision or hearing is impaired. Walk with a friend if possible.
- Stand on the sidewalk when waiting to cross a street—never in the street.

Fires

The death rate due to fires is highest among older adults. Common causes of fires include unsafe use of cigarettes; malfunctioning smoke detectors and fire extinguishers; problems with fireplaces, electrical outlets or space heaters; and accidents in the kitchen.

PREVENTION ✓

- If you smoke, make every effort to kick the habit. Research shows your risk from fires will be immediately reduced by one-third.
- Obtain fire extinguishers for your residence and learn how to use them. Also, install smoke detectors and keep the batteries fresh. Check these safety items every few months to make sure they're in working order.
- Keep your fireplace clean and make sure the screen is closed when you're burning a fire. Never leave a fire unattended.
- Don't overload electrical outlets, which can make wires overheat.
- Use space heaters carefully. Keep paper, furniture, curtains and combustible liquids away from the heater.
- In the kitchen, keep curtains, paper towels and wall hangings away from the stove and make sure burners are turned off when they're not in use. Keep your burners and oven grease-free and be particularly cautious if you are deep-frying; the grease can cause a flare-up of flames that results in a larger fire.

Planning escape routes

All the prevention in the world can't absolutely guarantee that a fire won't occur, so make plans—in advance—for how you will get out of your residence if a fire occurs. Carefully plan at least two escape routes out of every room and make sure those routes are free of hazards.

Crime

Unfortunately, older adults sometimes fall prey to thieves and other petty criminals—but there's plenty you can do to avoid potentially dangerous situations. The goal is to make it difficult for the crime to occur in the first place—before you become a victim.

PREVENTION ☑

At home

- Make sure all doors and windows have locks that are in good order.
- Install a peephole if you don't already have one, and use it. Never open the door to strangers or let them know you're alone.
- Keep the exterior of your home well lit, and bushes and trees trimmed to ensure good visibility.
- Don't give any information to strangers over the phone, and hang up on obscene or other nuisance phone calls.
- When you go on a trip, take steps to make your house or apartment look "lived in" while you're away. Stop delivery of mail and newspapers, or arrange for a neighbor or friend to pick up deliveries. Leave some shades up and/or lights on (or use an automatic timer) and arrange for someone to care for the yard.
- Have your Social Security checks deposited directly into your bank account; theft of Social Security checks is a prime source of crime against older adults.
- Get acquainted with your neighbors. Watch out for one another.
- Consider getting a dog. Even a little one can deter unwanted visitors while providing companionship.
- Attend a crime prevention program.

Away from home

- Avoid carrying large amounts of money or expensive personal items (don't wear flashy jewelry, for example) when out in public.
- Never carry a deadly weapon; it can be used against you. Instead, carry a whistle you can easily access and blow to scare away muggers, or carry a cane or umbrella you can use to defend yourself with, if necessary.

- Stay in well-lit, busy areas at night. If you have the feeling you're in danger, trust your instincts.
- Walk and act like you know where you're going.
- When you walk or drive, go with a friend or friends.

Finally, if your prevention methods are unsuccessful and you are accosted, don't resist: hand over your purse or wallet without hesitating. Purse and wallet snatchers are usually more interested in your money or possessions than in hurting you.

Scams

- No matter what your age, it always pays to be an informed consumer and stay alert to possible "scams."
- Never give out information—especially your credit card number—to anyone over the phone unless you placed the call. Ask for requests for confidential information in writing.
- Purchase home improvement services from respected, well-established companies. Ask for references.
- Carefully read and fully understand documents before you sign them. Have a trusted friend or family member provide assistance, if necessary.
- Be cautious of "good causes" and "hard luck stories." Select the causes you wish to support and only donate an amount that feels comfortable to you.
- Keep in mind that investment opportunities that sound too good to be true probably are.
- Evaluate insurance offers—especially unsolicited ones—very carefully. Call a trusted relative or financial advisor if you have any questions.
- If you feel at all unsure about a purchase, trust your feelings and don't sign anything until you're sure. Instead, buy yourself some time by saying: "Give me everything in writing. I want to review this with my attorney."

Abuse

Elder abuse can occur in assisted living centers, nursing homes, and even in your own home—usually by people hired to care for you. Sadly, even family members can be abusive.

Remember that no matter what your age, you have the legal rights to protect yourself from assault, abuse and harassment. Try to prevent abuse before it happens; recognize an abusive situation if you find yourself in one, and get help from a trusted source as quickly as possible.

PREVENTION ☑

Use caution when selecting care or other services to be delivered in your home or some other setting; quality can vary dramatically. Find out if staff members are trained and well-qualified, if cleanliness and safety are maintained at all times, how supervision of staff members is handled, and what your course of action is if you're not satisfied with the care. Ask for references and check them before you contract for any services. Encourage your caregiver (especially a family member) to take needed breaks and care properly for him- or herself. (See *Care for the Caregiver*, p. 377.)

Recognizing abusive behavior

It's safe to assume you are being abused if you are:

- Hit, slapped, pushed, shoved or in any way intentionally harmed or injured
- Verbally harassed, insulted, belittled, or continually criticized
- Neglected or placed in a situation that is unsafe or unhealthy

WHAT YOU CAN DO ☑

Immediately report any abusive behavior to the abuser's supervisor or sponsoring agency, friends and family, or the police. Be prepared to explain exactly what happened, the time and date of the incident(s), the name of the person who hurt you and anyone who may have seen it happen, and the kind of injury or discomfort you experienced.

Many older adults don't speak up when they find themselves in an abusive situation because they're embarrassed, afraid of being hurt even worse, feel like no one cares, or think no one will do anything to help. Try to remember, instead, that the person who is abusing you is breaking the law (even if it is a family member), and that speaking up may prevent the abuse of someone else. What's more—**you deserve to be treated with respect and kindness.**

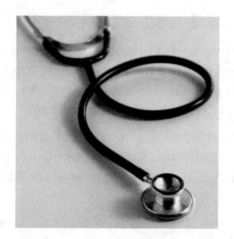

SECTION 6
Managing Illness

Managing Your Illness

Aging doesn't have to equate with illness. By exercising, controlling your weight, not smoking and eating a healthy diet, you can lower your risk of conditions once thought to be unavoidable. Physical and mental exercises help keep the body and mind fit, no matter what your age.

Genetics may play a role in increasing your risk of some diseases, such as certain forms of cancer. Other conditions, such as Parkinson's disease, rheumatoid arthritis and ulcerative colitis, seem to appear at random, without any means to prevent them.

The good news is that no matter what your situation, you can still take control at some level. You have the power.

You're in Charge

For starters, follow the steps to primary prevention. (See *Primary Prevention,* p. 364.) These lifestyle choices can help you avoid injury and many *acute* illnesses (illnesses that can generally be treated and cured) associated with aging, and improve your overall health.

It is important to remember that even with acute and *chronic* (ongoing) illnesses, you can live a productive life. Your attitude and adaptability can help you make the most out of your situation. If your mobility has been affected by arthritis, for example, you may feel depressed, isolated and threatened by a loss of independence. These feelings, although understandable, do not have to dictate your situation. You can make the choice to begin an exercise program to improve your agility; you can investigate aids designed to help with household chores; you can take advantage of community services that assist with meal preparation and special transportation needs. Making choices like these does not mean you've lost your independence—it means you have exercised it.

It's Never Too Late

Self-care, prevention and a healthy lifestyle are important throughout your life and it's never too late to start taking steps toward improving your situation. Studies repeatedly show that older adults who engage in exercise often regain or exceed the strength they had in their earlier years. The lung damage caused by years of smoking is slowed and eventually somewhat reversed by giving up smoking, even late in life. Cutting back on the fat in your diet can reduce your cholesterol levels, which can lessen the risk of stroke or the progression of heart disease. Managing stress, limiting salt intake, exercising and quitting smoking help to control high blood pressure. (See *Hypertension,* p. 190.) The choices you make to improve your quality of life are virtually limitless.

Steps to Taking Charge

- **Practice healthy lifestyle behaviors.** (See *Primary Prevention,* p. 364.)

- **Learn all you can about your condition or illness:**
  - Ask questions (particularly of your doctor or health care team).
  - Call a professional nurse phoneline or a national hotline.
  - Contact a community agency or national organization that deals with your condition or situation. (See *Tapping Your Resources,* p. 375.) These groups have a number of clearly written materials that can be sent to you for free.

- **Actively participate in your care plan:**
  - Consider yourself a partner with your doctor and health care team.
  - Encourage those in your family who help with your care to join your "team."
  - Don't assume your doctor knows how you feel. Communicate your health status to your health care providers when you feel it's necessary.

(See *A Self-Care Approach,* p. xii.)

Primary Prevention

Most people develop one or more acute illnesses during their lives. (See *Acute vs. Chronic Illness*, p. 365.) Primary prevention means avoiding or postponing sudden acute illnesses and injuries, as well as the onset of chronic conditions. The following chart shows some general guidelines that promote health while reducing the risk of an acute illness or injury.

Practice a Healthy Lifestyle

Eat a balanced diet low in fat and salt. Limiting fat and salt intake can reduce your risk of heart disease and high blood pressure, for example. A balanced diet also helps control weight, an essential element in the prevention of many diseases. (See *Eating Right*, p. 338.) Use alcohol moderately (one to two drinks a day or less) or not at all. (See *Alcohol Use*, p. 349.)

Develop and maintain a program of regular exercise, including aerobic exercise, to strengthen your heart. Regular exercise conditions your heart and lungs, keeps you fit and imparts a sense of well-being. (See *Staying Active*, p. 343.)

Make every effort to stop smoking and avoid inhaling secondhand smoke. (See *Smoking Cessation*, p. 346.) Smoking can lead to lung cancer and emphysema, and it makes you more susceptible to pneumonia and bronchitis. (See *Respiratory Concerns*, p. 166.)

Adhere to a schedule of regular screenings and vaccinations. (See *Preventive Exams/Tests*, p. 351; *Immunization Schedule*, p. 354.) Many illnesses can be detected early with routine screenings such as mammograms, Pap smears and prostate exams. A pneumonia vaccination, tetanus boosters and annual flu shots will limit your risk of contracting these illnesses.

Take steps to ensure your personal safety. (See *Safety*, p. 355.) Use your seatbelt, install handrails in your shower to prevent falls, make your home secure and take other actions to decrease the likelihood of injury.

Acute vs. Chronic Illness

Understanding the differences between acute and chronic illness will help you make wiser decisions about maintaining good health and preventing its decline.

Acute illness involves the sudden onset of an illness or injury. The progression and treatment for the condition are often predictable and a complete recovery— or a return to good health—is usually possible. Pneumonia and peptic ulcer are examples of acute illness. (See *Pneumonia*, p. 178 and *Peptic Ulcer*, p. 212.) The healthier you are to begin with, the faster your recovery is likely to be.

May be lifelong

Chronic illness is a condition that, once you have it, will likely continue for the remainder of your life. The disease's progression and treatment vary somewhat from person to person, making certain stages of the condition unpredictable, while other stages are more foreseeable. The challenge facing someone with a chronic illness is not how to return to full health, but how to slow or stabilize the disease's progression and deal with its lifelong consequences.

Examples of chronic illnesses are coronary artery disease (CAD), arthritis, diabetes, emphysema, stroke, osteoporosis and hypertension. (See index for specific topics.) Learning to manage a chronic illness effectively takes patience, courage and commitment, but the rewards are well worth the effort.

For more about these conditions:

Arthritis, p. 234
Asthma, p. 173
Back Pain, p. 243
Depression, p. 319
Diabetes, p. 226
Emphysema, p. 169

Heart Disease, p. 181
Hypertension, p. 190
Osteoporosis, p. 238
Parkinson's Disease, p. 100
Stroke/TIA, p. 93
Thyroid Problems, p. 230

Making Healthy Decisions

Remarkably, two of the most important aspects of managing a chronic condition are the way you make decisions and the way your perceive your health.

The more you believe you can control your life, the better you feel. The better you feel, the more control you believe you have. Your attitudes become self-fulfilling, and can spiral in either a positive or negative direction.

In spite of the challenges, ups and downs and disappointments that may occur, you'll have ongoing opportunities to call a lot of the shots. And the better prepared you are for these opportunities, the better your health and quality of life can be.

Understanding How and Why You Make Certain Choices

To manage any illness, understanding both yourself and the nature of the disease are critically important to improving your situation.

For example, do you believe you can make a difference in your health, or do you think things are pretty much out of your hands? Do you feel you and your doctor are on the same team, or are you anxious and distrustful about your medical care? Are healthy lifestyle changes important to you, or do you tend to discount them? Your answers to these and similar questions reflect your attitudes and significantly impact your decisions about health.

Different Types of Patients

The following information may provide you with insight about how and why you make health decisions the way you do.

Does this sound like you?

- You are proactively involved in your own health care and committed to practicing healthy lifestyle habits (such as eating a well-balanced diet and exercising). You trust your doctors.
- You regret some of the unhealthy habits you acquired when you were younger. Because these habits are so ingrained (smoking, for example), you feel unlikely to change (and stop smoking now). You see your doctors regularly, prefer specialists and are likely to try new over-the-counter (OTC) drugs.
- You describe yourself as rarely sick. You take medicine only when you have to and *don't* like to try new over-the-counter (OTC) drugs.
- You have very little faith in the medical system. Your worries concern health insurance and whether your doctors are well-informed in general, and knowledgeable about how different medicines interact in older adults.

In other words, if you are a proactive patient diagnosed with some aspect of heart disease, you may have fewer challenges trying to follow a low-fat diet than you may if you fall into one of the other three categories, simply because healthy habits (to some extent) are already part of your lifestyle.

It is beneficial to take stock of your attitudes about medical care as well as your confidence in managing your health. Knowing the level of difficulty you are likely to face (given your particular set of attitudes), can help you more readily accept yourself, and may prevent you from giving up on a lifestyle change that can greatly benefit your chronic condition.

Self-Managing Chronic Illness

The role of any good manager is to be responsible for decisions and see that those decisions are carried out. Managing your health is no different.

Setting Realistic Goals

Managing a chronic illness is never as simple as deciding what you want to do and just doing it. If you fail to set realistic goals (keep in mind that a chronic illness may mean giving up some options), or haven't learned certain skills needed to reach your goals, you may decide there's no way you can improve the situation. Setbacks could become overwhelming, and the situation will probably get worse.

- **Understand why you feel the way you do:** All chronic health problems share certain traits, including fatigue or loss of energy, sleep problems (pain and difficulty breathing are two causes), some physical disability, depression (worrying about the future, some loss of independence, feeling helpless), and lowered self-esteem (due to most of the points just mentioned).

- **Learn as much as you can:** Your chronic condition will have its own set of trends or stages. It's important to educate yourself about these so you will know what to expect and can prepare for the best ways to manage and adapt to the situation. Some of the most successful self-managers are described as thinking of their illness as a path—sometimes it's rough, sometimes flat; sometimes you can go fast, other times slow; sometimes it takes several different approaches to navigate the turns.

- **Practice problem-solving skills:** You will be faced with daily opportunities to make choices. (See *Making Healthy Decisions,* p. 366.) The process can become unmanageable unless you break it down into steps. As with any new skill, you'll find that this approach becomes more effective with practice, until you eventually adopt it as routine.

Problem-Solving Steps

- **Decide what you want to realistically accomplish.** For example, you've recently been diagnosed with emphysema and want to learn some exercises to aid your breathing.
- **Look for multiple ways to reach your goal or solve your problem.** You can ask your doctor for instruction; you can call the American Lung Association for information and resources within your community; you can obtain a list of exercises to teach yourself at home; or you can join a support group or class at a local hospital that offers classes and regular exercise sessions.
- **Select an option and try it, keeping in mind your chance for success is greatest where your interest is highest.** Because you'd rather exercise in the comfort of your own home and you don't drive, you choose a booklet to read about exercises you can do on your own.
- **Check your results.** After a week, you don't notice that breathing is any easier, and you're not sure you're doing the exercises correctly. You start to wonder if this was a good idea.
- **Substitute another idea or approach if the first one doesn't work.** You locate a breathing-exercise class for individuals with chronic lung conditions. It's nearby and also offers transportation, so you decide to participate and reevaluate your situation after a few sessions.
- **Reward yourself.** You congratulate yourself with a bouquet of flowers for having the determination to step out of your comfort zone.

You may find that the situation, for now, is unchangeable or unsolvable. That's important to know, and it's all right. Don't dwell on what you can't do, but start looking for another goal you can accomplish. Seek out a support group that deals with the same condition or issues you are facing.

Using Self-Management Skills

The decision to self-manage your chronic condition is a wise health care choice because of the benefits to you. You will enjoy the greatest benefits if your goals are to keep your daily functioning (work, chores, recreational and social activities) and your well-being (mental health, pain, perception of health status) at optimal levels, given your situation. By using self-management techniques to slow or prevent the progress of your current condition, your chances of limiting other illnesses and improving your overall health are good.

Steps to Self-Management

Develop and maintain exercise and nutrition programs. Even after the onset of atherosclerosis (see *CAD,* p. 181), a low-fat diet is important to minimize future heart problems. Eating right also helps you avoid complications of diabetes. (See *Diabetes,* p. 226.) Weight control can help lessen the symptoms of arthritis. (See *Arthritis,* p. 234.)

Monitor your symptoms. Do you feel better, worse or the same? How does a certain treatment affect you? Regular monitoring and reporting back to your doctor will help you detect subtle changes in your condition so you can take steps to lessen the impact of your symptoms or find alternative treatments.

Take the initiative to contact your doctor when you believe you need medical attention and keep your scheduled visits. Routine screenings, immunizations and checkups are as important as ever.

Follow your treatment plan to minimize medication side effects. Failure to comply with your doctor's instructions can have a serious impact on controlling your condition. However, if a treatment or medication is affecting you in an unexpected or adverse way, speak up. Often your doctor can adjust your care plan to be more suitable to your needs. Be sure your doctor and pharmacist know about any other prescriptions and over-the-counter (OTC) medications you may be using.

Work and communicate effectively with your doctor and/or health care team. Share information, ask questions and express your needs. (See *A Self-care Approach,* p. xii)

Find out about and use community and other support resources. Investigate ways to compensate for changes in your lifestyle. Learn how others are handling similar situations. Don't try to go it alone!

SECTION 7

Planning for the Future

Action Plan for Independence

If you're like most people, you genuinely value your independence. You enjoy the freedom of making your own decisions and going where you want, when you want.

As people grow older, there is sometimes a fear that this independence must be surrendered. The good news is that—with planning and a positive, realistic outlook—it is possible for many people to maintain a level of independence throughout their lives.

A key factor in preserving this freedom is planning. By anticipating the way your life may change and adapting to life's changes, you can most likely avoid hasty decisions that may be dictated by circumstance, and make better choices.

Important Questions

Use the following list to think about the future and how you can keep the independence you enjoy.

Where do you want to live?

Are you happy where you are now? Are family, friends and activities accessible? Are the weather and climate acceptable to you?

If you're pondering a move to a different city, you may want to plan it at a time in your retirement when you feel comfortable making new friends and adapting to new surroundings. You may also want to make a trial visit for an extended period before coming to a final decision.

What size of home can you maintain?

Older adults often decide to sell homes with large lawns and a lot of upkeep—and opt for smaller places. Those who live in the country may move into nearby towns where services are closer. City dwellers may want a smaller apartment, or one that's closer to friends or activities. Changes in your health may also create temporary or long-term requirements for changes in your living environment.

What are your financial resources?

Take a candid look at your resources. What are you able to afford, and how can you enjoy the lifestyle you want with the funds that are available to you? Develop a monthly budget based on your resources. If you're worried about your resources, look into governmental programs that may be available to you. Don't be embarrassed about tapping these resources—that's why they exist. Remember, too, that many of life's most enjoyable activities don't require money: chatting with a friend, curling up with a good book from the library, taking a stroll through the park, or gardening on a sunny afternoon.

Ask the "what if?" questions

Sometimes, it's helpful to consider some of the possible changes and then think of solutions before you actually need them. For example:

- **What if you could no longer drive your car?** Is there a local taxi company? What about buses? Is there a special shuttle service for older adults? Is it possible to walk to key services and activities? How comfortable would you be relying on friends for errands? What about shopping by phone or the Internet?
- **What if you need help with housework or yard work?** Can you make things simpler—by closing off several rooms, or by doing less yard work? Could you hire live-in help? Would a smaller place be easier to maintain? Is there equipment that would make things easier?
- **What if you need ongoing assistance?** What is available in the area? Do your friends have people helping them who seem competent? What services are available through local health care organizations, churches or social service groups?
- **If you were to become seriously ill, what kind of care would you want?** Several important tools—a Living Will and Durable Power of Attorney for Health Care—help you convey the kind of care you want even if you're too ill to communicate. These are explained more fully on page 378.
- **What if your spouse/partner were to die?** The simple fact is that if you're married or in a long-term relationship, one person will likely outlive the

other. It can be very reassuring to talk honestly with your husband, wife or partner about how one of you will cope without the other. Although this topic may be uncomfortable, talking about it often leads to deeply intimate and satisfying discussions.

The point of anticipating these possible situations is to think positively about solutions and how you can cope, long before an emergency or major change occurs.

What assistance is available in your area?

Do a little fact-finding to see which programs and services are available to you. Some good resources for information are senior centers, the local Area Agency on Aging, home health agencies, United Way, hospital geriatric departments, libraries, the local Visiting Nurse Association and religious organizations.

You'll soon discover a wide range of services that may include adult day care, assistance with shopping, employment and volunteer opportunities, home health aides, homemakers and chore services, housing assistance, legal services, mental health services, respite care for the caregiver and retirement planning.

Plans and Outlook

Share your thoughts with family and friends

Chances are your children or close friends would like to hear your ideas and plans. Try saying something like, "I've been thinking about the future, and here are some changes I plan to make as I grow older."

By sharing with people who are important to you, you can benefit from their ideas and suggestions and give them the opportunity to help you fulfill your plans.

Be positive and enjoy life

Thankfully, our culture is redefining what it means to grow older. No longer is aging thought of as a long list of surrenders—giving up various things long enjoyed. Instead, it's seen for what it really is: a time of reflection, of living as actively and fully as possible, and of drawing on the richness, experience and wisdom of a well-lived life.

Tapping Your Resources

A wide variety of services are available to help you maintain your independence. Think about the obstacles that could make your life more difficult and less enjoyable, then ask yourself what you need help with; how often the help is required (ongoing, hourly, daily or just one time); and whether obstacles are something you can solve by yourself with the right equipment or help.

Problem Solving

For example, an obstacle might be: "I want to stay in my home, but I don't have the flexibility and strength for the housekeeping that I once did." Ask yourself these questions:

- What needs to be done and why?
- How often does it need to be done?
- If there is a cost, how can it be paid for?

Then, think about solutions, which might include:

- Special cleaning tools that minimize the need for bending
- Closing off one room so it doesn't need to be cleaned
- Having bedding and towels cleaned by a laundry service
- Hiring a window-cleaning service for the outside windows
- Hiring someone to help inside your home on a regular basis

Older adults sometimes find themselves needing assistance with housing and house maintenance, daily grooming, medical care, and staying active and in touch with friends.

Community Services

You can take satisfaction in knowing that any problem you're likely to face has already been successfully solved by someone else. Services that are in place in a number of communities include:

- **Personal emergency response systems.** These types of systems let you immediately signal the local hospital, ambulance or emergency response system if you fall or need instant medical attention. (See *Be Prepared*, p. 18.)
- **Telephone reassurance programs.** Volunteers phone you regularly to make sure you're well, remind you to take medications or offer support in other ways.
- **Friendly visits.** Some organizations such as churches or local social service agencies will send people to visit, chat, play cards or keep you company.
- **Chore services.** These companies offer a modern-day equivalent of the "handyman" for yard work, general home maintenance or minor household repairs.
- **Meals services.** These programs deliver nutritious meals right to your home, often for a very modest fee or donation.
- **Companion services.** A variety of these services can help keep your home running smoothly, with housekeeping, essential shopping and meal preparation.
- **Home health aides.** Aides can supply all the help provided by companion services, and assist you with taking your oral medication as prescribed, dressing, bathing, etc.
- **Skilled home care.** Qualified health care providers bring even more expertise right to your home with help in medication management, specialized treatments and nutritional counseling. Home care providers can oversee other people providing services in your home and make recommendations for other assistance that might be needed.
- **Respite services.** These people "fill-in" to provide care while the regular caregiver(s) takes time away.
- **Hospices.** These special programs provide care to people who are dying, often in their homes. They help deliver medical care that reduces pain and makes life more acceptable, rather than providing intensive medical services. The hospice team might include a doctor, nurse, social worker, member of the clergy and volunteers.

Care for the Caregiver

Caring for a friend or loved one can be an opportunity to show your concern, but realize that it is also a big commitment. Don't overdo—and remember the emotional toll that giving care can take on you.

If you are considering being a caregiver, think about:

- **Physical ability and stamina.** Don't promise to do tasks that are beyond your own strength or energy level.
- **Time management.** Remember, you have your own life, too. Make a commitment that allows you the time you need for your life and its demands.
- **Emotional impact.** Providing care, especially for someone in your own family, can bring up a number of emotionally charged issues such as resentment or past family conflicts. Be aware that this often occurs and seek help if it becomes an issue.

WHAT YOU CAN DO ✓

- Join a support group and share stories, tips and ideas with others providing care.
- Schedule breaks in the routine (*respite care*) to get some well-deserved time away. This is vital since the likelihood of verbal or physical abuse increases as the caregiver becomes more depleted and resentful, and feels there is no option for relief. Overextended caregivers may find themselves acting in a way they could never imagine possible in ordinary circumstances.
- Scale down other demands on your time, if possible.
- Tap other resources. A loving family member should realize that, in addition to doing tasks personally, an equally beneficial service is looking to other family members for help, as well as utilizing professional resources.
- Become a creative problem solver. Look for new, fresh ways to get the assistance needed for both you and the person you're caring for.
- Watch out for guilt. Don't demand perfection of yourself and don't be motivated by guilt. If you've committed to something that you're not able to do, admit it honestly and seek help finding other resources for getting the job done.

Important Documents

No one likes to think about the possibility of being so ill or seriously injured that they can't communicate with a doctor directly about the kind of care they want. Unfortunately, that can happen. However, there are steps you can take to make sure your care is carried out in the way that you would choose if you are unable to make your wishes about medical treatment known.

When you make your preferences known now, you benefit from making decisions at a time when you can thoughtfully consider them. Plus, you take stress away from loved ones and family members, should they ever have to make medical decisions on your behalf in an emergency or end-of-life situation.

Decide in Advance

The two documents discussed below deal with medical situations where you are unable to communicate directly about the kind of care you want. They are sometimes referred to as *Advance Medical Directives*, because they set out your wishes in advance of your actually needing them.

The *Directive to Physicians (Living Will)* is a written statement in which you specify what type of care you want if you are terminally ill and dying, or if you are permanently unconscious. It helps guide the actions of your doctor, family members and others making decisions about your care.

The *Durable Power of Attorney for Health Care* is a legally binding document in which you give someone else the authority to make health care decisions for you if you're not able to make them yourself. If you do not have this document, the law specifies who will make decisions on your behalf. In some states this would be your spouse, adult children, parents or siblings (in that order).

It is not necessary to consult an attorney to complete these documents, although some people feel more comfortable having worked with their lawyer on these issues. Bear in mind that these documents may vary from state to state, so if you have moved or reside at more than one location, make sure that your documents are recognized in all places where you spend long periods of time.

Complete the forms and make sure that they are signed, dated, notarized and witnessed if required.

When You've Decided

Once you've finished them:

- Talk with the person to whom you've given durable power of attorney for your health care so they know their role in advance.
- Discuss your desires about care with this person, so they are best able to make decisions that reflect your preferences and plans.
- Give your doctor a copy of these documents.
- If you have a chart at a hospital, ask that a copy of these documents be added to your file, or bring a copy with you when you go to the hospital.
- Keep copies near other important or legal papers, so someone looking through your belongings can easily find them.

The Directive to Physicians and Durable Power of Attorney for Health Care are very important in an era when medical technology can artificially prolong life for weeks, months and even years.

You Can Always Make Changes

Most hospitals can provide you with pre-written and fill-in-the-blank forms for these documents. If you are using a pre-written form, realize that you have the right to change any of the language in the form. For example, the standardized form might say: "I consider artificially administered nutrition and hydration to be forms of life-sustaining treatment and direct that under my directions they be withheld or withdrawn the same as other forms of treatment." If you don't agree with this statement, you could cross it out entirely, or modify it by allowing hydration to be administered, or any other change you desire.

Bear in mind that the Directive to Physicians is focused on situations in which a person has an incurable injury, disease or illness certified as terminal by two doctors, and in which medical measures would only prolong the dying process. As long as you are able to communicate with your doctor, you'll be the one making the decisions about your own care.

One last point: Know that you can change, revise and update these forms as often as you like. Just make sure that all the key people have the most current copy.

Index